Brazilian Jiu-Jitsu:
Theory & Technique

Renzo & Royler Gracie

Brazilian Jiu-Jitsu: Theory & Technique

Renzo & Royler Gracie

with Kid Peligro and John Danaher

Photos by Ricardo Azoury

Invisible Cities Press

in association with

Editora Gracie

DEDICATION

Renzo Gracie: To my wife and children. To my father and my mother, who never laid their eyes upon me without a smile. Who loved me without conditions and who taught me to do the same. To all those who came before me and forged the Gracie legacy.

To those of my family who succeed me in name and deed
When I lie buried
Tell future generations that I lived and fought
According to my family's creed.

Royler Gracie: I want to dedicate this book to my father Helio Gracie, for without his labor, bravery, skill, and guidance neither this work nor the fate that drew me to it could have arisen. I also wish to dedicate it to the Gracie family as a whole, for without their combined efforts, past, present, and future, Brazilian jiu-jitsu could not have achieved the recognition and respect that it has. I also want to include Sheik Zayed, father and mentor to Sheik Tahnoon, and to Sheik Tahnoon himself, the visionary who has done so much for the sport and the children. Finally, to my wife and children, for all the love that we share.

John Danaher: To all my wonderful family, especially my beloved Mother.

Solitude begets the strength and depth
That society mocks.
Where does laughter and love return
But n the warmth of the hearth?

Kid Peligro: My work is dedicated to my friend Sheik Tahnoon bin Zayed for his inspiration, friendship, and advice. To Royler Gracie and Renzo Gracie for their lifetime of dedication to the art. To the Gracie family for giving us this wonderful sport, to heik Hazza bin Zayed for his friendship, to my parents for all their love and support, to my wife, Susanne, who is my greatest supporter and friend, and to all the current and future participants in this wonderful sport that is Brazilian jiu-jitsu.

Editor and Producer: Kid Peligro
Assistant Editor and Compiler: Luca Atalla
Corrections: Joao P. Tinoco
Designed by: Lia Caldas

All photos © Ricardo Azoury
except photo on page 14 (© Gustavo Aragão)
and photos on pages 2, 22 and 232 (© Luca Atalla)

Published by Invisible Cities Press in association with Editora Gracie

Invisible Cities Press
50 State Street
Montpelier, VT 05602
www.invisiblecitiespress.com

Editora Gracie
Rua Sebastião Afonso Ferreira, 236
Condomínio Santa Mônica—Barra
22793-260—Rio de Janeiro—Brasil
(21) 3326-1732

LIBRARY OF CONGRESS CATALOGING-IN-PUBLICATION DATA
Gracie, Renzo.
    Brazilian jiu-jitsu : theory & technique / Renzo & Royler Gracie with Kid Peligro and John Danaher ; photos by Ricardo Azoury ; [editor and producer, Kid Peligro].
        p.   cm.
ISBN 1-931229-08-2 (paper)
1. Jiu-jitsu—Brazil. I. Gracie, Royler. II. Peligro, Kid. III. Title.

GV1114.G73 2001
796.815—dc21   2001039395

Anyone practicing the techniques in this book does so at his or her own risk. The authors and the publisher assume no responsibility for the use or misuse of information contained in this book or for any injuries that may occur as a result of praticing the techniques contained herein. The illustrations and text are for informational purposes only. It is imperative to practice these holds and techniques under the strict supervision of a qualified instructor. Additionally, one should consult a physician before embarking on any demanding physical activity.

Printed in Canada
Sixth Printing

To Sheik Tahnoon bin Zayed.

Every revolution needs its leaders.

Every revolutionary, his allies and friends.

Through your untiring efforts in promoting Brazilian jiu-jitsu

and submission grappling you have helped change forever

the face of the martial arts.

Renzo and Royler Gracie, Kid Peligro, and John Danaher

Contents

Part 2: Technique   27

Blue Belt   29

The Making of a Book

I have been involved with martial arts for many years. As a kid I did judo, then karate, and finally Brazilian jiu-jitsu. I have had the great honor of attaining the rank of Black Belt in Brazilian jiu-jitsu and have dedicated the past ten years of my life to learning and appreciating every aspect of this beautiful sport. So it was with great enthusiasm and honor that I accepted Sheik Tahnoon's invitation to make this book. Our goals were the same, to make a book that would be as good as the sport itself. The book needed to reach people inside and outside the sport and to set a new standard so that people in remote areas where there aren't quality instructors available would be able to understand and learn this sport.

We first decided who was going to be in the book. That decision was easy. Two of the best in the world were available and willing to share in this dream and to open their knowledge and their hearts for everyone to share. We are referring to Renzo and Royler Gracie, who are considered to be experts in their field. Renzo and Royler are cousins and members of the famed Gracie family, accepted by all as the originators and ambassadors of this sport.

Next it was time to find a team that understands and loves the sport as much as myself, Sheik Tahnoon, Renzo, and Royler. We were fortunate enough to know one of the world's leading jiu-jitsu photographers and a black belt in the art itself, Ricardo Azoury. Then with the addition of a crack team of writers and artists, most of them Brazilian jiu-jitsu experts themselves, this book took shape. The process of putting together this work has been extremely demanding but equally rewarding, so I hope you enjoy reading it as much as we have enjoyed making it.

Kid Peligro

Preface

In the past decade there has been a truly significant paradigm shift in the martial arts. A series of mixed martial arts tournaments, pitting different fighting styles against one another with very few rules, was the catalyst for this revolution. The initial results showed in a very clear manner that *grappling* styles of fighting were far more successful than the more heavily favored *striking* arts. This was a shock to most people, since martial arts had generally been conceived of as concerned mostly with punching and kicking skills. Contrary to most people's preconceptions about real fighting, it was found that when there was no rigid set of sporting rules, almost all fights quickly went into a clinch, then to the ground. *It was on the ground, in a grappling situation, that the outcome of the fight was almost always decided.* To the traditional martial arts, this was a disappointing result to say the least. Long accepted theories of lethal strikes and deadly blows seemed to evaporate in the face of reality. The clear outcome of these mixed martial arts tournaments was that *grappling*, both in a standing position and on the ground, was absolutely crucial to success in real fighting. More than any other style of fighting—Brazilian jiu-jitsu became synonymous with success in these clashes between styles. Represented by the legendary Gracie family who created and refined Brazilian jiu-jitsu, the martial arts world was forced to sit up and take notice of this devastating martial art. An unfortunate result of these early tournaments was the martial arts became divided between grapplers and strikers. There is no need for such a distinction. Striking styles of martial arts need not, indeed, *can* not, turn their back on these recent changes and developments. This book is not intended for grapplers only, *but for anyone, regardless of martial arts style*, who wants to improve their fighting skill and versatility by learning the crucial element of grappling and ground fighting. The book is coauthored by two of the most recognizable and active members of the Gracie clan, Renzo and Royler Gracie. From the start this book was written with a clear aim in mind: to offer to the martial arts community at large a clear and accessible set of insights into the theory and techniques of the martial art at the center of the current revolution. In the dawn of a new century the martial arts is in a state of transition the likes of which has not been seen in recent history. After some initial misgivings and doubts it would appear that to a large degree the martial arts community has come to accept the change for what it is: a liberation that has dramatically and unforgettably altered our perception of real combat. It is the intent of the authors to introduce the reader to the key elements of their distinctive style of fighting—Brazilian jiu-jitsu. Each is well known for their technical perfection and experience, both as fighters and as teachers. It is intended to set the standard for instruction in this fascinating and highly effective martial art. Along with central theoretical and historical themes, Renzo and Royler demonstrate what they take to be the essential techniques of Brazilian jiu-jitsu, along with a selection of advanced moves.

Like any revolution, the change currently going on has its advocates and detractors. The initial result of the change was to divide martial artists into "grapplers" and "strikers," "modernists" and "traditionalists." Perhaps the ultimate direction of the martial arts revolution is that *all* martial artists, regardless of stylistic preference, can greatly benefit from learning the skills of grappling. Experience has revealed that grappling on the feet and on the ground is almost inevitable in real combat. Here in this book the knowledge that can turn this fact to your advantage—regardless of your current style or skill level—are outlined in detail by two of the world's greatest authorities.

The driving force behind this book is Prince Tahnoon of the United Arab Emirates' Royal Family. He is a very active and recognizable member of the grappling world, being the force behind the world submission wrestling championships held annually in Abu Dhabi—and himself a fine grappler. The result is a book that will serve as an authoritative guide to those martial artists who wish to learn Brazilian jiu-jitsu and grappling arts. In doing so they can only improve their capacity to successfully handle and overcome opponents in a real confrontation.

Big smiles and trophies: Royler and Renzo Gracie celebrate together their victory at the 2000 Abu Dhabi Submission Wrestling World Championship.

Introducing the Authors

RENZO GRACIE: It is a midsummer night on Manhattan's West Side. In a crowded martial arts school the students are going about their training. Most of the students are lean and muscular—their bodies a reflection of the arduous training they are pushing themselves through. The majority of them are professional martial artists, black belts in other, more traditional martial arts. The remainder are mostly security professionals, bouncers, policemen—people involved in the business of combat. Others are white-collar businessmen, doctors, and lawyers. Their faces share a mask of hardness as they train. In here, all people are measured by one standard— their skill in grappling. Reputation, appearance, and vocation are all irrelevant once you step on the mat. Something has brought them here to this unkempt school. The students separate into pairs and engage in grappling bouts, alternating bursts of great speed and strength with periods of heavy breathing and rest. Each strives to attain a dominant position, or, if possible, a lock or choke that will force the other to signal submission by slapping the mats upon which they wrestle. As they struggle with each other some students begin to stand out as more skilled than others. The exhausting nature of their exercise quickly drenches them in sweat. Off to the side of the mats a man periodically shouts out advice or encouragement. His voice exudes a Portuguese accent, yet his features are South American. He is Brazilian. When he talks, the students listen. Those that follow his advice as they grapple almost invariably overcome their opponents or at least escape whatever danger they were in.

"Renzo!" A student calls out to the man, using his first name in the same fashion you might speak to an old friend. In most martial arts schools this is unheard of. The teacher is always referred to in honorific or deferential terms such as "Sensei" or "Sifu." Renzo (pronounced Hen-zo) walks over, a boyish smile set on a good-natured, handsome face. "What's wrong, my man?"

Their talk is remarkably informal. There is no sense of hierarchy in their dialogue, no deference to idols. Despite this there is a strange sense of genuine respect on the part of the student. The man he is talking to has fought the battles, carried the Gracie flag aloft, and has the scars and videotape to prove it. There is no *need* for empty rituals of respect. No need for bowing and salutations. *The respect is there*—unspoken. It has a more genuine element to it than the tired clichés of respect in the martial arts. The student asks for advice on a technical aspect of grappling. The reply is given quickly. The advice is clear and direct with none of the vague metaphor that pervades so much of the martial arts world. When put into effect you can clearly see the way in which it is a rational response to the problem at hand. For a moment there is a look of "eureka" upon the face of the student. He looks up at Renzo with the same kind of joy and respect with which you might expect a student of mathematics to exude when a perplexing problem is explained to him by a brilliant professor.

Eventually Renzo makes his way over to one of the students who has been demonstrating great prowess on the mat, easily dominating the other students he has faced. Renzo strips down to his *gi* pants and kneels down in front of him. Though he is not a big man, his body is powerful looking, with thick neck and back muscles. These muscles are for fighting, not show. As you look more closely you see a collection of scars. Renzo wears them well, like a soldier wearing medals. They speak of past adventures and glory. For now, however, Renzo is absorbed entirely in the present. He shakes hands with the student and the two begin to wrestle. The student initiates with powerful, well-calculated movements while Renzo, still warming up, is surprisingly passive. Suddenly there is a flurry. It is so rapid that it is difficult to follow. Were an observer totally uninitiated in the ways of grappling, he still could not fail to be in awe of the speed and decisiveness of the movements. Quickly Renzo attains a dominant position and works to finish his opponent, who is defending gamely, but who is clearly outclassed. Each time Renzo finishes the student in a lock or choke they resume. As they grapple the rest of the students slowly stop their training and come over to watch. They are watching in awe the ideal toward which they strive. Renzo wrestles with a sense of élan, tactical brilliance, and abandonment that is far beyond these students—they can only stare in wonder. Soon the entire class has stopped and formed an impromptu ring around the combatants. It is strange to see the student, previously so dominant, now struggling to survive the onslaught. After a while the exhibition comes to a close. Renzo and student good-naturedly embrace and compliment each other. The crowd drifts away and training resumes.

This man is Renzo Gracie. He is one of the most well-known and respected members of the Gracie clan from Brazil, a family of fighters whose amazing record stretches back some sixty years but whose exploits have only become known outside Brazil in the past decade. The Gracies are largely responsible for what is without a doubt the greatest revolution in the modern history of martial arts. This book is about that revolution, investigating its theoretical and technical basis. Renzo operates a highly regarded martial arts academy in New York City, teaching his family's unique fighting system—*Brazilian jiu-jitsu*. His achievements in the world of mixed martial arts (MMA) fighting make him a revered figure. There are few people in the martial arts who would not recognize his face or name. In the field of MMA competition, he is the equivalent of a Mike Tyson or Evander Holyfield. Yet for all this he is a man of remarkable humility and kindness. In our age we come to expect highly successful athletes to behave in insensitive, even unpleasant ways, to abuse the privileges that their fame and wealth have given them. Yet Renzo Gracie, who can legitimately claim to be among the most dangerous men on the planet, exudes none of these ugly characteristics. On the contrary he is warm and courteous, is content with simple pleasures and deeply interested in intellectual matters. Though he fights for money, one always gets the impression that pride and a sense of family tradition are the basis of his motivation. At thirty-three years of age he has attained a fighting record and mastery that most can only dream of.

As Renzo begins to cool down he tells a story of an adventure from his early days in Brazil. With his strident gesticulations and voice he is a natural storyteller, relating the events with great verve and enthusiasm. His audience, mostly senior students, are rapt in their attention. Often the tales are informative, conveying some theme of combat that Renzo is teaching. Other times they are pure entertainment—invariably they are interesting and colorful. As the training winds down he offers glimpses into a life, family background, and theory of combat so fascinating and rich in content that it must now be told to a wider audience.

ROYLER GRACIE: In front of a massive throng of international martial artists, the face and future direction of modern martial arts is unfolding. In the Middle Eastern nation of Abu Dhabi, Sheik Tahnoon, a powerful and influential member of the local royal family, is hosting the third annual Abu Dhabi submission grappling tournament. In just three years this event has become the most prestigious event in the sphere of martial arts grappling, the unofficial world championships of submission wrestling. In an era where grappling styles have come to the fore in the martial arts, this event has captured the imagination and participation of more elite grapplers and onlookers than any other. Like the Ultimate Fighting Championship and its Japanese equivalent, Pride, this event is one of the seminal martial arts events of the turn of the century. Any man who claims expertise as a submission grappler must now come here and display skill among the elite. To excel here, among the world's best, is the most widely accepted path to legitimacy. Here, in the incredibly lavish headquarters of the Abu Dhabi Combat Club, presided over by the sheik himself, packed by an international squad of athletes, journalists, and spectators, alone, out on the wrestling mat, stands the lonely figure of Royler Gracie. It is a strange and memorable scene. In the background is a bizarre mix of muscular athletes flanked by trainers and talking in dozens of languages. Interspersed among them are traditionally dressed local Arab spectators, beautiful female assistants, and a mass of foreigners. A local drum and percussion band plays nonstop, thrashing out a broken rhythm of beats that ebbs and flows like a pulse with the action. It creates an air of Middle Eastern opulence and exoticism that is truly unique and unforgettable. It is here that Royler takes his lonely stand upon the mat. He is slim and fit looking, but strangely lacking in musculature compared with the other athletes. His face is now locked in the combat mask of the professional fighter. Tight-lipped. Unblinking. The countenance of determination and will.

For Royler Gracie the pressure now is intense. Last year, at this same event, making his Abu Dhabi debut, Royler had literally blasted through his elite opposition in the under 66 kg light-weight division. In a display that captured the attention of the grappling world, Royler attacked his opponents with furious abandon, bustling them off the mat, driving them into mistakes and confusion, constantly pressuring them with submission holds and attacks. That year he and his cousin Jean Jacques Machado were the two outstanding competitors. In the finals, Royler clashed with another great Brazilian champion, Soca, a man who himself stands at the top of the grappling world, the winner of the inaugural Abu Dhabi tournament. In an electrifying final, Royler caught Soca in a brutal ankle lock to gain an unexpectedly quick victory. Now, one year later, the two champions face each other in the finals again. Royler now has the chance to become the first man to win back-to-back Abu Dhabi tournament titles. To become the only repeat champion to this point. Soca has the chance to avenge last year's defeat and regain his world title. Royler's cousin and close friend, Renzo Gracie, will win his second title later in the day—but this is Royler's turn. The two men meet in the middle and shake hands. So much can change in a year. A fighter learns new moves to counter and thwart his opponents, improves his conditioning, studies his opponents in detail, probing for weaknesses. Soca will not be caught in an ankle lock this year. Like any great strategist, Royler does not remain strategically static. Last year he was a blaze of action, ruthless in his pursuit of submission holds. Now his opponents are expecting this. This year he has changed to a style emphasizing control and positional dominance to stay ahead of the pack.

Royler and Soca square off. Royler starts to attack from the word go; Soca has to put him in the guard. Now the onslaught begins. Royler methodically passes the guard and stays on Soca's side. He knows that the points do not start counting until the ten-minute mark, so he does a series of attacks attempting to submit Soca without losing his superior position. Just prior to the ten-minute mark, Royler the strategist lets himself be put in half guard. As soon as the ten-minute mark hits he passes the guard; points are scored. He puts knee on stomach; more points are scored. Back to side control and now mounts. As soon as the points are scored he jumps back to side control. Back to knee on stomach. Methodical, precise, relentless, and totally in control. He wins by a large score, perhaps the largest margin of the competition.

Soca, awesomely skilled as he is, cannot withstand Royler's onslaught. Here among the very world's best, Royler Gracie has prevailed for the second year running. Another

great victory in what must be one of the most prolific and successful competition careers in martial arts history. In addition to his double Abu Dhabi wins, Royler is four-time world Brazilian jiu-jitsu champion and multi-time winner of the Brazilian national and Pan-American jiu-jitsu tournaments. He regularly competes in the absolute division of these events, where there is no weight limit, and prevails against highly skilled opponents far larger than he. He has competed in and won a world Brazilian jiu-jitsu championship while virtually immobilized by food poisoning. He fights in MMA events against far larger opponents. Especially noteworthy in his second Abu Dhabi performance was the fact that in the course of winning the championship, *Royler never had a point scored upon him!* He is the everywhere man of Brazilian jiu-jitsu, competing in all the major tournaments. His involvement in the sport is massive—making him one of the sport's most popular and recognizable figures. Royler's fighting lineage is well known. He is a son of Helio Gracie and brother to perhaps the most revered Gracie of all, Rickson. For all his fame in the tournament scene, it is in the field of no-rules fighting that Royler first became known to most American martial artists. In the documentary series, *Gracies in Action,* Royler is featured in a number of clashes with other martial arts styles in order to determine their relative effectiveness. Royler showed stunning speed and ferocity in dismantling a larger Kempo karate expert.

The sheer ease of his performance embedded it into the consciousness of many progressive martial artists. The shock value of the video was immense. To a generation of martial artists raised on the idea that a single punch or kick from an expert would destroy an attacker, this scene was pure revelation. It amounted to the breaking of old myths and gods. It was a lesson in the reality of real combat and it carried with it the force of change and upheaval. The pattern of Gracie-style fighting was imprinted: take the fight quickly to the ground, gain control, finish the opponent. The ease with which this was done against the so-called masters of traditional martial arts was the stuff of revolution.

Royler gained immense respect as a fighter when a black-market video became available in the United States featuring him in a brutal and protracted fight with a Brazilian Luta-livre fighter. The opponent was immensely powerful and very skilled in a style quite similar to jiu-jitsu. In a harrowing, marathon fight, which at one stage saw Royler knocked out on his feet, Royler defended, then attacked, until the fighter had to quit, walking away from the fight after exhaustion and frustration had taken their toll. The grainy video image of that remarkable clash left an indelible image of Royler as a warrior and a champion in the minds of a great many martial artists.

Royler Gracie was born in Rio de Janeiro, Brazil. He is the fifth son of Grandmaster Helio Gracie. He started jiu-jitsu at the age of three, playing soccer in a gi in his family academy. As soon as he was old enough to compete, the young Royler started his illustrious competition career. He has been competing as a black belt for more than twenty years and has had more than three hundred matches in that time span. He has won the world championship four years running along with several national and regional titles. He was the most active sport jiu-jitsu competitor during that period, always ready to test himself against people of all sizes holding many different titles. Royler has a fire burning inside that propels him to achieve things no other person has achieved in the sport.

When one looks at Royler the most striking characteristic is his slight frame. This image is reinforced when he takes on opponents far larger than himself. His lack of brawn has made Royler the technician par excellence. He is totally dependent upon superior technique for victory. This technical perfection makes Royler one of the most skillful and adept of the Gracie clan. He is the pure jiu-jitsu man's fighter. Precise, technical, relaxed—always looking to employ technique and strategy against strength. As a result, Royler can teach anyone, even the physically ungifted and weak, to prevail in a fight. This makes him one of the most sought after instructors in the martial arts world. He is the living embodiment of the martial artist's dream of skill and technique overcoming strength and aggression. Eighteen years as a black belt instructor and leading member of the most famous grappling team in the world make him one of the foremost coaches in the world. His teaching schedule is brutal. Every day he rises early to teach private lessons through the length of the day, then the group class at night. Only a handful of people can legitimately claim the fighting and coaching expertise of this remarkable figure, arms now raised in victory, game face now replaced by the broad smile of success and glory.

JOHN DANAHER: Renzo Gracie laughingly points out that John Danaher's role as writer of the book was "a conspiracy on the part of the universe." How else can you account for the odd and conflicting set of attributes that made him the man uniquely qualified to put into words the ideas and themes that Renzo and Royler Gracie wanted to convey to the martial arts world? Danaher moved to New York from his native New Zealand in the early 1990s just as the Gracies were making their appearance on the world stage. His original goal was to study philosophy at Columbia University. The life of a graduate student is fascinating and enriching—but not financially! To improve his meager income, Danaher worked as a bouncer in several nightclubs and bars in New York for nearly a decade. Working as a security professional in a New York City nightclub has its share of hazards. Hard experience in the world of nightclub violence convinced him that the key to success in real-world altercations and subduing of violence lay primarily in grappling skill. Disillusioned with traditional martial arts, Danaher became an enthusiastic advocate of Brazilian jiu-

jitsu after being introduced to Renzo Gracie by a friend. Within weeks he was applying the techniques he learned in real-life scenarios on a regular basis. Juggling the study and teaching of philosophy at an Ivy League university with the quelling and removal of unruly bar patrons might seem an unusual contrast. However, it was this, along with intense and deep study of Brazilian jiu-jitsu from one of the very best practitioners in the world that made Danaher oddly well suited to write this book. The analytic and teaching skills honed in his extensive formal education created in Danaher the skill of breaking down and understanding technique and then being able to verbalize it to others. His obsession with technical detail and willingness to absorb his teacher's knowledge, along with frequent opportunities to put that knowledge to the test in real scenarios created a student with technical depth wedded to practical experience who could convey his knowledge in the clearest way to the martial arts reader. In time he became an instructor at Renzo Gracie's New York City Brazilian jiu-jitsu academy where he is a familiar face both teaching or training.

KID PELIGRO: When Sheik Tahnoon originally conceived the book project he chose to place ultimate responsibility for the production of the book in the hands of his friend and perhaps the best-known and most widely read martial arts writer in the world, Kid Peligro. Peligro is a black belt in Brazilian jiu-jitsu with two world titles in the masters division and a reputation for technical knowledge. His proximity to many of the very best grapplers in the world places him in a unique position to learn, assess, and disseminate the latest developments in this rapidly changing sport. Writing as the premier spokesman for the ADCC, the most respected web site and news source for contemporary martial arts, Peligro forged a reputation for journalistic excellence. He now writes for leading martial arts magazines in North and South America.

The problem confronting Peligro was that of successfully presenting in book form Sheik Tahnoon's vision: that of instituting a basic standard for instruction in Brazilian jiu-jitsu. There was no precedent for such a book. The entire project had to be created from the ground up in a way that would satisfy the general martial arts reader and the jiu-jitsu specialist. Having conceived an overall design for the book, Peligro assembled a highly qualified team of experts who could make the design a reality. Everyone involved in the project was an expert not only in their allotted task regarding the book's production, but also in Brazilian jiu-jitsu. The overall design of the book was worked out in close contact with Renzo, Royler, and Sheik Tahnoon. Having laid the groundwork for the project and selected the right people to construct it, Peligro oversaw the work in development. His agreeable nature, combined with a total commitment to the success of the project, ensured that the inevitable problems associated with the production of a large, authoritative book were overcome.

SHEIK TAHNOON BIN ZAYED AL NAYAN is one of the sons of Sheik Zayed, President of the United Arab Emirates. Sheik Tahnoon fell in love with the grappling arts while attending college in the United States. He started practicing Brazilian jiu-jitsu and quickly developed a passion for the sport. From then on he started to expand his horizons and learned several other martial arts. He is a certified black belt in Brazilian jiu-jitsu and an expert in Russian sambo, freestyle wrestling, and Muay Thai. Upon returning to his home country, Sheik Tahnoon created the Abu Dhabi Combat Club with the goal of having a center for the martial arts for his people to enjoy. He proceeded to invite experts from all over the world to teach and develop a world-class program for fighters. But he wasn't satisfied. His vision was not complete; so he proceeded to develop the ADCC World Submission Wrestling Tournament, a tournament in which the best and most famous grapplers in the world would compete against each other to select who was the best. The event has evolved to be considered the pinnacle of grappling competition worldwide and has been imitated across the globe. It has become so large and has enveloped so many people all over the world that it has spawned a whole new sport called submission grappling. Submission grappling has become a passion, and tournaments similar to the ADCC Submission Wrestling Championships have appeared all over the world and influence a generation of practitioners.

But Sheik Tahnoon's vision was still not complete. He wanted a book that would present the sport to all people, and inspire more people to practice the sport. He saw that Brazilian jiu-jitsu was expanding across the continents with no real guide or standard. The purpose of the book was to set a standard so that practitioners and laypeople all over the globe could be exposed to Brazilian jiu-jitsu and learn the philosophy and theory behind it. He wanted to leave a legacy for his children and his friends about the sport he loves so much. This book is the result of those dreams.

His Highness the Sheik Tahnoon Bin Zayed Al Nayan explains the rules of his Abu Dhabi Submission Wrestling World Championship, one day before the 1999 edition of the tournament.

Kid Peligro's involvement in the sport and martial art of Brazilian jiu-jitsu is huge. In covering the major events from MMA tournaments in Japan, America, and Brazil, submission wrestling in the Middle East, and Brazilian jiu-jitsu championships in North and South America, he is one of the most widely traveled and recognized figures in the martial arts. This, combined with more than a decade as a student and competitor in the sport and a very clear sense of the underlying purpose behind the book project made him the supervisor par excellence. The book's production quality is testimony to Peligro's skill in supervision and to the care and effort that this tireless jiu-jitsu enthusiast placed in the project.

Part 1: Theory

Tap-out! Renzo forces the powerful Japanese fighter, Kikuta-san, to signal submission in a tough MMA fight with a variation of the guillotine choke (demonstrated in the technique section).

The Current Revolution in the World of Martial Arts

The Fundamental Problem of the Martial Arts

Much is made of the differences between the various styles of martial arts. What is common to all styles of combat is a core problem that each tries to answer. *How can one successfully defend oneself against attack by a bigger, stronger, and more aggressive opponent?* All martial arts, if they are to be considered *martial*, must furnish an answer to this fundamental question.

To be sure, this fundamental question is often complicated by bringing in additional concerns, such as whether there is more than one attacker, whether the attacker is armed or not, and so on. Some styles claim that a martial art must address a great many questions, ranging from moral conduct to broad questions of lifestyle. Nonetheless, the core problem that any martial art worthy of the name must address remains—how can one best defend oneself against attack by a physically superior opponent?

In response to this common problem it would seem that every country and culture has offered a different answer. There are a vast number of different martial arts. While there are some obvious similarities between styles, one cannot help but notice the dramatic differences. An immediate query that arises in the face of these competing answers to the fundamental problem is this: *Which style gives the best answer to the fundamental problem of the martial arts?*

Most people are familiar with the broad stylistic differences. Korean styles generally favor high, powerful kicking attacks. Japanese and Okinawan karate emphasize low stances with powerful linear blocks and punches. Wing Chun kung fu advocates an upright stance along with low kicks and intricate hand-trapping skills. The list of styles is long and each has its distinctive features.

A very different response to the fundamental problem of the martial arts is offered by the *grappling* styles. Unlike the vast majority of fighting styles, which have favored kicking and punching as the best route to victory, grappling arts focus on getting a hold on your opponent and using this grip to take him down to the ground. Once on the ground the opponent can be controlled in a pin or submission hold. Judo, sambo, and Olympic wrestling were for years the most well-known grappling styles.

There is little question that for most of the period after World War II, when martial arts first became very popular in the West, grappling arts were a distant second in popularity to the more spectacular-looking striking arts. Indeed, wrestling was for many years not even considered a martial art all. Judo, despite its prestige as an Olympic sport was not taken seriously as a fighting art. Sambo, the national grappling style of the former Soviet Union, was barely known in the West until the 1990s.

So then, we are struck by the many different responses to the fundamental question of the martial arts. The question that begs for an answer has always been: *Which style answers best the fundamental problem of the martial arts?* This was the unavoidable question that for many years everyone asked, but no one tried seriously to answer.

Determining the Respective Merit of Styles through Mixed Martial Arts (MMA) Competition

There would seem to be a very simple way to determine which martial arts were superior to others. One could take fighters who were well qualified in their field and match them against fighters from other styles with no rules or interference to mar the result. One could then see if there were any styles that consistently outperformed the others over a period of time. This would furnish an empirical answer to the question of which style was the better one. While this might seem an obvious way to resolve the problem, it was not until the 1990s that mixed martial arts (MMA) competitions, pitting different styles against each other with very few rules, began in North America. Unbeknownst to most martial artists, such MMA events had been going on for years in South America. These however had been ignored, possibly because for generations Asia had been seen as the source of martial arts expertise. The early MMA events were bare knuckle, with either no time limit at all or a very long time limit, no weight categories, and *very* few rules—only prohibitions on eye gouging and biting. This was as close to a real fight as civil society would allow. Different stylists flocked to the events to represent their art.

Analysis of the Early MMA Events

Most people's *expectations* of the early MMA events were simple enough. These expectations represented decades of misinformation and unjustified assumptions that had crept into traditional martial arts precisely because they had drifted so far away from the real combat that MMA events offered. The vast majority of martial artists assumed that whoever kicked and punched harder than everyone else, while taking less punishment, would win by simply blasting his opponents into bloody defeat. To the utter amazement of the martial arts community, this was not at all the case. The vast majority of the fights followed a very similar pattern. Both combatants would begin with punches and kicks then quickly go into a clinch. Then, either by accident or design, they would fall to the ground. Those fighters with expertise in grappling actively sought to take the fight to the ground while the others simply wound up there despite their intention not to. To the shock and embarrassment of most martial artists, once a fight went to the ground, most of the supposedly highly skilled martial artists were utterly lost and flailed about helplessly, utterly unsure how to cope with this unanticipated situation. Victory after victory was won by those fighters versed in grappling. A number of points quickly became clear. First, people trained only in standing striking skills were very vulnerable to being taken down to the ground, where their striking was almost useless. Second, grapplers could force strikers to play their grappling game (by closing the distance into a clinch or takedown) far more easily than strikers could force grapplers to play a striking game. Third, skill on the ground was a far more reliable indicator of success in MMA combat than striking ability. Fourth, submission holds—locks and strangles that force an opponent to give up or face severe injury to the joints or unconsciousness—were the most efficient route to victory, far more so than strikes.

Over time a combination of spectator demands and political pressure forced the addition of more rules governing MMA events. In spite of new rules, weight categories, rounds, and time limits current MMA events still carry much of the flavor of the early MMA shows. The skill level of the combatants has risen tremendously. No longer does one see naive entrants who know nothing of ground grappling. The emerging trend of current MMA events is the "complete" fighter, one well versed in both grappling and striking, comfortable on his feet, in the clinch, defending and initiating takedowns, and, crucially, on the ground.

Brazilian Jiu-Jitsu in MMA Competition

Of all the many fighting styles represented in early MMA competition, none had a more decisive impact than Brazilian jiu-jitsu. Due to its unanticipated success against other styles, Brazilian jiu-jitsu went from obscurity to international renown in a staggeringly short time. The biggest MMA events in North America, the Ultimate Fighting Championship, Extreme Fighting, the World Combat Championship, and Martial Arts Reality, were all dominated by practitioners of Brazilian jiu-jitsu. Especially surprising to most viewers was the fact that the Brazilian jiu-jitsu fighters were almost always considerably smaller than their opponents. In addition, the victories were relatively bloodless affairs. The Brazilian fighters did not have to resort to bludgeoning their foes into defeat. Rather, they quickly took them to the ground and then caught them in various strangles and locks, forcing them to give up. In the few cases where Brazilian jiu-jitsu fighters were themselves taken down by their opponent, they were able to use their highly refined ground-grappling skills to win fights from *underneath* opponents. This was quite radical at the time, for most people had the notion that the man on top in a fight was almost assured of victory. Unfolding before everyone's eyes was the realization of the martial arts dream—*to see a fighting style that allowed a smaller, weaker man to overcome and defeat a larger, stronger, skilled opponent with a minimum of violence and blood*. Early response to this success on the part of the martial arts community was varied. Some claimed that MMA competition was immoral or somehow contrary to the spirit of the martial arts. Others gave grudging admiration of the results but claimed that the new style would not work in a real street fight where there was a danger of weapons and multiple opponents. Progressive martial artists, however, quickly took note of the results and sought to learn Brazilian jiu-jitsu, either as a style they wished to emulate, or at least so they could learn how to counter the devastating moves and techniques that were wreaking havoc in MMA competition. In either case, progressive martial artists were anxious to learn this new art. This was the shot heard around the martial arts world—the revolution had begun.

An Analysis of the Success of Brazilian Jiu-Jitsu in MMA Competition

Previous to the first MMA events in North America, few people would have considered Brazilian jiu-jitsu a style likely to dominate the others in open competition. It is worth asking *why it was the case that Brazilian jiu-jitsu was able to do so well against other styles in such a consistent fashion*. Answering this question can illuminate much that is important in fighting theory. Even a cursory analysis of the early MMA events quickly reveals a number of factors.

Brazilian jiu-jitsu could succeed regardless of whether the Brazilian jiu-jitsu stylist took his opponent down and landed in a top position or whether he was himself taken down and had to fight from underneath. In the unpredictable and chaotic action of real fighting this proved a great advantage. When facing a far larger opponent it was often the case that fighters quickly found themselves on their back and had to fight from there. The Brazilian jiu-jitsu fighters were very successful at this, often surprising their bigger, stronger opponents.

The *training methodology* of Brazilian jiu-jitsu allowed its practitioners to use the same strategy and techniques that they used in actual fights at full power on a fully resisting opponent. By constantly training in the same way they fought, the Brazilians were very comfortable once the action started—actual fighting had few surprises for them. The crucial role of training method is a subject to which we shall return later in more detail.

The *point system* utilized in training and Brazilian jiu-jitsu competition is designed to reflect the most important elements of a real fight. Points are awarded according to how well a student moves into positions that allow him to dominate and finish an opponent in a *real fight*. This ingrains in the student the principles and body movements needed to do well in actual combat. For example, anyone can see that there is an obvious advantage to pinning your opponent down from on top of his chest. From there you can hold him down and strike him at will while he can do little in return. This fact is represented in the Brazilian jiu-jitsu point system by rewarding the attainment of this dominating position with the maximum of four points. This gives direct encouragement to the student to always seek this dominating position as he or she trains until it becomes an ingrained habit—one that will prove exceedingly useful in real combat.

The *lack of restrictions* upon students of Brazilian jiu-jitsu as they train and compete in their sport prepares them well for the reality of actual combat. *Real* combat is totally without restrictions—you can do whatever you please to attain victory. In contrast, *sporting* combat is full of rules, restrictions, and referee intervention. For example, in boxing the referee stops the action as soon as the fighters enter a clinch. In Thai boxing the action is stopped as soon as one fighter goes to the ground. In Olympic wrestling one cannot apply submission holds at all. In judo one can only do so to the elbow joint (along with strangles). In Brazilian jiu-jitsu there is stunningly little referee intervention. Once a fight begins the referee does little more than count the points and keep the fighters inside the circle. The fighters can apply submission holds to the ankles, knees, hips, spine, neck, shoulders, wrists, and elbows. Also, strangles and muscle crushing is allowed. This lack of intervention and restriction prepares students for the unrestrained nature of real combat.

The *fighting heritage* of Brazilian jiu-jitsu was a crucial element in the success of Brazilian fighters in MMA competition. The Gracie family came from a long tradition in their native Brazil of fighting in MMA events. This experience gave them a good idea of what to expect when fighting with very few rules. In contrast, their opponents were largely heading into the unknown.

The possession of a simple, yet highly effective, combat-proven strategy married to highly refined technique imprinted in the student through daily training was a massive advantage. Most of the early entrants to MMA events had no real overall strategy as to how they would defeat their opponents other than a vague notion of smashing their opponents into submission. To their surprise they found this was far more difficult than anticipated, especially once they were locked in a clinch and fell to the ground. The Brazilian jiu-jitsu fighters, on the other hand, were always working within an *overall strategy*. They sought to close the distance to their opponent as quickly as possible to limit any potential damage. From there they took the fight to the ground, where they could nullify their opponent's skills. Once on the ground they were constantly looking to improve their position, advancing step by step toward their goal of getting to a position from where they could finish their opponent with a submission hold. This gave the Brazilian fighters *a clear sense of direction at all times in the fight*. In addition *they had the technical knowledge to implement that strategy in an efficient way*. There was never any question of what they ought to be doing at any time in the course of the fight. This immediate sense of purpose and strategy was in marked contrast to the confusion and indecision of their opponents, most of whom had no idea what they ought to be doing at any point in the fight once they were in a clinch.

Brazilian Jiu-Jitsu as an Answer to the Fundamental Problem of the Martial Arts

We have seen that the core problem at the heart of the martial arts is that of protecting oneself against attack by a bigger, stronger, and more aggressive opponent. MMA events gave the best available means of evaluating the different responses to that problem. The evidence furnished by these MMA competitions was very clear. Grappling was a potent element of real fighting that had been almost entirely neglected by the martial arts community. Traditional martial arts based upon standing striking and kicking skills proved incapable of dealing with grappling attacks that bound the strikers in a tight clinch and took them to the ground, where striking power was largely negated. Foremost among the grappling arts was the hitherto unknown Brazilian jiu-jitsu whose success was as unexpected as it was clear-cut. The record showed that Brazilian jiu-jitsu was undoubtably one of the very best answers to our fundamental problem.

In the face of this success, it is worth asking: *What is the answer of Brazilian jiu-jitsu to the fundamental problem of the martial arts?* A clear statement of that answer can be offered now.

Contrary to the advice of most martial arts, Brazilian jiu-jitsu does not advocate engaging in a standing striking battle with your opponent. Such a strategy exposes one to too high a risk of losing to a bigger, stronger opponent, since he will hit harder than you can as a result of his greater size and weight. In addition, experience has shown that such

striking cannot be relied upon to stop and defeat an opponent who is determined to charge into you and grapple. The traditional doctrine of "one strike, one kill" is simply not borne out by experience. A much safer option is to close the gap and enter into a clinch, from where you can prevent your opponent from punching you while at the same time using grappling skill to off-balance your opponent and control his movement. From here you can either strike your opponent with knees and elbows (preventing him from doing the same by off-balancing him and controlling his body through grappling technique) or take the fight to the ground. Once in a clinch it is very likely that the fight will go to the ground, either by design (one fighter deliberately takes the other down) or by accident (one or both fighters trip and fall). A common misconception is that Brazilian jiu-jitsu *always* advocates taking a fight to the ground. In MMA events this is true, since you are engaged with only one opponent and the floor surface is favorable. In some street fights the Brazilian jiu-jitsu student might well decide to resist going to the ground, perhaps because he fears being kicked on the ground by his opponent's comrades, or because the ground surface is hazardous. In such a case he or she can stay in a standing clinch and fight from there or break the clinch and look to escape. What Brazilian jiu-jitsu recognizes as a hard fact of life that many traditional martial arts do not, is that *in a real fight it is usually not a matter of choice whether you end up on the ground—*it just happens—regardless of your stated intentions. The weakness of the answer given to the fundamental problem of the martial arts by most styles is that they do not take into account the actions and intentions of the opponent, or the wild and chaotic nature of real fighting. Part of Brazilian jiu-jitsu's answer to the fundamental problem of the martial arts is that fighting on the ground is not a choice, but is almost always made necessary by events. *Ironically, the people who are best qualified to keep a fight standing are grapplers, since they spend a good deal time practicing clinching and takedowns.* This makes them skilled at resisting takedown attempts when they so desire.

Nonetheless, the kind of positional dominance and control sought after by Brazilian jiu-jitsu practitioners is best attained on the ground, where most people do not know how to move and where body weight and the floor can be used to thwart an opponent. Hence the preference for taking a fight to the ground when circumstances favor it.

The essential idea behind Brazilian jiu-jitsu's answer to the fundamental problem of the martial arts is this: *You must constantly strive to put yourself in a position where you can control your opponent as much as possible. Thus allowing you to do maximal damage to him while exposing yourself to as little potential damage as possible.* This is the answer in a nutshell. In practice this generally means getting into a tight clinch as quickly as possible, thus preventing your opponent from striking you effectively. From here you can control him by holding his head or upper body while off-balancing him, or better yet, slipping behind him. If you desire to stay standing you can attack with knees, elbows, and standing submission holds. If you decide to take the fight to the ground, or if you end up there anyway, you will seek to maneuver yourself into a controlling position where you can strike your opponent far more successfully than he can strike back and then finish with a submission hold. The coldly efficient theoretical core of Brazilian jiu-jitsu is the idea that you should seek always to place yourself in a position where you can damage your opponent while he cannot damage you. The myriad techniques of Brazilian jiu-jitsu are designed to enable a fighter to bring about this goal. This strategy can only be realized by *grappling* with your opponent. After all, you cannot control your opponent without grabbing him in some way. This is half of the reason why Brazilian jiu-jitsu advocates grappling as the answer to the fundamental problem of the martial arts. The other half is the unavoidable fact that regardless of your intentions it is almost impossible for you to stop your opponent from grappling with you if he attempts it. The record shows that in a real fight he almost certainly *will* attempt it. This is why Brazilian jiu-jitsu advocates grappling as the most important part of its answer to the fundamental problem of the martial arts.

Ground Fighting and Self-defense

Ever since the advent of mixed martial arts events with very few rules, martial artists have been forced to acknowledge the crucial role played by grappling, both on the ground and standing. One often hears the adage, "If you do not know how to fight on the ground, you do not know how to fight." In contrast to this recent enthusiasm for grappling, one also hears the opinion that whatever the pattern of fighting in a mixed martial arts event, in an actual street fight the ground is the last place you would want to be. Many people reason that putting oneself on the ground in a street fight is tantamount to suicide. By doing so you expose yourself to the danger of being kicked into defeat by other people, of being badly cut up and bruised on hard pavement, of being eye gouged, bitten, suffering attacks to the groin and other dangers. Thus there is a split in opinion between those who advocate grappling for self-defense purposes and those who claim it is suitable only for MMA events. Brazilian jiu-jitsu takes a clear stand in this debate. Followers of the Brazilian style *do* advocate grappling for self-defense purposes. Nonetheless we must be clear that this does not mean that Brazilian jiu-jitsu practitioners *always* advocate taking a fight to the ground. Of course there will be times when common sense suggests that avoiding a ground-grappling situation is the sensible thing to do.

People tend to underestimate the versatility of Brazilian jiu-jitsu because when they see it in action in mixed martial arts events, ground fighting plays the major role. However, Brazilian jiu-jitsu has a great range of techniques in a standing clinch situation that allows a student to defeat an aggressor without going to the ground. Some of these techniques will be directly addressed in this book. Moreover, by constantly working on takedown practice, the grappling student becomes very adept at countering attempts to take him down. Ironically, this makes grapplers the best qualified among martial artists at remaining on their feet during an attack if they should elect to. Fights go to the ground either by accident or by design. If you should accidentally trip and fall while locked with an attacker any shortcomings in ground fighting will likely prove disastrous. At other times, grappling makes perfect sense, an option you can deliberately choose. There is no more effective means of overwhelming an aggressor than to take him to the ground where he can be controlled and dominated. This control gives you a tremendous range of options to apply, depending on the contingencies of the situation. One can be surprisingly gentle or very brutal toward one's attacker when holding complete control over him—grappling gives you the choice. Should you not desire to go to the ground, whether for fear of multiple attackers or the fear of the hard cement pavement, you can use your grappling skills to avoid being taken down or to engage in standing grappling in the clinch. Do not think that Brazilian jiu-jitsu is entirely limited in its outlook toward self-defense. It does not mindlessly claim that you should always go to the ground. On the contrary. It will save you if you should be taken to the ground and it can allow you to dominate and control an attacker if you should choose to take the fight to the ground. However, it also gives you the tools to remain standing and to fight from there, should that be your choice.

Critics of grappling for self-defense purposes also claim that foul tactics, banned in mixed martial arts events—tactics such as biting, groin grabbing, and eye gouging, significantly undermine the street effectiveness of grappling. Doubtless such tactics can have some effect in a real fight, but one should not overestimate their role. If your attacker is close enough to engage in biting or eye gouging, then you are close enough to do the same to him. Moreover, you can use your grappling skills to gain a superior position from which your biting and eye gouging will be far more devastating than his. There are numerous counters to such foul tactics. A person well versed in grappling can readily adapt his body's position to protect his vulnerable groin and eyes during a real fight. Accordingly, these threats represent more of a nuisance to the experienced grappler than a real threat.

Probably the most common complaint with regard to grappling as a viable means of self-defense is that grappling is useless against multiple opponents. The argument is that in locking with one attacker, one is easily attacked by his partners in crime. This is entirely true. Grappling skills will not allow you to destroy several attackers at once. Brazilian jiu-jitsu makes no claim to teach a method of overwhelming mass attacks. Should you be heavily outnumbered, Brazilian jiu-jitsu will not save you. *It is the contention of the authors that no other style of empty-hand fighting will save you either.* The martial arts world is full of overinflated claims. One of the most common is that one unarmed man can defeat many aggressive, dangerous attackers at once. The irony is that many of the stylists who made such grandiose claims proved entirely incapable of defeating even a single attacker when put to the test in mixed martial arts competition. Such claims are the stuff of fantasy and belong more to the realm of martial arts movies than a book concerned with real fighting.

History

Accounts of the histories of most martial arts are often marred by a lack of any genuine historical evidence to vindicate the claims being made. Too often the "evidence" is merely anecdotal or legendary accounts that would be unacceptable in any other sphere. In addition, petty nationalistic concerns often creep into the tale. Each style is linked to a particular national or cultural tradition that the author is keen to eulogize. Such nationalism has no place in an attempt to establish an effective style of combat.

Our historical account of Brazilian jiu-jitsu is aided by the fact that most of the events are fairly recent and quite well documented. The actual history of the events and personalities is a long and fascinating tale. However, the focus of this book is on the theory and technique of Brazilian jiu-jitsu, not the precise history of its foundation. Instead of offering a detailed survey of the historical facts, we shall look at the themes and elements that emerge from the history of Brazilian jiu-jitsu and contribute to its effectiveness as a fighting style. Thus we offer a *historical analysis* rather than history per se. Our analysis seeks to discern what factors in the history of Brazilian jiu-jitsu made it so successful in MMA competition.

Most people involved in the martial arts are familiar with the basic story of Brazilian jiu-jitsu. How a Japanese jiu-jitsu expert, Maeda, came to Brazil as part of a diplomatic mission to found and establish a Japanese colony. He befriended Gastao Gracie, a man of Scottish descent who had influence in local political circles. Maeda offered to teach Gracie's sons jiu-jitsu. The Gracie boys became very proficient in jiu-jitsu, opening their own schools and developing their own additions and modifications to the techniques they had been taught. As a test of their technique, the Gracies fought many matches against other styles with great success.

In this manner they came to learn which techniques worked and which did not. They based their developing martial art on their combat experiences over generations. As succeeding generations of Gracies grew into the "family trade," the wealth of experience continued to grow until a move to the United States by many senior members of the Gracie family and jiu-jitsu's astounding success in North American MMA events brought overnight recognition and stardom. So much for the broad outline. We need to get into specifics if our analysis is to have worth.

The Japanese Legacy

The origins of Brazilian jiu-jitsu stem from Japan around the beginning of the twentieth century. Jiu-jitsu had existed for centuries in Japan. Its earliest origins are not entirely clear. India is often regarded as the original source of jiu-jitsu although there is insufficient evidence to verify this claim. Ancient Japanese texts make reference to various grappling styles, and there are many scrolls depicting ancient jiu-jitsu technique that is quite recognizable to a modern jiu-jitsu student. *Jiu-jitsu* translates as "gentle art" or "soft art." The term would appear to be something of a misnomer, for jiu-jitsu was a fighting art with direct links to the bloody battlefields of feudal Japan. It encompassed punches, kicks, painful pressure point attacks, throws, strangleholds, and joint locks. The term "gentle art" was meant to convey the guiding idea that lies beneath *all* jiu-jitsu, both classical Japanese and modern

Royler Gracie attacks Vinícius Magalhães to win his first jiu-jitsu world title in February 1996.

Brazilian—the idea of using one's strength in the most efficient way. Rather than resisting force with force, the idea is to yield to force and then use an opponent's strength against him, *using efficient technique in an intelligent fashion to overcome raw strength and aggression*—this is the philosophical core of jiu-jitsu. It is by following this principle that a smaller man can hope to defeat a stronger, bigger man. *This* is the sense in which an art teaching eye gouging, strangulation, groin strikes, and so forth can be termed a "gentle art." Many different *ryu* or schools of jiu-jitsu had emerged in Japan, each with its own particular emphasis. Some concentrated on throws, others on ground grappling, others on striking. As long as Japan maintained a feudal society based on warrior virtues, jiu-jitsu was elevated in importance. However, the massive sociological changes that swept through Japan when feudalism was dropped in favor of modernization along Western lines totally undercut the need for jiu-jitsu. With the demise of the samurai and of the martial tradition they stood for, demand for jiu-jitsu dropped away, contributing to the demise of classical jiu-jitsu in Japan. By the mid– to late nineteenth century, jiu-jitsu was in serious decline. Many of the old masters had to eke out a living as physical therapists, using their knowledge of human anatomy to help them. Others fought in show matches for money. Many came to be regarded as a public nuisance, as a violent and unwelcome hangover from a past era.

The Influence of Jigoro Kano

Jigoro Kano (1860–1938) took up the study of jiu-jitsu as a means to improve a frail physique and in response to persistent bullying in school. After immersing himself in study he became very proficient in several classical styles of jiu-jitsu, especially Kito ryu and Tenjin Shin'yo ryu, eventually taking over teaching responsibilities at his dojo. While studying jiu-jitsu, Kano saw several problems that had to be overcome. Some of these were sociological. Jiu-jitsu was losing popularity at the time Kano began study. There was some danger that it would die out completely if care was not taken to preserve the techniques. In addition, Kano had reservations about the kind of people training in jiu-jitsu (many of them were seen as little more than thugs who gave jiu-jitsu a bad name) and the motivations they had for training. The public's view of jiu-jitsu and its practitioners as violent and archaic was worrisome. Kano also saw problems in the very nature of classical jiu-jitsu. *It was really just a collection of isolated techniques.* There was, Kano perceived, no overall strategy or guiding principle behind it. Rather than offering the student a comprehensive guide or strategy as to how he should act throughout the dynamics of a fight, classical jiu-jitsu was simply an accumulation of "tricks" designed to overcome an

opponent through the efficient use of the body. Another major problem that Kano saw in classical jiu-jitsu was the teaching method. Classical jiu-jitsu was taught almost entirely by *kata*— pre-arranged, choreographed sequences where two training partners followed a pattern of movements without resisting each other. "Live" training (sparring) was done in only a few schools and only at the highest levels. This was made necessary by the fact that classical jiu-jitsu contained many dangerous moves, eye gouges, groin strikes, hair pulling, and so forth. Obviously these cannot be practiced at full power without seriously injuring your partner. Accordingly kata was the means of instruction. This meant that students never got the feel of applying their moves on a resisting opponent. Obviously you cannot expect your opponent in a real fight to cooperate with you as you try to apply techniques on him, so the training in classical jiu-jitsu appeared artificial. The weakness of training only in kata can be seen easily enough. Kata is to real fighting as riding a stationary exercise bicycle is to riding a real bicycle. They may appear similar, but proficiency in riding the stationary exercise bicycle is no guarantee of skill in riding the real bicycle. In response to these problems, Kano sought to rejuvenate classical jiu-jitsu with a complete overhaul.

The Genius of Kano

The originality and genius of Kano in the history of the martial arts and of grappling in particular lay in his insight concerning the need for a radical revision in the way students trained the techniques they were shown. Kano was not a great innovator in technique; most of what he knew in terms of technique was taken from old jiu-jitsu schools. His great innovation lay in the way he taught and trained his students in those techniques. The most crucial element that Kano instituted in his Kodakan School was randori, or live sparring. The idea was for two students to train "live" with each other, each trying as hard as he could to apply technique on the other. By this means students could become familiar with the feeling of applying technique on a live, resisting human being. This, as you can imagine, is far more difficult than applying technique on a cooperating training partner in some choreographed kata. Such live training develops far greater physical and mental agility and speed in the student and prepares them well for the tiring and unpredictable movement of real combat. In order for randori to be possible, Kano saw that the dangerous elements of jiu-jitsu would have to be removed. One cannot engage in daily sparring sessions with full power strikes, hair pulling, and eye gouging! To prevent unacceptable attrition through injury, Kano removed strikes and "foul" tactics from randori. Joint locks were limited to the elbow (this was deemed safer than locks to the legs, spine, neck, wrists, and shoulders). In this way students could grapple at full power with little risk of injury, thus gaining crucial expertise in applying techniques on an opponent who was fighting back at them.

The Paradox of Randori

The practice of removing the dangerous elements of a martial art so students can train harder might strike the reader as strange. After all, wouldn't a martial art be more *deadly* and *effective* if students were taught and practiced the really dangerous, painful moves such as those used in classical jiu-jitsu? Does it not *weaken* a martial art to remove such techniques? Herein lies the true innovative genius of Kano. Counterintuitive as it might seem, Kano saw that a martial art can be made *more* effective by the removal of "dangerous" elements so that students can train at full power on resisting opponents with the techniques that remain. What Kano realized is that *the effectiveness of a martial art is not determined solely by its repertoire of techniques, but also by the training method by which it instills those techniques into the students.* The importance of this insight cannot be overemphasized. It represents one of the biggest breakthroughs in the history of the martial arts. Only when an effective means of imprinting the techniques into the minds and movements of the students is utilized is a genuinely effective fighting style created. This is only possible when students apply their techniques at full power on a fully resisting opponent. There is something paradoxical about the idea of a martial art being made more combat effective by the *removal* of dangerous techniques. *Kano saw that a fighter who constantly trained at full power on a resisting opponent in live combat with "safe" techniques would be more combat effective than a fighter who always trained with "deadly" techniques on a cooperating partner with no power.* We should note immediately that "safe" technique does not mean "ineffective." The "safe" techniques that Kano retained were "safe" only in the sense that they can be used safely in live training so long as students agree to stop when they have been successfully applied. In a street fight they could be used to snap a man's elbow or strangle him until unconscious. Training in this fashion represented a massive advance in the history of grappling.

Kano Vindicated

Kano opened his own school, the Kodokan, in the early 1880s and utilized his teaching method. He called his martial art judo to differentiate it from classical jiu-jitsu. His choice of name was interesting. *Ju* in "judo" is the same character as *jiu* in "jiu-jitsu." (Jiu-jitsu is actually an old and mistaken way

to represent the Japanese characters. "Jujutsu," or perhaps "ju jitsu," is the correct version. However, "jiu-jitsu" is the traditional spelling in "Brazilian jiu-jitsu" so we have retained it.) *Ju* means "gentle" or "soft." *Do* means "way" and has connotations of a broad lifestyle or quasi-religious vision. Rather than being merely a series of techniques, judo was supposed to be a complete way of life, with moral, spiritual, and social overtones as well as combat effectiveness. The Kodokan attracted many highly talented students and quickly rose to prominence in Japan. Around 1886 the Tokyo police force was looking for an effective martial art to train its members. Various schools of classical jiu-jitsu, including some of the most well known and highly esteemed, vied for the honor of being chosen to train the police force. An open martial arts tournament was to be held to determine the respective merit of the entrants. Victory would be only by perfect throw, landing an opponent flat on his back, or by submission. The tournament was not like a modern-day MMA event since there was no striking. It was more like a grappling tournament. The Kodokan students faced off against the most powerful classical jiu-jitsu ryu in Japan. When it was over, the Kodokan had won decisively winning nearly all the matches. This was a remarkable result, given that the Kodokan had been in existence for about four years and whose sensei was only in his mid-twenties. The lopsided result was the death knell for classical jiu-jitsu, and Judo became the prominent fighting form. Kano's innovative training methods had been vindicated.

Maeda

One of Kano's best students was Mitsuyo Maeda (1878–1941). He had originally trained in classical jiu-jitsu but switched to the Kodokan at age eighteen, where he was well known for his outstanding skill. Kano was very interested in spreading judo throughout the world, possibly as part of his desire to make it an Olympic sport. He sent several representatives to the United States to demonstrate the sport. Two were sent to the East Coast. One was an older man, Tomita, one of Kano's first pupils and a veteran of the 1886 Tokyo police tournament. He was a fine technician and teacher, but no longer a great fighter. Along with him was sent Maeda, as the one who would do the sparring, if necessary. Initially things did not go well in America. In a demonstration at the West Point Military Academy (not the White House, as is often thought) an impromptu challenge was issued to both men by a powerful-looking football player. Maeda immediately accepted. The charging football player took Maeda down. In the West grappling matches are normally decided by a "pin." Holding your opponent on his back for a short time signifies victory. In jiu-jitsu and judo, however, so long as you hold your opponent between your legs you are not regarded as being pinned even though you are on your back (since in this position you can still control and defeat your opponent). Some people regarded the football player as the victor since he took Maeda down and "pinned" him. Maeda, however, kept fighting and quickly secured an arm lock, forcing the football player to submit. The confusion over the outcome made people want another match. Tomita was a higher rank in judo than Maeda and the Americans mistakenly assumed this meant he was a better *fighter* (he was in fact a much better *teacher* than a fighter, as well as being well past his prime). Accordingly they wanted the football player to wrestle Tomita. Honor demanded that Tomita accept the challenge. To Maeda's dismay, Tomita was easily taken down and this time he really *was* pinned. Tomita could only squirm under the big man's pin—it was a humiliating defeat for judo. After this embarrassment, Tomita and Maeda split, Maeda staying on the East Coast, Tomita going to the West Coast. Anxious to uphold the dignity and reputation of judo, Maeda tried to set up a professional fight in which he would take on an American boxer or wrestler. Living and teaching in Princeton, New Jersey, and also in New York, Maeda trained for a fight in the Catskills, in Upstate New York. He was to fight a talented local wrestling champion. Maeda won, restoring honor to judo and jiu-jitsu.

The relative obscurity of judo and jiu-jitsu made teaching in New York a difficult way for Maeda to make a living. Nonetheless, his skill and success in challenge matches added to his reputation and his confidence in the effectiveness of his fighting style. So confident did Maeda become that he challenged to a no-rules fight the world heavyweight boxing champion of that era, Jack Johnson, a man who many regard as the greatest heavyweight of all time. In doing this Maeda started a tradition that Helio Gracie and his sons would carry on. Helio challenged the top heavyweight boxer of his time, Joe Lewis. In the modern era, several Gracies have challenged current boxing icon, Mike Tyson. Johnson did not respond, setting a tradition among top heavyweights not to respond to such challenges!

Maeda was a world traveler. After his time in North America he toured Central and South America and also Europe. By taking many professional challenge fights, Maeda clearly went against the strict moral codes of Kodokan judo. Probably because of this, Maeda described his fighting method as "jiu-jitsu" rather than "judo." There are other likely reasons why he switched the nomenclature of his art. Maeda had in fact studied classical jiu-jitsu before he studied judo under Jigoro Kano, who was regarded as an outstanding student of Tenshin Shin'Yo jiu-jitsu. When he began fighting challenge matches, he almost certainly began using techniques that were not allowed in judo training but which were part of his old jiu-jitsu curriculum. In addition, Maeda was an intelligent and thoughtful innovator. He added techniques and took out those he considered ineffective. He molded his fight-

ing style to deal with the two most common types of opponents encountered, Western boxers and wrestlers. In terms of technique, he was moving away from pure judo. One thing is clear, when Maeda taught people during these long overseas voyages, he insisted on calling his art "jiu-jitsu." Maeda spent his time instructing police units and private citizens in jiu-jitsu its and advertising his skill in a huge number of challenge matches. His tremendous record made him a legend in Central and South America. He fought also in England and Spain. It was in Spain that he took on the name "Count Koma," by which he is often known.

In the early 1920s, Maeda returned to Brazil and became heavily involved in the Japanese government's attempts to start a colony in northern Brazil. This was the era of imperial Japan. Japan was interested in starting colonization projects overseas just as the leading Western nations had done. One of the countries chosen for colonization was Brazil. Maeda was chosen to help with this colonial project. His own good experiences in Brazil and his bad experiences in North America (where there was much anti-Japanese sentiment) convinced him that Brazil, not North America, was the best place for Japanese colonization. He immersed himself in the project with great zeal. The colonial project was a very difficult one (in fact it ultimately failed). One local man who used his political connections to help Maeda was Gastao Gracie, whose family had emigrated to Brazil from Scotland. The friendship that grew between the two men led to an offer from Maeda— *he would teach his jiu-jitsu to Gastao's sons.*

Maeda and the Gracies

Carlos Gracie (1902–94), the oldest of the Gracie brothers, became one of Maeda's students. A fascinating question to ask is *what did Maeda teach Carlos?* Information is scarce about Maeda's teaching method and the technical changes he made to jiu-jitsu and judo as a result of his combat experience. We have seen that Maeda insisted on describing his art as jiu-jitsu rather than judo and his probable reasons for doing so. Maeda does note that he had to modify his technique for MMA competition. He discerned, for example, the principal weaknesses and strengths of his main opponents, Western boxing and wrestling, and fought in a way that negated their strengths and exploited their weaknesses. His principal fighting method involved throwing a low kick or elbow to set up a clinch from where he would throw his opponent to the mat. Once there, he focused on ground-grappling submission holds to finish the fight. This general strategy seems very similar to that used by modern Brazilian jiu-jitsu fighters.

The main lessons that Maeda appeared to transmit to Carlos were these:

1. Grappling skill could, with minor modifications, be made into a highly effective combat style, which could negate the strengths of other styles and exploit their weaknesses. Maeda was living proof of this. The usefulness of his many challenge matches and MMA experience was beyond doubt. Maeda had learned much from them about which techniques and strategies were truly effective in real combat. By rejecting Kano's moral prohibition on professional MMA fights Maeda had greatly advanced the effectiveness of grappling as a fighting style.

2. The need for live training (randori) as the means to successfully inculcate technique into students in a way that they could utilize in real combat. This came from Maeda's training with Kano. We shall soon see that the Gracies greatly extended and improved upon this lesson.

3. Actual technique of jiu-jitsu.

4. The basic strategy of taking a striker to the ground, thus removing his greatest strength (his punches and kicks) and exposing him to your greatest strength (grappling submission holds).

Carlos was in fact a student of Maeda's no more than four years and possibly as little as two years. He opened his own school in 1925, but there is conflicting evidence as to how long he had studied jiu-jitsu before opening his school. In such a short space of time he could only have learned a limited amount of technique. Bear in mind also that Maeda was himself very heavily involved in the colonization project at the time he is thought to have trained Carlos and appears to have traveled frequently. It would thus appear that the teacher/student contact between Maeda and Carlos was not extensive as is commonly supposed. Consequently, *most of the technical knowledge of jiu-jitsu had to be developed and discovered by the Gracies themselves over the years*.

Maeda continued his travels around Brazil and the other countries, leaving the Gracie brothers to work out the myriad precise details of their martial art over time. Maeda had given the Gracie's *the basic technical start they needed, along with an overall strategic vision of how a grappler could control and dominate a fight that had been well tested in the cauldron of real combat. In addition he imparted a very good training methodology and a philosophy of using real combat as the ultimate test of stylistic effectiveness*—this was the legacy Maeda gave to the Gracies in the relatively short time he taught Carlos.

The Development of Brazilian Jiu-Jitsu

The Gracie brothers had several advantages that enabled them to make quick advances in the development of their art. One of these was *numbers*. There were four sons who were all heavily involved with jiu-jitsu. This meant there was never a lack of training partners with whom to practice and refine technique. The four brothers had a *huge* number of children, most of whom became avid students and teachers of jiu-jitsu. They in turn had many sons who likewise went into the family trade. Add to this the many close students of the family and you can see that the Gracies were like a research team whose field of study was unarmed combat. Another advantage was *time*. The Gracies taught jiu-jitsu for a living and so could devote all their time to study and research. Helio Gracie, for example, is known to have spent a staggering amount of time in refining and adjusting technique over many years, always seeking the most efficient use of strength and resources. Another was lack of *physical size*. The Gracies were all very small men. Ordinarily one would not think this an advantage for a fighter, but this lack of physical stature forced the Gracie boys to refine technique to an extraordinary degree, making them place great emphasis on technical perfection as the key to victory. Another great advantage possessed by the Gracies was their *autonomy*. It is very common in traditional martial arts to have a strong sense of tradition. Modifications to a style are often seen in a negative light, as a watering-down of the original insights of the ancient masters. Since the Gracies operated largely on their own, they did not have to answer to anyone but themselves. Never having to pay homage to tradition meant that they had absolute freedom in adding and rejecting technique. Effectiveness, not tradition and veneration of the past, was the only criterion of inclusion. These advantages aside, the development and success of Brazilian jiu-jitsu has deeper elements that we now need to investigate.

The Genius of the Gracie Clan— Overcoming Kano's Limitations

The classical jiu-jitsu and judo that Maeda taught to the Gracies had several revolutionary elements. Not only was Maeda showing the *techniques* of jiu-jitsu and judo, but also the new training method of randori, or free sparring. The innovative genius of the Gracies lay in their extending and modifying the *technique, training methodology,* and *strategy* of Japanese jiu-jitsu and judo and creating a new and revolutionary martial art in the process. Part of this story involves the rejection of certain limits that Kano had imposed upon martial arts training. We have seen already that Kano was interested in much more than physical fighting technique. As a public educator he was interested in the moral and social development of citizens and thought that judo training could be part of that development. Judo was to be made safe so that all citizens could participate.

In trying to make a martial art part of an acceptable

moral and social education that the whole citizenry could engage in Kano created a wonderful social project but had to impose such strict limitations upon the dangerous elements of fighting that his judo suffered as a combat style. Kano took out *too much* of the dangerous elements of fighting and grappling training. To prevent injuries in training, only submission holds to the elbow joint were permitted, along with strangleholds. Pressure against the face was made illegal. Striking was only practiced in ceremonial kata, never as part of live training. Students only trained in a gi. As a spectator sport with Olympic aspirations, a greater emphasis was put on aesthetically pleasing throws than on effective ground grappling. The result was an ever growing bias away from ground grappling. Competitors had only a very short period on the ground before the referee would intervene and stand them back up. As part of the moral code, fighting with other styles in challenge matches was forbidden. Under such tight restrictions it was difficult to continue making improvements as a *pure combat* style.

The social, moral and aesthetic demands were a hindrance to progress in developing the combative efficiency of grappling. The Gracie clan saw the negative effect of these limitations and rejected them outright. Their concern was not with social education but *combat efficiency*. Following Maeda's lead they engaged in challenge matches and MMA events as a means of further developing the efficiency of their style. Interestingly, when the Gracies first came to North America and continued their tradition of challenges and MMA combat, many martial artists criticized them on the basis of the very same moral, social, and aesthetic grounds that the Gracies had rejected years ago as a hindrance to the development of a combat-effective style.

Another improvement that the Gracies set about making lay in the actual techniques they developed. We have seen that this was partly due to the fact that their small stature required more efficient use of leverage to get techniques to succeed. This is only part of the story, however. The fact that Brazilian jiu-jitsu had a very different rule system and strategy from its parent arts meant that many new situations and predicaments emerged in the course of training and combat. These all had to be resolved by the invention of new technique or the modification of old ones. This process of invention and modification took *years* of painstaking research and continues today. To give a simple example, in judo if one player is caught in an arm lock from underneath by the opposing player and he succeeds in standing up, the referee stops the action and both players resume from a standing position. Consequently there is no great need for a technique to defend an arm lock from underneath, since by merely standing up you will be saved by the referee. In a real fight, however, the arm lock from underneath can be successfully applied even when the opposing player stands up (this often happens in modern MMA events). In recognition of this fact,

in Brazilian jiu-jitsu the match continues when one player stands up while caught in an arm lock from underneath. As a result there is a direct need for a set of techniques to escape such an arm lock. These had to be invented by the Gracies over time. In this way, changes in the rules required additions to the inventory of technique.

A third very significant change that the Gracies incorporated was a dramatic freeing up of the restrictions imposed by Kano on randori. We have seen that Kano had instituted "live" randori training in the Kodokan and that was largely responsible for the dramatic success of his style against classical jiu-jitsu styles that only trained with kata. Kano had, however, as a result of his concern over safety in practice, severely limited the kinds of grappling moves students were allowed to train with. All leg locks, neck cranks, spine locks, shoulder locks, wrist locks, muscle crushing, and cross-facing were illegal. These, however, are very effective combat techniques. By removing them students lose a good deal of combat effectiveness. Also if they encounter someone who does use them, their lack of familiarity with the techniques will make them very vulnerable. By adding these techniques to randori training the Gracies made their art much more combat effective. Live sparring had much more combative feel to it with the removal of these restrictions on technique.

The single greatest innovation that the Gracies incorporated, and one that is perhaps more than any other responsible for the success of Brazilian jiu-jitsu in MMA events, was the development of a simple, yet devastatingly effective, general combat strategy, and the adoption of a sport point system that reflected that strategy. Following the experience of Maeda, the Gracies had realized the effectiveness of taking an opponent to the ground in a real fight, thus removing the danger of strikes to a large degree. At the same time the opponent is in an environment with which he is unfamiliar and with which the Brazilian jiu-jitsu student is *very* familiar. Accordingly the skill of taking an opponent down to the ground is a very useful one. This fact is reflected in the sport point system instituted by the Gracies. A clean takedown scores two points. Once a fight goes to the ground, experience has shown there is a clear *hierarchy of positions* that the two combatants can enter into. Some positions offer great advantages in terms of the ease with which you can strike or submit your opponent. Others are potentially disastrous, offering your opponent too many advantages. Still others are roughly neutral, neither side having a clear advantage. For example, if you are underneath your opponent you can still exert considerable control over him so long as you keep him between your legs. From here it is even possible to submit your opponent or sweep him over into an advantageous position. In addition it is difficult for him to strike you effectively, as you can use your arms and legs as barriers to his strikes. If, however, your opponent were to get past your legs to a position on your side, he would have gotten past your best line of defense into a position where he can strike you, submit you, or progress on to still better positions. This success on his part is rewarded in the point system, gaining two points. If he were to place his knee on your stomach and sit up he would gain a truly dominant position from where he can strike you at will and enter easily into a host of submission holds. Under the point system this is recognized by the awarding of three points.

There are many ways to score points in Brazilian jiu-jitsu. Each represents a positional change that would prove advantageous in a real fight. By training and competing under this system of points, the strategy that has proven so effective in real combat is ingrained into the training and grappling habits of students, making their everyday randori training very good preparation for a real fight. The most decisive way to win is by submission. No matter how far behind in points you might be, if you make your opponent surrender, you win. Again, this is a reflection of real combat. Submission is gained by stranglehold or joint lock. This strategy of constantly striving to work your way up the hierarchy of positions until you get into a position from which you can dominate, pressure, and finish your opponent is the innovative core of the Brazilian system. It is the most directly combat-realistic point system of any grappling style. Once this training methodology is adopted and ingrained it is only a short step to prepare a student for MMA competition. All the basic strategic and technical habits have already been established.

The Historical Record

The record shows that the innovations and improvements to jiu-jitsu incorporated by the Gracies have created a combat style with unequaled success in MMA competition. Since the early days of Carlos and Helio, through the second generation, Carlson and Rolls, through the current generation, Rickson, Rorion, Royler, Royce, Ralph, and Renzo (among others), the Gracies and their students have experienced tremendous success in open MMA events and challenge matches that has brought them worldwide recognition. Our historical analysis has revealed some of the major reasons why this success came about.

Brazilian Jiu-Jitsu as a Martial Arts Research Program

Our analysis of the historical development of Brazilian jiu-jitsu reveals the degree to which the Gracies were engaged in a massive research project to discover the most effective form of unarmed combat available. They had large amounts of time, enthusiasm, autonomy, and innovative genius. Over genera-

tions they accumulated a staggering amount of information and knowledge, all of it tested in real combat. This was a privately operated research program unprecedented in the history of the martial arts.

The development proceeded along scientific lines. A large group of researchers (the Gracies and their students) tried to answer a clearly delineated problem (the fundamental problem of the martial arts). Those researchers were not content with mere theorizing but sought empirical proof of their theories and showed a willingness to abandon and modify theories in the face of hard evidence. The research program was not marred by ideological, moral, nationalistic, or aesthetic distractions but remained at all times an objective and focused investigation into the problem at hand.

Contrast this to the history of traditional martial arts where research so often proceeds along the most *irrational* lines. Here we typically see a research program without a clear problem. There is often a confusion of martial and social concerns. Is it a way of life or a fighting style? A moral guide or a guide to combat?

The "research team" is usually a single person or tiny group, working in isolation. Accordingly there is little opportunity for the interchange of ideas that comes from working within a large, highly motivated group of researchers. The more minds you have engaged in a project, the more likely that someone will introduce new ideas, challenge old ones, and promote growth.

There is an unhealthy fetishism of authority in the traditional martial arts. Age and tradition are venerated to a degree that stifles progress. There exists an irrational faith in ancient ideas for no other reason than the fact that they are ancient. Also there is a fetishism for legend and myth. Otherwise rational people will accept the most outlandish tales of superhuman feats—one man defeating ten, doubtful metaphysical theories—as part of their art.

Such irrational elements have no place in a modern martial art. The historical development of Brazilian jiu-jitsu is refreshingly free of such lapses into irrationalism.

Royler Gracie trains for one more vale tudo fight in his Humaita Academy, Rio de Janeiro, November 1999.

Training

Starting Training in Brazilian Jiu-Jitsu

We have talked at length of the theory and history of Brazilian jiu-jitsu. We now need to take a turn toward more practical concerns—namely the question of how someone beginning the art can train properly so as to make the fastest possible progress. Many people begin training in Brazilian jiu-jitsu with a strong background in some other grappling art such as judo, sambo, or wrestling. This certainly makes the task a little easier. For others, however, the beginning is more difficult since they have no experience of grappling. Such a person might well approach the first training sessions with a number of questions. First: *What do I need to begin training?* You will need at the very least a training partner. Brazilian jiu-jitsu cannot be practiced alone (although there are many valuable exercises and drills that you can do alone). It is strongly recommended that you practice on mats to save wear and tear on the body. A grappling gi, or kimono, is certainly recommended for reasons we will look at later. You will be able to get all of these by joining a school.

Second: *What can I expect in class at a Brazilian jiu-jitsu school?* Obviously different people run their classes in different ways. Nonetheless, there is a broad pattern of training that is common to most schools. Class begins with warm-up stretching and calisthenics. In some schools this is very light, but in others it is a long, arduous workout. Then comes a period of practicing throws and takedowns from a standing position. Then the heart of the class—technical demonstration and practice of ground-grappling technique. This is followed by open sparring (randori). Usually this open sparring begins in a kneeling position so students can focus on the ground work.

Third: *What is expected of me?* Brazilian jiu-jitsu is known for its informality. Generally there is little bowing and rigid class structure. You can train at your own pace to a greater degree than most martial arts. Students are expected to push *themselves* hard rather than being pushed by someone else. This kind of self-discipline is always more impressive than having discipline imposed upon you by another person.

Fourth: *How will I benefit from studying Brazilian jiu-jitsu?* The most obvious benefit is gaining knowledge of one of the most effective means of self-defense available and the resulting confidence this will build into your character.

Most martial arts claim a wide range of benefits over and above self-defense. One often hears claims that the study of traditional martial arts helps to build "discipline," "spiritual development," "righteous character," and various other desirable traits. Since Brazilian jiu-jitsu was largely promoted due to its success in actual combat, it was generally taken to be a *pure fighting style* with no additional benefits over effective self-defense. Indeed, Brazilian jiu-jitsu was often portrayed as the style of choice for people who had no other interest save fighting. However, Brazilian jiu-jitsu offers the practitioner a wide range of additional benefits.

Brazilian jiu-jitsu is an individual and a social activity. Unlike a team sport, you face your opponents alone, both in training and competition. This forces one to become self-reliant. You cannot blame others for whatever failure you experience, nor can others take credit for your successes. Thus the student grows in terms of individual responsibility. Brazilian jiu-jitsu is a social activity insofar as you cannot succeed without a group of training partners upon whom you depend for your development. You have to learn to get along without them. Anyone who cannot fit into a group working toward a common goal and become a respected member will quickly find himself without training partners and unable to progress.

There is a tremendous emotional growth that comes with the study of Brazilian jiu-jitsu. This is a result of having to confront and overcome the inevitable failures and mistakes that will occur in the course of your training and competing.

The study of Brazilian jiu-jitsu is a great way to develop virtues of character that will stand one in good stead in a wide variety of contexts. It teaches perseverance, since it takes great time and effort to develop your skills to the best of your ability. There is nothing more humbling than training in Brazilian jiu-jitsu. Initially you will be easily defeated by everyone who has trained longer than you. This can be a very disheartening experience, especially if you began with a high opinion of your fighting skills! You quickly learn that there are no secret techniques that will substitute for hard work and sweat. Thus a strong work ethic is cultivated.

An important trait that results from diligent training in jiu-jitsu is that it teaches the student to judge others' ability by their actual substance, rather than superficial elements, such as external appearance. When we look at a potential adversary or opponent we are often misled or distracted by unimportant features. For example, we expect a dangerous opponent to look a certain way—to have a brawny physique, an intimidating face, an aggressive and frightening demeanor. Yet these superficial features are not a reliable guide to fighting ability. Training in Brazilian jiu-jitsu teaches you to look beyond these unimportant surface features and judge the opponent by his actual ability. You soon learn that some people with very mild external features can be terrors on the mat and that others who look frightening are easy to defeat.

Perhaps the most important lesson afforded by the study of Brazilian jiu-jitsu is that of tackling problems through the use of strategy rather than brute strength and aggression. In order to succeed in training and competition you must overcome the myriad problems created by an opponent who

is doing everything in his power to frustrate your efforts and succeed with his own. Initially you try to do so by sheer strength. This inevitably fails against a more skilled opponent. In response to that failure you must apply the strategy and techniques of jiu-jitsu. There is a tremendous sense of *problem solving* in the sport. For every problem in a grappling situation there is a rational solution. You may often feel that the battle is as much intellectual as physical. You must employ strategy and tactics to overcome practical problems.

There are, then, a great many benefits to the study of Brazilian jiu-jitsu over and above learning to fight. Like any other martial art it can foster positive changes in character that have good effects in a much wider set of contexts than fighting.

The Belts and Grading System of Brazilian Jiu-Jitsu

Most martial arts have a system of belts or similar ranks by which a student may assess his level of development. Brazilian jiu-jitsu, tracing its roots back to Maeda's influence, shares the Japanese system of colored belts. The belt system begins with white belt and progresses through blue, purple, brown, black, and various degrees of black, up to red belt for those whose influence and fame takes them to the pinnacle of the art. Compared with other styles, there are a relatively low number of belt grades in Brazilian jiu-jitsu. Most styles have different grades within a belt color, so that one can be a third-stage orange belt, for example. This plentitude of belt levels ensures that students have a sense of constantly moving forward, since they are often being given a new level. By way of contrast, the student of Brazilian jiu-jitsu must often endure long years holding the same rank. Few make it even to purple belt, with black belt being truly elite status.

What distinguishes the Brazilian system from others is its extreme *informality*. There is no precise, agreed-upon set of rules that determine who is a blue belt, who a purple belt, and so forth. Part of the reason for this is the complete lack of forms, or kata (pre-arranged, choreographed sets of movements containing the idealized movements of the style in question, typically a collection of kicks, punches, blocks, and the like performed solo), in the Brazilian jiu-jitsu system. Most martial arts put a lot of emphasis upon learning these katas. When one has learned a set of katas, this is often taken to be indicative of progress, indicating that the student is ready for promotion. Lacking a curriculum of kata, the Brazilian style must look to other indicators of progress. One might try to differentiate grades in terms of numbers of moves that a student knows. Such a method is clearly inadequate. It is often pointed out that a purple belt knows almost as many moves as a black belt—he simply does not perform them as well, or combine them as well, or at the correct time. Also, some fighters do very well with a small collection of moves that they can apply well in any situation—should they be ranked lower than a another fighter who knows a lot of moves but applies none of them well? A more objective method is to test fighting skill. If one fighter always defeats another when they grapple, this might be taken as firm evidence that he deserves the higher rank. Yet it is not always so simple. What if he is far heavier and stronger and this is the only reason that he prevails in sparring sessions? What if he is technically inferior? You can see that there are no easy answers to the question of what criteria we can offer for a given belt ranking. Rather, the extreme informality of the Brazilian style is a direct reflection of the fact that it is impossible to provide clear-cut rules as to how people ought to be graded. The most we can do is provide very general criteria. The individual decision must be left to an experienced instructor who will take a range of criteria into account. For example, the size and strength of the student, depth of technical knowledge, ability to apply it in sparring sessions and competition, how he compares with students of other ranks both inside and outside his school, his ability to teach, and so on. In general Brazilian jiu-jitsu takes a very *conservative* stance toward promotion. This is a direct reflection of the fact that it is primarily a fighting style. It makes no sense to promote someone to a high rank if they cannot fight well—after all, should a highly ranked fighter be defeated it is a bad reflection on the school. So then, the two principal features of the Brazilian ranking system are its *informality* and its *conservatism*. Having said this, we can now go on to say a little about the grading process as it is applied to the actual belts.

In this book a guideline for belt requirements is offered. This is offered only as a rough guide, a set of minimum requirements for a given belt level. The fact is, *there is no substitute for training under an experienced coach in an accredited school*. One might well memorize all the techniques offered here for blue belt level, even practice them with a friend, then go to a Brazilian jiu-jitsu school and be trounced by the white belts! To really know a given move one needs to learn not just the basic movements, but be able to perform them on an opponent who is resisting as hard as he can. This comes not from a book, but from time spent on the mat in hard training. A true sense of your level of development is had by training and competing with other practitioners and drawing comparisons with your own game. Still, a rough guide can be offered to those who lack the benefit of a good local school or who seek a general guide to the grading process.

White Belt to Blue Belt

Of all the belt grades this is the least controversial. The step up to blue belt is the beginning of a long road. The white belt often obsesses over technique, hoping to learn as much as possible so as to do better against his classmates. This is a healthy attitude; the fact remains, however, *that the transition to blue belt is not merely a matter of acquiring a set of techniques*. One must always remember that Brazilian jiu-jitsu is more than a large set of moves. Rather, it is a set of moves *woven into an overall strategy*. The most basic general strategy of Brazilian jiu-jitsu can be stated very simply. One takes the opponent to the ground where he can be easily controlled, seeking to find a dominant position. From that dominating position, one looks to apply a finishing technique that will bring the fight to an end in the most efficient manner. All the myriad moves of Brazilian jiu-jitsu fall within that simple strategy. The blue belt is one who has taken that strategy to heart, who tries to follow it as he trains, *who lets that general strategy guide the application of the techniques he has learned*. It is important to realize that that basic strategy remains the same through all the belt levels; *the difference between belt levels is merely a reflection of the increasing sophistication and technical expertise with which the basic strategy is carried out*. You can see, then, *that the essence of a blue belt lies in the adoption of this strategic element along with the beginnings of the technical expertise to carry it out upon people of a reasonably high level, that is, other people who have been judged as blue belts*.

In this book we will offer a series of moves that are commonly judged appropriate to blue belt level. A series of moves that is sufficiently complete to allow the hard-training beginner to successfully attempt to employ this overall strategy in training and in self-defense situations. Given our earlier statement of the general strategic vision that lies behind Brazilian jiu-jitsu, one can see that the blue belt will require at a minimum a means of taking his opponent down, of escaping from bad positions, of attaining and maintaining good positions, and of efficiently finishing an opponent once a good position has been attained. This is precisely what this book will attempt to offer, bearing in mind that the techniques will have to be practiced against someone of blue belt level.

Minimum Technical Requirements

Self-Defense Techniques	5
Throws	1
Guard Passes	1
Submissions	3
Sweeps	2
Escapes	2
Combination Attacks	1

Blue Belt to Purple Belt

It is often claimed that purple belt is the first really big hurdle over which the practitioner of Brazilian jiu-jitsu must climb. There is a good deal of truth to this. It is one of the most time-consuming belts. Typically it takes about the same time to gain a purple belt in Brazilian jiu-jitsu as it does a black belt in most other styles (around four to five years of hard training). By the time the student has attained a purple belt, he has a working knowledge of most of the moves of the system and has determined which of these are his favorites—the moves that he relies upon for his own personal game plan. As a blue belt student progresses, learning ever more techniques, he comes to a level where he can easily counter the moves of less seasoned blue belts. His technical knowledge is at a higher level than theirs. This allows him to anticipate and counter their moves easily. Since he is battling with higher-level opponents he must employ a greater number of moves than a standard blue belt. Moreover, they must be employed in a more precise fashion.

Along with these changes come changes in style. The purple belt uses moves in *combination* much more readily than a blue belt. Rather than struggling to employ a given move on a fiercely resisting opponent, the purple switches to another, complementary technique that completes the job with far less effort. His deeper knowledge of technique is what allows him to do this. In this book we will attempt to show how a series of new techniques can be added to the arsenal of a blue belt, which, through hard training, can take him to the next level. A selection of moves, widely taken to be representative of purple belt level, will be shown. When these are added and combined with those of the blue belt level, drilled constantly and made part of grappling training, they can take the student up to purple belt.

Minimum Technical Requirements

Self-Defense	5
Throws	1
Guard Passes	1
Submissions	3
Sweeps	3
Escapes	1
Combination Attacks	1

Brown Belt

Brown belt is the beginning of the truly elite rankings. Typically it takes five to six years of hard training to attain this level. You may well ask, "If purple belt level signifies techni-cal expertise and black belt level technical and practical expertise, what does brown belt signify?" Brown belt is really an intermediary step. It provides the bridge between purple and black belts. Often it marks the student's first steps in teaching techniques to beginners. The brown belt is expected to have a deeper knowledge of technique than a purple belt, along with greater practical ability. On a more mundane level, if a student is regularly dominating other purple belts both in sparring and competition, this is strong evidence that he is ready for promotion. So the chief function of brown belt level is to provide a smooth transition to black belt. Of course the brown belt uses a greater number of techniques than the lower belts—this is a reflection of his longer training time. Some of these moves are high level; all of them are performed with the crispness appropriate to that high level. A series of moves taken as representative of brown belt level are shown here.

Minimum Technical Requirements

Self-Defense	5
Throws	1
Guard Passes	1
Submissions	3
Sweeps	1
Escapes	1
Combination Attacks	2

Black Belt

In virtually all the martial arts, black belt denotes the highest level of achievement. Brazilian jiu-jitsu is no exception. By the time the student attains a black belt his knowledge and skill are of the highest class. In addition, his depth of knowledge makes him a fully qualified teacher. Rather than merely knowing how to perform the moves, the black belt is expected to know *why* a given move works. That is, he understands the biomechanical principles that underlie the move. The principles of leverage, of body control and mechanics. This deeper knowledge makes him a far better teacher than someone who merely recounts a series of moves. Moreover, such knowledge allows him to invent new moves and combinations and so develop a more personalized jiu-jitsu.

It is important to see that there is no resting place in jiu-jitsu. While black belt represents the highest common belt (there are degrees of black belt, but we shall not go into this), this does not mean the student can stop learning. Always there is more to learn. Indeed, new techniques crop up all the time. The dedicated student always tries to keep moving forward. There is a definite "feel" that goes with each belt rank. When you grapple with a black belt the feeling is usually one of relaxed technique, of one move flowing into another, of extreme technical precision. Listed here are a series of moves taken to be representative of black belt level.

Minimum Technical Requirements

Self-Defense	1
Throws	1
Guard Passes	1
Submissions	2
Sweeps	1
Escapes	1
Combination Attacks	2

More on Belts

When one considers the question of progress up through the belt rankings in Brazilian jiu-jitsu, it becomes evident that there are four separate elements that must be considered. The first is the strategic element. This refers to the overall strategic game plan that is embodied in Brazilian jiu-jitsu. We have seen that this involves taking the fight quickly to the ground, where an opponent can be controlled much more readily, attaining and maintaining an advantageous position from where an efficient finishing hold can put a quick end to the fight. This strategic element stays the same through the ranks. Once learned it does not progress much further. Progress is really made in the remaining three elements. The first is the technical element. This is the learning of new techniques to deal with problematic situations. As the student trains he comes to encounter more and more techniques, increasing his grappling vocabulary, so to speak. In addition, training brings about increases in another element, the practical element. This is the student's ability to actually make a technique work in sparring, competition, or self-defense. It is one thing to know of a technique, it is another to be able to make it work under severe stress.

The last element has never been emphasized in Brazilian jiu-jitsu. This is the fitness element. As a student trains more and more, his body will adapt to the pressure. While white belts quickly become exhausted, the higher ranks go for hours without rest or becoming fatigued. To be sure, this is mostly due to superior technique, but it cannot be denied that grappling training is very demanding physically. Constant practice definitely hardens the body.

Different Types of Training

There are two main types of training and competition in Brazilian jiu-jitsu. The most common is sport Brazilian jiu-jitsu.

This is pure grappling with no punching or kicking. Most people engaged in the sport are involved only in this kind of training. Most competitions require the competitors to wear a gi, but there are other tournaments that do not. The other is *vale tudo* ("anything goes") training and competition. Here there are very few rules and striking of all kinds is allowed. This kind of MMA competition is what made Brazilian jiu-jitsu famous. *It is strongly recommended that you become very well versed in sport grappling with a gi before beginning any vale tudo training.* You need to build up your technical grappling base before you add punches and kicks into the equation.

In this book the moves are demonstrated with both Renzo and Royler wearing a kimono, or gi. The gi used in Brazilian jiu-jitsu is a heavy, reinforced cotton jacket, pants, and belt, very similar to that used in judo. It is made strong enough to cope with the tremendous stress of grappling training. Generally practice in Brazilian jiu-jitsu is done while wearing the gi. This may seem strange, since Brazilian jiu-jitsu prides itself on its street-realistic nature. Attackers are usually not considerate enough to first put on a gi before engaging in combat! Nonetheless, regular training with the gi has several benefits. The gi is heavy and somewhat constricting. It can be uncomfortably hot. This develops a definite fortitude in the jiu-jitsu student. It makes him used to discomfort and more able to endure the hardship that is part of tough training. More importantly, the gi gives the opponent a great many handles by which he can hold, control, lock, and even strangle you. While wearing a gi it becomes much more difficult to escape locks and holds simply because your opponent has so much to grab hold of. This forces you to escape in the technically correct manner, rather than just relying on brute strength and slipperiness. *Thus students who regularly train in the gi often attain a higher technical level than those who do not.* Also, wearing the gi makes one aware of the danger of strangles and chokes. It forces the student to properly defend his neck at all times and thus *sharpens his defensive skills*. Moreover, in a real fight, there is often pulling and grabbing of clothes. Training in the gi prepares you for this. Nonetheless, some training time should be given to training without the gi. Such training has a different feel. Most of the moves of Brazilian jiu-jitsu, with a little common sense, can be adapted to use without the gi, but the game generally has a faster dynamic.

Making Technical Progress

Most people who begin a martial art are anxious to make the fastest possible progress—students of Brazilian jiu-jitsu are no exception. One great advantage of jiu-jitsu is that no great athleticism or strength is required to attain a high level of proficiency (though it is always to your advantage to work hard on your conditioning and strength training). This means you are not required to develop extraordinary flexibility or strength before you can perform techniques well. The basic route to technical progress in Brazilian jiu-jitsu consists of a consistent training regimen based upon three main elements.

1. Learning the techniques and strategy of Brazilian Jiu-Jitsu.

2. The use of drills to practice those techniques and strategies until the technique can be performed flawlessly on an unresisting partner.

3. Applying the techniques and strategy on a resisting partner in live sparring.

By incorporating these three key elements of training progress can be made very quickly. As soon as you learn a given technique and try to apply it on your opponent, he will try to counter you. If the technique is unknown to your opponent and you apply it well, chances are he will not be able to counter you. Eventually, however, he will learn to resist you successfully. In order to keep ahead, you must learn new techniques, or new combinations of old techniques—some kind of innovation or expansion of your grappling arsenal is needed. You can see the pattern that is emerging here. As your opponents learn to counter your moves, new ones become necessary in order to retain whatever advantage you have. For example, as a beginning blue belt, you might have one takedown that you know and apply well. With time, however, your training partner will learn to counter it. In order to be able to keep taking him down you must learn new ways to apply the takedown or to learn a whole new takedown. Should he learn to counter your new technique, then you must progress again.

The deeper point that is beginning to emerge here is this: *You are only as good as your training partners make you.* If your training partners are weak or incompetent, there will be no pressure on you to improve your technique. This fact reinforces the crucial importance of training at a good school so as to have a healthy supply of quality training partners. Your progress through the belts is largely dependent upon them and the tough competition they provide. *The technical progress you make is largely contingent upon the quality of your training partners.*

How Many Techniques?

Now we come to the thorny question of how many (and what) techniques are necessary to make "good" progress. This question is impossible to answer in any great detail. The most we can hope for is a rough guide. Some very good fighters have a surprisingly low number of techniques. They make up for it

with an excellent sense of when to apply them and how to do so in any situation. One point is clear: When you watch a jiu-jitsu player in action, even at higher levels, *it quickly becomes obvious that the actual number of moves he regularly employs while sparring is dramatically lower than the number of moves he knows in theory.* The importance of this point should not be overlooked. *It is not so crucial to know a vast number of moves as to know in depth several moves for each position.* Accordingly, this book will not list a vast array of techniques for the belt levels. Rather, it will focus on *completeness.* It will look to supply the student with several moves for each of the positions he will encounter in a ground-grappling situation, building as the belts go higher. Moreover, the moves selected are meant to combine with each other, so the student can create his own combinations to confuse his opponent and keep his innovative edge. They are intended to help the student implement the complete strategy that lies behind Brazilian jiu-jitsu. What is needed for that is not an encyclopedia of moves so much as a short but complete guide to how to successfully carry out the strategy of taking your opponent to the ground and getting a good enough position to finish the fight.

How to Encourage Technical Progress

Most of the sparring training in Brazilian jiu-jitsu consists of both combatants starting on their knees and then commencing to grapple. Each tries to gain some kind of positional advantage from where they can attempt to force their opponent to submit. This is an excellent manner in which to train. It develops great skill and confidence in applying the techniques that you have learned in a "live" clash. One problem, however, is that you can quickly develop a predictable "pattern" to your training. Most people discover that some moves and positions suit them better than others. So, for example, big people tend to be able to force their way into a top position. Small, flexible people tend to spend most of their time underneath their opponents in the guard position. Consequently most people find a "comfort zone" where they feel most at home. They stick to a small set of "tried-and-true" moves and positions. Staying in such a comfort zone can, in the long run, inhibit technical progress and have a limiting effect upon your training.

There is nothing wrong with having favorite positions and moves. However, to make technical progress you will need to move out of the comfort zone and incorporate new moves. You can try placing yourself in positions you do not normally enter into or like and force yourself to defend and work your way out of them. Try picking a small set of submission holds that you rarely use and only allow yourself to employ those holds until you become good at them, thus widening your submissions arsenal. Force yourself to practice escapes by letting your partner start mounted on you. In this way you will be exposed to a much wider array of grappling situations, forcing you to expand your technical base to deal with them.

How to Conduct Yourself in Training

While a key element in the success of grapplers in real fights is their exposure to the pressure of constantly subduing and defeating a live opponent in training, *this does not mean that training should consist of all-out grudge matches in which the sole aim is to make your opponent submit*. The spirit in which you approach training is crucial to your progress. Rather than focusing only upon defeating the person in front of you, try hard to apply technique in a skillful, relaxed manner. If raw power and strength is the only means by which you prevail, something is wrong. If you are strong, try hard to resist the temptation to rely upon your strength. Aim to utilize the technique in the most precise manner possible. Do not stick with the same moves. Rather, try to use new ones, even if it means failing in the beginning. Training is a time for experimentation and learning, not win-at-all-costs. Let yourself be put in disadvantageous positions so that you can familiarize yourself with them and work on your ability to escape. Operate with a feeling of *finesse* rather than brute power.

No one enjoys being forced to submit while sparring, however, you must accept this as part of training. The truth is, you will learn far more during the sessions where you are forced to tap out than those where you force others to tap out. Failure forces us into self-analysis. From this self-analysis we learn what we did wrong, we question ourselves and think about how we might improve. *By forcing us to think hard about our game and its weaknesses, the failure of today will lead to the success of tomorrow*. Victory, on the other hand, teaches us little. Accept the idea that you will regularly be forced to submit in training, especially when trying new techniques. Do not let it concern you. Focus instead upon progress, of which setbacks and failure are an essential part.

The Crucial Importance of Fundamentals

Many of the techniques shown in this book concern the most fundamental and important moves and concepts in Brazilian jiu-jitsu. There is often a tendency for students to accumulate as many techniques as possible in the shortest time. Often there is an assumption that there is a great tactical advantage in knowing a greater number of moves than opponents.

Some students show a distinct preference for the more spectacular moves, hoping that these will lead to success. These are natural enough sentiments. However, it cannot be emphasized strongly enough that *the key to success is mastery of the fundamentals*—this is true at any level of Brazilian jiu-jitsu. To say that a technique is *fundamental* is not to say that it is *simple*. Students soon learn that there is no technique that is simple per se. *The degree of difficulty of a given technique is largely a reflection of how good one's opponent is.* Even the simplest moves are very difficult to perform upon a skilled opponent. Conversely, "difficult" moves seem easy against a beginner. Champion jiu-jitsu players are those who pay great attention to the fundamentals of the sport. This is true even of unorthodox champions. Underneath their unique game plan you will invariably find strict observance of fundamental concepts.

Sparring

A very large percentage of training time in Brazilian jiu-jitsu is taken up with live sparring. You and your training partner engage in live training, employing the techniques of jiu-jitsu to the best of your ability in an effort to make your opponent submit. This gives a considerable advantage to the practitioner of Brazilian jiu-jitsu. By constantly being exposed to the pressure and demands of live training with a resisting partner he or she becomes very used to the idea of restraining, dominating, and finishing a resisting opponent—which is exactly what will be demanded of you in a real fight. Because the more extreme elements of a real fight (such as biting, eye gouging, hair pulling, and striking) are removed from training you can partake in such live sparring on a daily basis without fear of constant injury and damage. As you grow in skill and confidence you can periodically add in striking to test yourself and your defenses.

In Brazilian jiu-jitsu live training normally begins on your knees rather than from a standing position. This allows you to get right into your ground grappling without distraction. Starting on your knees also greatly reduces the likelihood of injury in training. However it should be noted that time must be devoted to standing grappling training also. While it is a fact that the vast majority of fights *end up* on the ground it is also true that most fights *begin* in a standing position. Consequently it is crucial to set aside time to practice standing grappling as well. This includes takedowns, throws, defending takedowns, clinching, and standing submission holds. However in your day-to-day training where ground grappling is being emphasized it makes good sense to begin sparring on the knees. The idea in sparring is to utilize the overall strategy and techniques of Brazilian jiu-jitsu to force your opponent to submit—just as you would in a real fight.

You want to work yourself into progressively better positions from where you can control your opponent and then use some kind of finishing hold to force a submission.

As you train you must try very hard to think strategically rather than simply muscle your way to victory. Try to stay as relaxed as you can and to employ the moves outlined in this book. In this way you will become a technical fighter rather than a brawler. As you grow in confidence you can even give your opponent an advantage by deliberately falling into a bad position and trying to work your way out. By this means you can become very adept at escape. Initially your wrestling sessions will be exhausting as you substitute strength for technique, but as you progress technically you will become smoother and more efficient in your grappling style.

The Key Positional Strategy of Brazilian Jiu-Jitsu

One of the keys to the success of Brazilian jiu-jitsu in MMA events is its emphasis on attaining and maintaining good position at all times in the course of a fight. By doing this you nullify the offense of your opponent while setting up your own offense. This is a very high-percentage approach to fighting. It seeks to lower the chance of your opponent successfully attacking you while maximizing the chance of your attacks striking home.

Often there is debate over which of the two main skills in grappling, positional skills or submission skills, is the more important. Submission skill pertains to the ability to finish your opponent (make him submit) with some lock or choke. Positional skill is concerned with the ability to attain and hold a dominant position in a ground-grappling situation. If you had only submission skills, it would be difficult to successfully employ them, since these generally require you to be able to attain and hold a good position long enough to apply them. On the other hand, if you had only positional skill and lacked submission skills, you could control your opponent but would lack the means to cleanly and efficiently end the fight. Clearly then, both are needed. While positional skills lack the glamorous nature of submissions, they are just as essential, indeed, it can be argued that they are the more important of the two, since it is almost always the case that gaining a good position is prerequisite to submitting an opponent. Moreover, it is extremely difficult to successfully employ a submission hold on an opponent who is dominating you in terms of position. Considerations like these often give rise to the view that "position precedes submission." In order to outline this positional strategy we need to look at the basic positions of ground grappling.

Renzo Gracie spars on the mats of the Abu Dhabi Combat Club before the eyes of His Highness the Sheik Tahnoon Bin Zayed Al Nayan, February 1999.

Basic Positions in Ground Grappling

The Mounted Position

Attaining the mounted position is one of the most sought-after goals by experienced ground fighters, especially in a real fight. This occurs when one fighter is on top of his opponent, astride his chest, with both knees on the floor. The reason this position is so sought after is simple enough: from the mounted position, you can hit your opponent with virtual impunity. Consider the following simple experiment. Mount a friend; sit up straight and form a fist. Touch your fist to your friend's jaw. Now have your friend reach up with his fist and try to touch your jaw. You will soon find that unless there is a vast disparity in height between the two of you, your friend will not be able to reach your jaw while you can easily reach his. Obviously this amounts to a totally decisive advantage if the two of you were to begin exchanging blows. Moreover, you will find that your blows, coming down, are much stronger, since you can utilize shoulder and hip action from the top position while your opponent, pinned underneath you, cannot; thus his punches are sadly lacking in power. In addition to being able to punch at will, the man on top can attack with a wide array of submission holds while the man on bottom has virtually no realistic opportunity to respond with his

Renzo Gracie goes for an arm bar during the final of the 1998 Abu Dhabi Submission Wrestling World Championship.

man on top holds his opponent's head with his right arm, he can roll his right shoulder across his opponent's jaw to prevent any possibility of biting, all the while being able to punch with his left hand. Thus while tactics such groin grabbing, eye gouging and biting have a definite nuisance value, they are not serious counters to the mounted position.

Another claim made by detractors of the mounted position, and indeed, of Brazilian jiu-jitsu in general, is that the person holding the mounted position is very vulnerable to being attacked by multiple opponents. You might be mounted on one man, doing very well, and yet be set upon by his friends and kicked and beaten. Since this is such a common criticism and applies to all the ground-fighting positions, we shall address it now. There is no doubt that if you are mounted, or indeed, grappling in any position, one is vulnerable to being attacked by multiple opponents who will take advantage of the fact that you are locked up with one opponent and press home their numerical advantage with kicks and punches. To claim that this problem is unique to grappling styles is patently absurd. If Mike Tyson were boxing one man in the ring when suddenly two more boxers jumped in and attacked him, he would be in as much trouble as a grappler in a similar situation. Multiple opponents present as much of a problem to strikers as they do to grappling styles. Whether you are a striker or a grappler the same problem presents itself, that as you focus attention on one man, another will attack, either hitting, holding, or dragging you down. Such attacks are extremely difficult to contend with and non-grappling styles have not shown any more effectiveness in dealing with them than grappling styles such as Brazilian jiu-jitsu. People who can take on and defeat multiple opponents are rather like ghosts: everybody *talks* of them, but no one has seen them.

own submission attempts. Thus the mounted position offers a potentially devastating advantage to the person who attains it.

There are many ways for the person on top to hold and control his opponent. One arm can encircle the opponent's head, the other is held out wide, hand on the ground, to make a wide base that makes the opponent's attempts to roll out very difficult. If the opponent is wearing a jacket, one hand can reach inside his collar so as to threaten the opponent with various chokes. In addition, your legs can be used to stabilize the mounted position by crossing the feet under the opponent's buttocks or by grapevining around the opponent's shins.

If your opponent has mounted you, the onus is on you to escape. It is useless to attempt submission holds and strikes from this very disadvantageous position. Your focus should be on escape to a better position, such as the guard position. Such escapes will be covered later.

It is often claimed that the mounted position is not as effective as it appears in mixed martial arts competition. Some people claim that in a real fight your opponent could simply bite, eye gouge, or groin grab his way out of the mounted position. While these methods do have a degree of effectiveness, in a real fight, one has to realize that they are not an effective counter to the mounted position. Consider groin grabbing, for example. In order to attack the groin from the bottom of the mount you have to reach down with at least one hand, thus exposing your face to a barrage of punches. Moreover the attacking hand is easily trapped by the man on top and followed by punches. As for biting and eye gouging, the man on top has such superior control that he is in a position to reply with his own bites and gouges that will prove far worse than those he receives. In addition, it is relatively easy for the man on top to position himself in a way that precludes biting or gouging by his opponent. For example, if the

The Across-side Position

One holds across-side when lying across the opponent's upper body. There are a number of ways this can be done. The more popular methods will be demonstrated. The principal virtue of this position is its great stability. It is a great means of holding and controlling even the strongest opponent. In addition, a great many submission holds can be used from across the opponent's side. While not nearly as well suited to striking an opponent as the mounted position, one can strike effectively from across-side, principally with knees to the opponent's head and ribs and short head butts to the face. Having attained the across-side position, experienced grapplers have the option of simply consolidating by holding position, attempting submission holds, or moving on to attain the mounted position.

Headlocks appear to fall into the category of across-side hold-downs. However, the use of headlocks in Brazilian jiu-jitsu is generally not encouraged. They offer a great opportunity to the opponent to escape and attain a dominant position on you. Some escapes from headlocks will be covered later.

If one is being held down in the across-side position, the best strategy is to escape by either putting the opponent back in the guard position, or getting to your knees underneath him. Attempting submission holds or strikes on an opponent who is holding you down in the cross-body position is very unlikely to succeed. Escape to a better position, such as the guard, is a far better strategy.

Knee-on-Belly Position

The knee-on-belly position, as the name implies, is attained by popping up from the across-side position and placing the knee of the leg closest to your opponent's hips upon his belly, the other leg out straight for balance and support. Your hand can grab your opponent's collar and belt, or, if he is not wearing a gi, can base out on the floor or his chest. There are several advantages to this position. It offers almost the same punching and submission advantages as the mounted position, yet is easier to attain than the mount, though not quite as stable. It is easy to slide into the mounted position from knee-on-belly and back again, the two positions complement each other well. Often when your opponent attempts to escape your mount you can switch to knee-on-belly to frustrate him.

In a street fight, knee-on-belly offers the advantage of being able to get up quickly off the opponent and stand up, should you feel threatened by sneak attacks. Most beginners feel unstable while holding this position and consequently do not employ it as often or as confidently as they should. The important thing to realize is that the great advantage of the knee-on-belly position is *mobility*. This great mobility can be utilized to hold the opponent down. As your opponent tries to escape, you can jump over him to the other side, or spin around his head and take knee-on-belly on the other side. Thus rather than holding him down with weight and power, you do so with mobility and speed. Should your opponent gain the knee-on-belly position on you, you must think in terms of escape to a better position. As was the case with being on the bottom of the mount or across-side position, attempting to apply a submission hold or strike while on the bottom of knee-on-belly position is foolhardy. The most common escapes involve turning *into* your opponent (never away, as that would expose your back) and getting to your knees.

Renzo works hard to pass the formidable guard of Jean-Jacques Machado. Both men are displaying tremendous technical skill. Jean-Jacques is attempting a sweep from the open guard (demonstrated in the technique section). Renzo resists by spreading his base wide and keeping his back straight.

strikes at will. The best situation is where you are behind your opponent, either on top of him or underneath him, with both of your feet locked into his hips. Do not cross your feet, as this makes you vulnerable to a foot lock; just keep them pressed against the front of his hips. The function of these "hooks" is to keep you in place as your opponent tries to dislodge you. These "hooks" give you a great deal of control over your opponent and give you the time and control to apply chokes and other submission holds. Once you have gotten behind your opponent in a ground-grappling situation, one of your first objectives should be to get your hooks in place, so as to facilitate controlling and then finishing your opponent. The fact that in a sporting jiu-jitsu match, achieving the rear position with both hooks in scores the same as achieving the mounted position (four points—the highest possible score for any given position) indicates just how highly valued this position is. While it is generally best to get your hooks in whenever you get to your opponent's back, it is possible to control and finish him without your hooks in place.

Should your opponent get to your back you must think in terms of escaping to a better position. Unless your opponent makes a very basic error, such as crossing his feet, you have virtually no submission holds to use against him and little chance to strike him effectively. We shall look at some such escapes later.

On Your Opponent's Back

It is very advantageous to get into a controlling position behind your opponent. This is because your opponent cannot strike you and has virtually no chance of applying a submission hold, while you can attack with chokes, arm locks, and

The Guard Position

One of the most distinctive features of Brazilian jiu-jitsu is the prominence of the guard position. This is where you have our opponent between your legs while you are on your back or buttocks. Normally you might think of this as a very disadvantageous position, since your opponent is on top of you and appears to be able to punch, strangle, or head butt you at will. However, when you hold your opponent in guard you have a great many submission holds available to you that can enable you to efficiently finish the fight while on your back underneath your opponent. In addition, various sweeps can be readily used from the guard position that enable you to attain a still better position (such as the mount). Moreover, a skilled user of the guard position can make it extremely difficult for his opponent to get off any really powerful punches or head butts. Thus in spite of being underneath, the skillful user of the guard can employ this position to defend himself and work into either a submission hold or a better position. The guard is often thought of as a defensive position; however, skilled users of the guard position often employ it in a very offensive manner, taking the fight to their opponent and attacking at every opportunity. It need not be thought of as a purely defensive or passive gesture. The initial description of the guard as any position where you are on your back or buttocks with your opponent between your legs was intentionally loose. The guard position comes in many forms. You can lie back and cross your feet behind the opponent's back. This is often referred to as the "closed guard." You can uncross your feet and place them on the opponent's hips, biceps, under his thighs, or on the ground. Anytime your feet are uncrossed we shall refer to as the "open guard."

The great virtue of the guard position is that it enables a smaller, weaker man to take on a far larger and more aggressive opponent and win. Whenever you fight someone far larger and stronger than yourself, it is normal enough to end up underneath him in the course of the fight. For most people this is disastrous, yet the skilled jiu-jitsu practitioner can take advantage of this situation and by intelligently employing the guard position control and finish the fight. The guard is also of great value when fighting someone who is more skilled in takedowns than you. Even if you are taken down to your back you can fight from the guard position. This emphasis on the guard position is one of the most representative features of Brazilian jiu-jitsu and gives it a very distinctive look.

It is often claimed that the guard position is vulnerable to leg locks. A skilled user of leg locks certainly represents a danger to the inexperienced or careless user of the guard position; however, there are ways to defend your legs against such attacks. While leg locks are legal in Brazilian jiu-jitsu competition, competitors are often wary of using them, since they have a higher-than-normal risk attached to their use. They tend to either succeed spectacularly or result in losing position when the opponent counters.

When you find yourself in your opponent's guard (that is, he wraps his legs around you), you have the option of striking him. This, however, is often not very effective, since the opponent can often defend himself very readily using the guard. You can try to gain a submission hold on the oppo-

nent, usually in the form of a leg lock, though there are others. This is acceptable. However, the difficulty of applying a submission hold or strike against an opponent who holds you in his guard makes the best option that of getting out from between your opponent's legs and working your way past his legs to a more advantageous position such as across-side or knee-on-belly. This process of getting past the opponent's legs to a better position is referred to as "passing the guard," and it represents one of the most important positional skills in Brazilian Jiu-Jitsu.

It often happens in the course of attempting to pass an opponent's guard that you get to a position where your opponent has his legs wrapped around only one of your legs. You do not quite have a full across-side position on him, since he still has one of your legs trapped, nor does he have full guard on you, since one of your legs is out and you are getting close to across-side. This position is referred to as "half-guard." It represents a neutral position where neither man has a major advantage. Both can employ submission holds from here. The man on top is generally looking to continue passing until he gets a clean across-side position, the man underneath is principally looking to put his opponent back in guard, though both men have other options.

A Practical Example of Brazilian Jiu-Jitsu Positional Strategy

Say you that are confronted by an aggressive and belligerent person. As the dispute between he and you escalates, he suddenly rushes at you, swinging wildly. You grab each other. His strength and aggression momentarily overwhelm you and you both fall to the ground. Your opponent's momentum enables him to fall on top of you. This scenario is one of the most common in a real fight. The initial aggression on the part of your attacker and the shock it creates in you gives him an initial advantage. It begins with blows but quickly enters into a clinch with both combatants going to the ground. In most cases the fight would now be won by the larger, more aggressive attacker. He has landed in a dominant position and can now pummel you into a bloody and painful defeat. Let us see how positional strategy can be used in a very practical way to get out of this potentially disastrous situation, regain the initiative, and win the fight.

As you fall and your opponent lands on top, the initial shock is quickly replaced by the realization that you must escape from this terrible position with all haste. You realize that you have virtually no chance of defeating your opponent from this position, either with submission holds or strikes. Your mind is thus set on one thing—escape to a better position. Before your opponent can sit up and let loose a torrent of punches you bridge hard into a move you have practiced since beginning jiu-jitsu, the "upa" (described later). As you roll your opponent over you receive one cuffing blow to the forehead, nothing serious. You make a mental note that this is nothing compared with the dozens of blows you would have received had you not known how to escape and that this was the inevitable result of making the initial mistake of allowing the opponent to fall mounted on top of you. As you come up on top of your opponent between his legs, you consider your next move. You realize that your opponent is not skilled in jiu-jitsu and that consequently being in his guard (being between his legs) is not a great danger. You could probably win the fight merely by punching him from where you are. You decide against this, however, as you realize that punching from your present position is far less efficient than from other positions that you can attain. Also, there is always the danger of him kicking you in the face along with the risk of hurting your hands in a slugging match. You briefly play with the idea of putting him in a leg lock, as he obviously has no idea how to defend his legs from attack. The idea of breaking the man's knee seems too harsh; there are less devastating ways to subdue your attacker that seem more appropriate to this situation—you want to subdue him, not cripple him. Accordingly, you decide to "pass the guard," that is, to get around his legs to "across-side," where you lie across his chest. You work your way past his legs, controlling him as you go (explained later), and finish up across his side. As you attain this dominant position you think about moving on to a still better position, the mount. Suddenly your attacker erupts beneath you, perhaps sensing the danger he is in. He thrashes madly under you, twisting left and right and threatening to overturn you. You decide the best option is to consolidate your current across-side position, since it is more stable than the alternatives. You hold on until you feel your opponent weakening. As this happens you become aware of a commotion behind you. People are arguing loudly and you fear that your opponent's friends are about to intervene. Quickly you pop up to a knee-on-belly position that enables you to simultaneously control your opponent and look up to check your surroundings. People are arguing as to whether they should call the police or break up the fight. You sense that you are not in any danger of being jumped so you slide your knee down to the floor and take the mounted position. Now your opponent goes berserk again; he twists to his side. You let him go and get behind him, sliding your "hooks" into his hips as you do so. You now have total control of you opponent. He thrashes about wildly but to no avail. You decide against striking him, though you easily could—it would not look good if the police showed up with him bleeding profusely and you with not even a scratch! Consequently you decide to employ your finishing skills. You apply a simple choke (explained later) and put your opponent quietly to sleep.

As you get up off your senseless opponent people look at you in shock. You have just defeated a larger and more

Royler triumphant! Victory in the 1999 Abu Dhabi Submission Wrestling World Championship under 65 kg division.

aggressive opponent in spite of getting off to an awful start, all without bloodshed and tears. Your attacker was subdued quickly and effectively with injury only to his ego. This was done by the application of simple positional strategy and technique combined with finishing skills.

By keeping this overall strategy in mind as you grapple with your partner you can greatly increase your progress in the sport.

An Inherent Advantage of Grappling Training

In the debate over whether grappling styles of martial arts are a viable means of self-defense there is a very important factor that is often overlooked. When you engage in free-grappling training with a partner you are employing the majority of the methods of combat that will be used in competition and in the street at close to full power. Moreover, you are confronted with an opponent who is employing all his skill, knowledge, and strength to resist and defeat you (within the limits of a grappling session). The result is that you rapidly become used to applying your techniques and knowledge in a "live" situation. This is a *tremendous* advantage. Just as you could never hope to become a champion swimmer without ever actually getting wet, you can never hope to become a fighter without ever coming to grips with an opponent who is actively trying to thwart and defeat you.

Because grappling training does not allow striking or foul techniques, you can engage in it *far more often* than martial arts that do. If you spar hard every day in boxing training, the likelihood of injury is unacceptably high. The risks are even higher for martial arts that allow bare-handed fighting and foul tactics. You could not spar in that fashion without daily injury. By prohibiting dangerous moves, you can concentrate on the moves that grapplers will utilize in a real

fight on a daily basis with a far lower chance of injury. The result is that grapplers can progress very rapidly in learning to implement techniques on resisting partners. There is a certain irony in this. By removing the more dangerous elements of fighting—punching, kicking, gouging, biting, and so on, you can concentrate on the techniques you hope to use in a real situation against live opponents. Moreover, you can reasonably expect to do this on a daily basis without great fear of injury. *The resulting familiarity with applying your techniques full power against a person doing everything in his power to defeat you is a great advantage in a real fight.* Of course you have to adapt to the obvious differences that will emerge in a real fight. The opponent will probably be trying to punch, kick, scratch, gouge, and bite you. However, the familiarity with active resistance will make the transition relatively easy. You will be comfortable with the feeling of a struggling, resisting opponent. After modifying your style in the appropriate ways, you can use that experience of hard daily sparring to your advantage.

One would think that by removing the more dangerous elements of training, such as striking and foul tactics, a martial art would become *weaker*. Experience shows the opposite is true for the reasons outlined. *Success in fighting is directly related to the degree to which a martial art exposes its students to the pressures of real combat.* Because grappling training is safe enough to engage in at full power on a regular basis, it can expose the students to a greater amount of the pressures they can expect in a real fight. This is an advantage that can not be overlooked and one that was witnessed in the clash of styles in the early days of mixed martial arts competitions. Styles with apparently lethal elements that were considered too dangerous to use in regular training did poorly, precisely because they had never been exposed to the cauldron of live training against resisting partners.

So much for the theoretical elements of Brazilian jiu-jitsu. It is time to look at the techniques.

Part 2: Technique

Blue Belt

Royler Gracie works methodically to pass his opponents guard on his way to
winning his first World Brazilian Jiu-Jitsu Championship, February 1996.

Tying up the belt

Most practitioners of Brazilian jiu-jitsu wear a traditional gi (kimono) while training. A gi is compulsory in most tournaments. The advantage of wearing a gi in training is that it makes movement and escape much more difficult than normal. Since your opponent can grab the gi at will in a very strong grip, free movement becomes quite limited. The friction generated by the gi makes it nearly impossible to use brute strength to pull out of submission holds. This forces you to apply proper technique in escaping, making you a more technically sound fighter. In addition the wide array of strangleholds that the gi creates forces you to become very adept at defending your neck—a crucial skill for a grappler. Any time you don a gi you greatly multiply the possible number of moves and techniques that you and your opponent can use. This is because there are many techniques that require a gi to be effective. Since you have a much wider array of moves available both you and your opponent quickly get into the habit of applying moves in long combinations, of thinking of many options as you grapple. The gi also is physically uncomfortable and hot. Once you learn to stand the discomfort, grappling without the gi seems so much easier. The gi consists of long pants, a heavy jacket, and a belt. The jacket is much thicker than the form of jacket worn in karate and other striking martial arts. This is because it is subject to great stress in grappling training. It is double weave, reinforced heavy cotton with a very heavy collar. The gi comes in several different sizes. Some experimentation may be required before you find the ideal size for you (bear in mind that the gi will shrink when washed and dried). Here we look at the proper way to put on the gi and tie the belt.

1

Royler puts on the pants (they have a drawstring that you pull tight and then tie with a common bow) and jacket. Fold the left side of your jacket over the right side. Most manufacturers place a small company logo on the front left side of the gi that will be visible when worn correctly. Take your belt in your right hand and hold it in the middle so that there is an equal length of belt on both sides.

2

Holding the belt in both hands, place the middle of the belt in the middle of your stomach beneath your navel and bring both ends around your back.

3

Wrap the belt all the way around your back and back to the front of your stomach (the belt is quite long and will do this easily). This means in effect that the belt goes twice around your stomach.

4

Cross the ends of the belt, right side in front.

5

Thread the right side of the belt end over and then around both loops of the belt under your navel.

(!) Now simply loop the left end of the belt over and around the right and pull tight. This completes a simple square knot.

6

Pull both ends of the belt to tighten it.

7

Ready to go!

002 Rolling and breaking a fall

The art of rolling and breaking a fall is a crucial one to learn in the study of jiu-jitsu. There are many throws and takedowns in jiu-jitsu. When inexperienced people are thrown they are often hurt. Fear of injury often makes people reluctant to partake in throwing practice. There is a proper way to fall that virtually removes the risk of injury. Once you develop the ability to roll and fall properly there is little fear in being thrown. Rolling practice is also an excellent way to warm the body up before intense grappling training.

1

Renzo starts in a standing position. He has one side of his body forward.

2

Renzo bends down to a position where both hands can touch the floor. His knees are bent.

3

Renzo passes his lead arm between his legs and tucks his chin down. His weight is supported on both feet and his other (rear) hand. He begins to lean forward in the direction of his lead leg.

!

A good way for beginners to drill this move is to have a partner pull the hand through the legs as shown and gently push on the lower back. This will give you the feeling of the correct roll.

4

Pushing off with his legs, Renzo rolls over his lead shoulder. Notice how his head is tucked in. The feeling here is very relaxed. Do not tense up as you roll.

5

As Renzo rolls over to his back his rear arm comes forward. He uses it to slap the mat. The harder he rolls, the harder he will slap. This is the classic finishing position to all the breakfalls. Whenever you are thrown, this is the position you want to land in, slapping the mat as you land. This slapping motion both helps in breaking the fall and ensures that you do not make the common mistake of extending an arm and landing on that braced arm. This is a common cause of injury to those people who do not know how to fall. As you gain confidence you can go faster and faster. Eventually you will be able to sprint forward and leap into the fall. Once you feel confident you can allow people to throw you with little to fear. Start with the basic hip throw outlined in this book, as this throw allows the thrower to control your descent.

Escape from the mounted position, "Upa"

There are few worse scenarios in a real fight than being pinned underneath your opponent's mount. Sitting astride your chest, your adversary is free to strike you as he wishes. His strikes can utilize the full rotational power of his hips and shoulders, generating tremendous power. Your shoulders and hips, on the other hand, are pinned to the floor, making your attempts to strike back weak and ineffective. Moreover, your opponent can easily enter into a vast array of devastating submission holds, arm locks, neck cranks, and strangles while you lack the necessary position and leverage to respond. If you do not know *exactly* what to do, the chances of you emerging without serious injury are slim indeed. One of the most fundamental and important means of escaping the mounted position is the "upa" method. This involves rolling your opponent onto his back. The chief advantage of this method compared with others is that it can take a wild-punching street fighter off your chest and onto his back, where he is unlikely to have the technical skill to resist you. Against a skilled grap-

pler, however, the completed "upa" technique still leaves you locked in the guard position. Still, this is far better than being pinned under the mount. The "upa" escape combines extremely well with the "elbow escape" (outlined later in this book). Whenever "upa" fails, it almost always generates enough space to allow you to switch easily into an elbow escape. Whenever your opponent resists the elbow escape by pinching his legs together (thus narrowing his base) he becomes vulnerable to "upa." In unison, these two techniques can get you out of all but the tightest mounts.

The "upa" is based upon a simple, yet very effective principle. The idea is to trap your opponent's arm and leg on one side of his body and then to roll him over on the side of his trapped limbs. Since he cannot base out with his trapped arm or leg, he has no means of preventing himself from being rolled over. Your opponent can hold you in many ways while mounted. No matter how he holds you, there is always a simple method of trapping his arm and leg on one side of his body as a prelude to rolling him over. Here we look at a case where you opponent is holding you down at the neck or chest area.

1

Royler is mounted on Renzo, holding him down with his hands at the chest or throat.

2

Renzo's first concern is to get control of one of Royler's arms. How he does this is dependent upon the way Royler holds him. In this case Royler's hands are on Renzo's chest/throat. The best grip is to reach across and grip the opponent's wrist (your palm faces toward your legs). If you are gripping your opponent's left arm, your left hand comes across to grip the left wrist and vice versa. Your other hand grips the same arm at the elbow. Now you have trapped one of your opponent's arms with two of yours.

Here you can see the grip that Renzo employs to trap his opponent's arm. You must be able to secure this grip very quickly. You have very little time when pinned under the mount in a real fight.

3

Renzo's next concern is to trap his opponent's leg on the same side that he has trapped the arm. Failure to do so allows an experienced opponent to post out his leg and resist being rolled over. To trap the leg, Renzo simply brings his foot up and places it just outside his opponent's foot on the same side as the trapped arm.

The trapping action of the foot can be seen clearly here. Make sure there is contact between your ankle and his foot/ankle; space allows your opponent to escape.

4

Using the power of both legs, Renzo bridges straight up, his hips coming high off the floor. This off-balances Royler and pitches him forward.

5

Having brought Royler forward, Renzo turns over on the shoulder on the same side as Royler's trapped arm and leg. The key point here is that Renzo does *not* roll his opponent directly over to one side. Rather, he takes him forward and to the side. A good way to perform this correctly is to look over the shoulder that you are bridging (which will be the one on the same side as your opponent's trapped arm and leg). Now push and bridge in the same direction that you are looking.

6

Renzo continues to bridge over his shoulder, taking Royler over very easily. The power you can generate with this move is very impressive. Done correctly, it can take a very heavy opponent over with ease.

7

Renzo finishes in Royler's guard. From here he must continue the fight. Notice that Renzo immediately places his hands on Royler's biceps to prevent Royler from striking him or attempting a quick stranglehold as he goes over.

004 The Upa drill

In any grappling style there are certain movements of the body that are essential to success in that style. Brazilian jiu-jitsu is no exception. We have seen already the elbow escape drill—a series of movements that mimic those employed while performing an elbow escape. Another very useful drill is the upa drill. You will remember that the upa is one of the basic escapes from the mounted position. It consists of trapping your opponent's arm and leg on one side of his body and then arching your body so that your hips come off the floor, taking your opponent forward and over to the side of his trapped arm. This movement of arching your body (often referred to as "bridging") is essential to many escapes in Brazilian jiu-jitsu. Whenever you are trapped under an opponent's mount or across-side pin, this arching movement is extremely useful—indeed, it forms the backbone of many of the best escapes. It makes perfect sense, then, to practice the movement as much as possible so that when you are pinned under an opponent you can easily explode into an arch and perform an escape. You do not need a training partner to perform the basic movement. Time spent in this solo drill will be amply repaid when you come to wrestle with your partner.

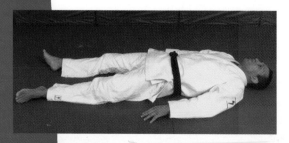

1

Renzo starts in a supine position.

2

He then adopts a good defensive position when trapped under a pin. His hands are tight to his chest, elbows tight to his sides, making it difficult for his opponent to trap an arm and gain a submission hold. Renzo draws his knees up, both feet on the floor, giving him the potential for a strong push off the floor with both legs.

3

Pushing hard with the strength of both legs, Renzo thrusts his hips off the floor and turns to one side. *Only his feet and one shoulder remain on the floor.* A crucial point here is that Renzo looks in the direction he arches. *He does not turn directly to the side.* Rather, he arches up and over his shoulder in an 11 o'clock direction.

4

Continuing his drive, Renzo powers up onto the shoulder he is arching over and throws his leg (the one on the opposite side toward which he is turning) over the other leg.

5

Renzo continues turning until he is flat on the ground, face down. If he had had an opponent on top of him he would now be on top of his opponent, having taken him over from the mounted position.

6

To finish the drill, Renzo comes up to his knees and regains his base. You can drill this movement for long periods. Try to imagine an opponent on top of you while you bridge your way out.

Defense against the two-handed front choke

One of the most common forms of street aggression is the two-handed front choke. The aggressor grabs your throat with both hands and squeezes hard. While this can be very intimidating, especially when done in a quick and powerful way, there is a relatively simple counter. Since it is easily countered, experienced fighters generally refrain from this move.

However, it is so common among unskilled attackers that it is important to learn the counter.

When people use the two-handed front choke in a real fight they usually try to push you against the nearest wall, driving you backward as they apply it. Practice the move with this in mind.

1

Royler grabs Renzo in a classic and common form of unskilled aggression—both hands on the throat, squeezing hard. This is uncomfortable. An attacker with very large hands and a particularly strong grip can even cause you to pass out with this kind of hold. In addition, the attacker can use this grip to push you against a wall and dominate your movements; hence, it is important to be able to escape quickly and efficiently.

Renzo's first concern is to relieve the pressure of the attacker's fingers sinking into his throat. He immediately tenses his neck muscles to reduce the pain and pressure.

2

To begin the escape, Renzo drops his level by bending at the knees and ducking his head straight between Royler's outstretched arms. The only thing preventing Renzo from moving forward in this way is Royler's thumbs. In a battle of strength, Renzo's entire upper body will always defeat Royler's thumbs!

Note how Renzo initially reacts to the choke by dropping his level to establish a secure base, making it difficult for his opponent to shove him around. He does this by bending at the knees, not the waist.

3

Now Renzo can bend forward at the waist, his head going straight down between Royler's arms. Then he steps back with his right foot and quickly swings his head back to his right to break out of the hold. The move works very efficiently for a simple reason: the attacker's hand position cannot prevent Renzo from moving forward and down to initiate the move. Renzo can easily push past the attacker's thumbs to come forward and drop his level. Moreover, the attacker cannot prevent Renzo from circling his head and trunk backward with the grip that he has on the throat. The double-handed grip on the throat has no pulling power, so Renzo pulls away easily once he has come forward and dropped his level.

The single-handed wrist grab (palm up)

Street attacks are very often preceded by grabs. Aggressors grab clothing, arms, the neck, even hair. One of the most common forms of grabbing is of the wrists. People with a very strong grip can use this grab to dominate a victim, dragging their victim around or immobilizing the arm to set up punches with the other hand. Faced with this kind of aggression, you need to be able to break out quickly. Bearing in mind that the people who most favor this form of attack tend to be big, powerful people with extremely strong gripping power, the escape must not rely upon strength, since you can reasonably assume your attacker is superior in this regard to you.

1

Renzo grabs Royler's left wrist with his right hand.

2

In response to Renzo's right-handed grip upon his left wrist, Royler quickly steps back with his right foot. This creates space between him and his attacker. This space will be useful when he comes to escape. Royler clenches his fist and rotates his left wrist under and inside Renzo's right hand. His left palm turns up to the ceiling as he does this movment.

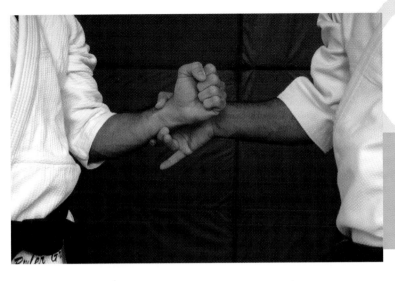

The key to this movement is the idea of turning your left wrist under and inside your attacker's right wrist. This directs your escape toward the weakest part of your attacker's grip—the thumb. From here it is easy to retract your hand out of the strongest grip.

3

Once you have gotten to the position shown in the detail photograph, escape is simple. Jerk your hand back toward yourself, using the space you have created between you and your attacker.

Practice breaking the grip as quickly as possible. The longer the aggressor holds you, the more time he has to do damage with his other hand. Once having escaped, do not leave your arm hanging out so he can grab it again. Retract it and be ready to defend yourself.

Single-handed wrist grab (palm down)

Another way for your opponent to grab your wrist is with his palm down toward the floor. This grip can also be used by a big, strong attacker to dominate one of your arms. Since his hand is palm down, a different means of escape is required.

1

Renzo begins by grabbing Royler's left wrist with his right hand. Renzo's right palm is down. This renders the escape method used in position 006 ineffective.

2

Royler quickly steps back with his right leg. This opens up space between him and his attacker. Royler immediately rotates his left palm up to the ceiling. To effect the escape, Royler must pass his left wrist under and outside Renzo's right wrist.

Once again, the crucial point is that Royler direct his escape to the weakest part of his attacker's grip—the thumb. To do this, Royler turns his palm to the ceiling and rotates his wrist under and outside Renzo's grip. Now Royler's escape will be directed toward the weak area between Renzo's thumb and fingers.

3

Royler utilizes the space he has created between himself and his attacker to jerk his hand back to safety. Once again, do not leave your arm hanging in a way that allows your attacker to grab it again. Once having completed the move, bring your hands back close to you.

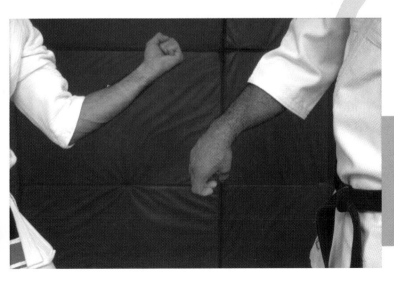

Note how Royler pulls up and to the left to effect his escape in an efficient manner.

As with any wrist grab, escape against a particularly strong grip can often be aided by faking escape in the wrong direction, then quickly snapping out with the correct escape.

Two-handed wrist grab

A common scenario in a defense situation is the double-handed wrist grab. Here your opponent uses both his hands to grab one of your wrists in the same manner in which one would hold a baseball bat. At first this grip seems intimidating and hard to break, due to the fact that it uses the strength of two hands against one of yours. There is, however, a simple solution.

1

Renzo grabs Royler's left wrist with both hands, as though gripping a baseball bat. Notice that in this case you have eight fingers holding the bottom side and just the two thumbs holding the top. Therefore the path of least resistance would be in the direction of the two thumbs, and that is where the escape will be directed.

2

Royler reaches with his free hand (the right) and grabs his trapped (left) hand. As he does this, he steps back with his right foot, opening up space between him and the aggressor. This space will be utilized later.

Royler grips his hands right palm under left fist, a very strong and mechanically efficient grip. Note that he does not use his thumbs when he grips

3

Having gotten his grip and stepped back with the right foot, Royler pulls his trapped left hand straight back toward his chest. The space between the two men that was created when Royler stepped back with his right foot allows for a very strong pull. The sharp pulling action of both hands allows Royler to easily slip out of the aggressor's grasp.

Movements that allow you to escape grabs of this kind are best done with short, snappy, jerky motions rather than slow pulling motions.

009 The offensive hip throw

The basic hip throw is one of the most versatile takedowns in the jiu-jitsu repertoire. It is relatively simple to perform. It can be employed with or without a gi. It is easy to control the fall of the opponent, and it can be used in a great variety of situations. Here Renzo demonstrates its use as a straightforward attack.

1

Renzo and Royler square off.

2

Renzo quickly reaches forward and grabs Royler's elbow.

3

Renzo pulls the arm in tight to his body.

4

Stepping around to the opposite side of the arm he has grabbed, Renzo throws his other arm around Royler's waist. Note how tight to his opponent Renzo is. In a tight clinch position like this, Renzo is in no danger of being hit.

5

It is now a simple matter for Renzo to place the foot that was behind Royler, around in front of Royler. Note the relative foot position. Renzo's feet are right in front of Royler's feet, facing the same direction. Renzo pushes his hips across in front of Royler's hips and bends his knees to lower his level.

(!) Note the way that Renzo pushes his hips across in front of his opponent. A common mistake here is to have your feet too far apart. Keep them around the same width as your opponent's, about shoulder width.

6

Renzo straightens his legs and uses the arm around Royler's waist to bring Royler over his hip in one smooth motion. There should be a feeling of ease here. The mechanical efficiency of the throw is impressive.

7

Renzo can control Royler's descent easily, letting him fall as hard as he wants to. At the completion of the throw, Renzo is left in a totally dominant position.

Defense against a single-handed lapel grab

Very often physical aggression begins with the protagonist grabbing the victim as a prelude to the assault. Sometimes it is used simply as a means of intimidating a victim. Either way, you should be able to deal with what is a very common form of attack.

1

Royler reaches out with his right hand and grabs Renzo's lapel. This gives Royler a good deal of control over Renzo. He can use his grip to pull Renzo around and control his movements while he strikes with the other hand. He can also use this grip to initiate a throw. It is a very common sight in real fights to see one man grab with one hand to control his opponent as he strikes with the other. In America the prevalence of such technique in the violent sport of ice hockey has led to the label "hockey fight" to describe this situation.

2

Renzo recognizes the danger of allowing an opponent to control both the movement and distancing of a fight and looks to escape immediately. He grabs Royler's right wrist with his left hand and begins to bring his right hand under Royler's right arm.

3

Renzo steps his right foot out wide past Royler's right foot. It is important to step wide since you must allow sufficient room for yourself to step through the space between your foot and the opponent's body. At the same time Renzo brings his right arm in a scooping motion under Royler's right arm so that his right hand is holding Royler's right arm at the tricep or elbow.

4

In one quick and fluid motion, Renzo back steps through with his left foot. To do this he briefly turns his back on his opponent while maintaining the grip on Royler's arm and steps back with his left foot into the space between himself and his opponent. The step with the left foot must be long enough to take you behind your opponent.

5

Renzo pushes with his right hand on Royler's right elbow. Since Royler is in a mechanically disadvantageous position it is difficult for him to resist. Renzo slips his head out from under Royler's arm, taking a position behind Royler's back with a tight shoulderlock. By pushing Royler's right wrist up his back, Renzo can tighten the lock.

Front collar choke

The front collar choke is a very efficient means to make an opponent submit in training and competition. In a street fight it can be used to render an attacker unconscious. Usually this choke is employed in a ground-grappling situation. Typically it is used from the mounted position, knee-on-stomach, or while one has an opponent in the guard position. It can also be used in a standing situation. For demonstration purposes, Renzo and Royler will be standing. Chokes that rely upon the collar are often thought of as useful only in a sporting situation, where contestants wear the gi. However, many popular forms of street attire give excellent opportunity to employ collar chokes in the street.

1

Royler reaches for the right side of Renzo's collar with his left hand. He opens the collar out wide.

2

By opening the collar in this fashion, Royler can easily slip his right hand, fingers first, deep inside Renzo's right lapel. Note that for this particular version of the choke, Royler's right palm is facing up toward the ceiling, his thumb is outside the lapel. Royler makes sure his right hand goes in as deeply as possible, all the way to the back of Renzo's neck.

3

Royler now passes his left hand under his right, palm up, and gets a good, deep grip on Renzo's left lapel. Once again, the grip is fingers inside the collar, thumb outside.

🛈 Notice the depth of Royler's grip, especially with the initial hand that goes in, in this case, the right hand. The deeper the grip with the first hand inside the lapel, the easier the choke will be. Note that once Royler gets his hand in position, fingers inside the lapel, thumb outside, he clenches his hand in a tight fist.

4

Royler's two hands are in ideal position now to begin the strangle. Both palms are facing the ceiling, his hands closed into fists. Royler begins the strangle by rotating his two fists toward each other. This has the effect of pressing the wrist bones against the carotid arteries that run along the side of the neck. The resulting lack of blood flow to the brain can easily bring about unconsciousness if the person being strangled does not signal submission.

5

Royler does not strangle his opponent at arms length. Rather, he pulls his opponent in tight to his chest as he applies the strangle by pulling down with both elbows and rotating his fists toward each other. By pulling his opponent down to his chest, Royler prevents him from defending the choke. In addition, in a street fight, he prevents his opponent from punching him as the strangle is being applied.

The classic finishing position for the choke. Royler pulls his opponent down tight to his chest. His opponent must now submit or pass out. Though this move is usually referred to as a "choke," it does not work by blocking the opponent from breathing, rather it cuts off blood to the brain—a far more efficient and quick method of attaining victory. As such, it is perhaps more properly referred to as a "strangle."

The key to the front collar choke is to get the first hand in as deeply as possible. Failure to do so will inevitably result in a poor strangling effect. The simplest way to ensure adequate depth with the first hand is to use your other hand to open your opponent's lapel wide, thus creating an open path for your hand to enter all the way to the back of the neck.

012

Defense against standing side headlock

Headlocks are perhaps the most common technique used in street attacks. While skilled grapplers can make good use of them, most people use them in ways that are not particularly effective. To the inexperienced fighter even a poorly applied headlock can be intimidating. Strong men often use them to dominate weak and inexperienced opponents, grabbing around the head and using the control that this affords to manhandle their victims. Often people hold with one arm around the head and punch with the other. Headlocks can be used in both standing positions and also on the ground. While even poorly applied headlocks can be uncomfortable and even frightening, there are several easy counters. Here we look at a counter to a common form of standing headlock.

1

Royler rushes in and grabs Renzo in a side headlock, a very common form of attack. Such an attack is not advisable but is so common that learning a simple defense to it is essential.

2

Royler throws his right arm around Renzo's neck and head and locks his hands together. This is often a prelude to being punched with the left hand, so quick action is essential. Renzo quickly places his left forearm across Royler's jaw. This prevents his attacker from pulling him in and down, enabling Renzo to maintain a fairly upright stance.

3

Renzo drops his level while keeping his back straight. His right hand reaches under his attacker's near thigh close to the knee.

4

Renzo lifts powerfully, using the strength of his legs. He gains lifting strength by driving his hips in under his attacker. This enables him to easily pick Royler up off the ground. The key to the lift is popping your hips under the attacker and then thrusting them in and up, looking up as you do so.

5

Renzo takes his attacker all the way up. Since the lift relies upon good body mechanics, the use of leg strength, and getting the hips close to and under the opponent, you can easily lift even a very big person. The fall is a very heavy one for the opponent.

6

Renzo now has the option of putting the attacker down as hard or gently as he wants, depending upon the situation. Clearly if he were to drop the attacker on pavement it would be devastating. One of the great advantages of grappling in a self-defense situation like this is the tremendous flexibility it offers. The same move can be used in very different ways depending on the context. Renzo has the option of putting the attacker down in a number of ways, ranging from the gentle to the truly frightening.

7

Some people are immensely strong and when they apply a headlock it can be very uncomfortable. Be confident, however, that the side headlock will not seriously harm you, no matter how uncomfortable it might be. It will not cause you to pass out or break anything. Do not panic.

013 Defense against the rear bear hug

A very common form of attack in a street fight is for an assailant to approach from behind and grab around your arms, locking his hands together. This has the immediate effect of trapping your arms, making any kind of defense very difficult. Quite often this method is favored by multiple attackers as it allows a second attacker to hit you with impunity. What is needed is a means of escape that is quick, since it is likely that the reason you are being held is to enable a second man to hit you. Moreover, it should be devastating enough that the fight is taken out of your assailant, enabling you to concentrate on the other attacker.

1

Renzo grabs Royler from behind and locks his arms around Royler's arms. Royler's arms are trapped.

2

Royler's first reaction is to simultaneously drop his hips down and snap his hands up so that his arms are bent at ninety degrees and the forearms parallel with the floor. By lowering his level straight away, Royler makes it very difficult for Renzo to lift him and throw him around. By bringing his hands up, Royler makes it impossible for Renzo to slide his arms down to Royler's wrists and trap Royler's arms even more efficiently. More importantly, he prevents Renzo from grabbing around the waist and controlling his hips.

ⓘ Note the position of Royler's arms. They are bent at ninety degrees, palms up. Notice also that by dropping his hips Royler has placed his center of gravity beneath Renzo's.

3

Royler now turns his (right) foot out and slides his hips to the same side as the out-turned foot. Renzo cannot prevent this movement of the hips since Royler has prevented him from bringing his arms down to Royler's waist. By turning the heel of the foot out and turning his hips in toward his opponent, Royler creates space between his hips and those of his opponent.

4

In one quick move Royler steps his other leg behind Renzo's legs. He steps through the space created by the initial turning out of the other foot. At the same time Royler bends down and grabs Renzo behind both knees with both his hands. Note that Royler does not grab the pants. Rather, he cups his hands directly behind the tendons of Renzo's knees.

5

This is an immensely strong lifting position. Royler straightens up using the strength of his legs. He combines this with the lifting action of his arms, bringing Renzo's legs up to the side.

6

Note the extreme elevation of the throw. The leverage here is tremendous. Renzo is lifted high over Royler's hips and lower back.

7

The fall is a heavy one for the opponent! Renzo crashes hard into the mat. Note the way Renzo is breaking the heavy fall by preparing to slap the mat with his free arm. In a self-defense situation it is unlikely that the opponent will rise quickly from such a fall.

8

Royler finishes in classic style, controlling Renzo's arm. If circumstances require it, he can easily go straight into an armlock or begin striking from this dominant position.

Thrusting choke, "Amassa Pão"

The thrusting choke is a very simple submission that requires the use of the gi collar. It can be used very successfully from the mounted position, especially when combined with the arm bar. You attack first with the thrusting choke, then, as your opponent goes to defend his neck with his arms, you switch to the arm bar. Another good time to use the thrusting choke is while inside your opponent's guard. This represents one of the few times you can attempt a submission hold while locked in your opponent's guard. There is some danger here, however. Your opponent can counter by attacking your arms as you attempt the thrusting choke. Then it might well be *you* who ends up submitting! Rather than use the thrusting choke as a direct submission hold, many experienced grapplers use it as a simple means to force their opponent to open their guard. In order to attack your extended arms, your opponent must open his guard, at which point you cease the choke immediately and begin passing his guard. Here we see the thrusting choke applied while inside someone's guard, as a direct and simple form of submission hold.

1

Royler finds himself locked in Renzo's closed guard. He grabs Renzo's lapels at the lower chest

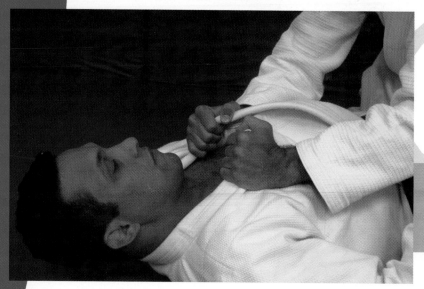

Note the fashion in which Royler grabs the lapels. His thumbs are up toward the ceiling, fingers inside the gi lapels, his knuckles pointing at Renzo.

2

Renzo pushes one hand hard across Renzo's throat while pulling back with the other hand.

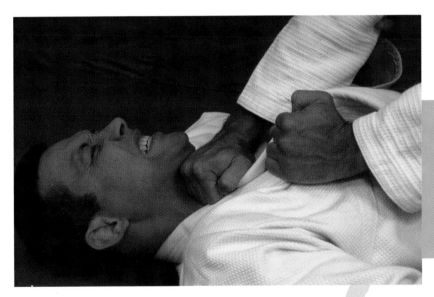

Note the hand position. The primary choking hand drives across the throat cutting off air and blood. It is as though Royler is trying to drive his fist down to the ground over Renzo's shoulder. By pulling back on the other lapel all the slack is removed from the gi, resulting in a very tight choke.

Defense against the thrusting choke

There is considerable power in the thrusting choke. Failure to defend it can quickly result in defeat. It is tempting to counter by attacking the extended arm as your opponent leans forward to choke you. However, as we pointed out before, it may well be that your experienced opponent is merely using the thrusting choke to get you to open your guard so as to begin passing. Here we show a defense that does not rely upon you opening the guard.

1

Royler applies the thrusting choke while in Renzo's closed guard.

2

Renzo pushes back hard with his hips, arching his back. He turns his head to look in the same direction as the force of the choke in order to relieve the pressure. At the same time he puts his hands on top of the hands of his opponent, his fingers gripping under his opponent's fingers.

3

Renzo's main concern is the choking arm thrusting forward. He uses his grip under the fingers to peel Royler's choking hand back and away from his throat, turning his chest and head back to face his opponent.

4

Having thwarted the choke, Renzo pulls his lapels apart and grips them to prevent the same choke being reapplied.

016 Defense against the front-thrusting kick

A very common and effective form of attack in both the street and vale tudo competition is the front-thrusting kick. Often the opponent uses it like a jab, testing range and distance, or as a distraction for some other form of attack. Other times it is used as a direct attack to knock an opponent down. Your opponent can strike with either the ball of the foot or the heel.

1

Renzo and Royler square off.

2

Renzo chambers his leg by cocking the knee high.

3

Thrusting his foot straight out, Renzo aims for Royler's midsection, one of the preferred targets for the front-thrusting kick. Royler steps back just enough to avoid the force of the kick and catches the foot of the kicking leg. The key to catching a fast-moving thrusting kick is to have one hand *under* the kicking leg. When the kick is retracted, the foot will always go downward. If your hand is there it will always be able to intercept and trap the opponent's foot.

(!) Note the way in which Royler has taken hold of Renzo's foot. Both hands are cupped under the Achilles' heel. This affords a natural handle with which to control the foot.

– 60 –

4

Royler switches his hand position to enable him to drive Renzo's kicking leg up to the ceiling.

(!) Here you can see the way Royler grasps the trapped foot. The hand of his forward arm maintains the grip under the Achilles' heel. The other hand is open, the palm pushed into the sole of the opponent's kicking foot. It is this hand in the sole of the foot that is used to push the opponent's leg upward.

5

Royler drives into his opponent as he pushes the kicking leg straight up. This easily destroys his opponent's balance, making it easy to take him down to the ground. If your opponent is very flexible and capable of a full split, he will still go down due to the forward drive into the opponent. If necessary you can even sweep out his supporting leg with your own leg.

Passing the guard

One of the most distinctive features of Brazilian jiu-jitsu is the extensive use of the "guard" position. Used intelligently, the guard position can allow a smaller man to control, frustrate, and finish a bigger, stronger opponent from a bottom position. Your opponent holds you in his guard when he has you positioned between both his legs. If his legs are wrapped around your waist and his feet crossed behind your back, he has you in a "closed guard." Inexperienced ground fighters generally assume that when they are held in someone's guard they have a superior position, given that they are on top. In fact this is not the case. By holding the person between his legs the man on bottom has considerable control over the top man. From there he can employ a great many submission holds and strikes. In addition he can frustrate the attempts of the top man to strike him. Due to the difficulty of attacking a person who is using the guard position against you, it is generally best to break out of the guard and get to a better position from where you have a far better chance of striking or submitting your opponent. This task of getting around the opponent's legs to a better position is referred to as "passing the guard." *It is a crucial skill for the grappler to learn.* Given the overall strategy of seeking a better position from which to dominate and submit the opponent, this skill is of paramount importance. To be sure, there are some submission attacks you can employ while held up in someone's guard; most of them are attacks to the opponent's legs, but in general passing the guard is the strategy to follow.

There are a great many ways to pass the guard. The method shown here is one of the most basic. This method has certain limitations that will be discussed, but it remains one of the best ways to teach beginners the fundamental skills required to pass the guard. The crucial skill that it develops is that of "stacking" the opponent as a prelude to passing his guard.

1

Royler has Renzo locked in his closed guard. Renzo does not want to stay here since he can be attacked with many different submission holds. Renzo begins by sitting up straight and placing his hands upon Royler's biceps. By immobilizing Royler's arms, Renzo can make it difficult for Royler to attack with chokes, locks, and strikes. Renzo maintains good posture. His back is straight, head up.

2

Renzo posts his left leg out wide and turns his hips a little toward the left. He keeps his head up and back straight. By turning his hips a little, Renzo opens up a narrow space between his left inner thigh and Royler's right inner thigh.

3

Renzo passes his left hand through this small gap and pushes his left arm through so that it is deep under Royler's right leg. Renzo is sure to sink his level down as he passes his left hand through the gap. By lowering his hips he keeps his base strong. It would be difficult for Royler to sweep him over. Note that while in this position Renzo is somewhat vulnerable to being struck in the face by Royler's right hand. This is the first limitation of this guard-passing method, a limitation that makes it less appropriate for a no-rules fight.

(!) Sometimes it can be tough to create a sufficiently large gap through which to pass your hand. You want to avoid leaning over, out of balance, in a frantic attempt to dig your hand into the gap. By doing so you expose yourself to the danger of being swept over by your opponent.

4

Sometimes you are confronted by an opponent with immensely strong legs. It can be very difficult to break his feet apart. Rather than struggle and strain against his strength, grab your left shin close to the ankle with your left hand and shuffle your left foot away from yourself. Do not step with your left foot as this will destroy your balance. Simply shuffle it out; your foot never leaves the floor. This will break apart the feet of even the strongest opponent.

5

Renzo has shuffled his left foot out wide, breaking Royler's feet apart and putting him in great position to pass the guard. The key detail to note here is that Renzo has put himself in a position where his left *shoulder* is under Royler's right thigh. This is very important. It is *not enough* to merely get your bicep under the thigh and lift with the strength of your arm. You must get down low and hoist your opponent's thigh up onto your shoulder. This will give you tremendous power to drive forward and pass. Lifting with the arm alone is tiring and ineffective, as it allows a skilled opponent to scoot his hips out to the side and attack you.

6

Having gotten his shoulder under Royler's thigh, Renzo reaches with his left hand to grip Royler's left lapel. Grab with the thumb inside the collar, fingers outside, palm down to the floor. A deep grip is desirable. If your opponent is not wearing a gi, grip his left shoulder at the trapezius muscle. An experienced opponent will very often use the *triangle choke* at this point (the triangle choke is covered in another section). This is a definite danger. Renzo can counter this danger by pulling his right elbow back tight to Royler's right hip. This immobilizes Royler's hips and makes the triangle choke rather difficult to perform.

7

Drive with the strength of your legs to bring your opponent's knee up to his nose. This movement is referred to as "stacking." It is a very important concept in passing the guard. By stacking your opponent you prevent him from being able to attack you or even defending himself. It is an uncomfortable position for the man on bottom.

8

Once Renzo has brought Royler's knee up to his nose in a tight stacking position, he walks around to Royler's right side and drives forward with his hips and stomach to clear Royler's legs out of the way. He now finds himself past the legs and lying across Royler's side in an excellent position.

9

Renzo further secures his position by placing his right hand on the floor next to Royler's left hip. This is a simple means of preventing Royler from bringing his right knee in and putting him back in the guard position. Renzo places his left elbow on the floor next to Royler's left ear. This affords him excellent control of his opponent's head. By pulling his left elbow tight toward his left hip Renzo makes movement and escape very difficult for the bottom man.

Beginners often are in a rush to perform the movements required to pass the guard. There is no great hurry. Slow the movements down and concentrate on a slow and deliberate stacking motion that shuts down your opponent's defense. Before you even attempt stacking your opponent, make sure your shoulder is deep under his thigh, not merely resting on your bicep.

Scissors sweep

The scissors sweep is a simple, yet highly effective means of unbalancing and sweeping an opponent who is kneeling inside your guard so that you can take a superior position.

It can be done as a direct attack on a static opponent or as a counter to an opponent who is actively attempting to pass your guard.

1

Renzo is kneeling inside Royler's guard. Royler reaches across to grip Renzo's right lapel with his right hand. Royler's left hand grips Renzo's right sleeve at the elbow. If Renzo were not wearing a gi, Royler would hold behind Renzo's neck with his right hand and the elbow with his left.

2

Here we show a situation where Renzo actively attempts to pass the guard. Royler could attempt the same move even if Renzo did nothing.

3

Royler responds to Renzo's passing attempt by quickly opening his guard and turning over to his left side, retaining his collar and elbow grip. It is crucial that Royler turn to his side; the move will not work if he is flat on his back. Royler's left leg is on the floor, foot turned out, his calf in contact with the outside of Renzo's right knee. Royler bends his right leg and brings the right knee into Renzo's stomach area.

Note the position of Royler's right leg. The knee is in the middle of Renzo's stomach, his right shin is along the line of Renzo's belt. The instep of the right foot is tight on Renzo's left hip, functioning as a tight hook. This will enable Royler to exert considerable sweeping power by scissoring his legs in opposite directions.

4

Royler sharply scissors his legs. His left leg sweeps Renzo's left knee, his right leg extends. At the same time Royler pulls forward with both hands to further off-balance Renzo. Renzo topples over to his back.

5

Wasting no time, Royler immediately comes up to take top position. He throws his right leg over Renzo's stomach to take the mount. Note that he has not released his grip on the gi.

6

Royler stabilizes his position by pulling up on Renzo's left arm, making a counter on Renzo's part very difficult. He is now in an excellent position to attack with chokes and armlocks.

Attacking from the mounted position "Americana"

One of the most basic, yet effective attacks from the mounted position is the "Americana" lock, often referred to in America as "the keylock." This lock puts tremendous pressure on both the shoulder and elbow joints and has the potential to cause serious injury to those joints. It can be performed while mounted, half mounted, or across your opponent's side. Here we see an application from the mounted position. The lock itself is very simple to apply. The key to successful use is setting up the lock.

1

Renzo is mounted on Royler. In a real fight the simplest way to set up the Americana lock is to begin punching. As your opponent puts up his hands to protect his face, you immediately switch to the lock. Obviously you cannot employ such a method while training with your friends. Here Renzo is faced with a problem: Royler is keeping his arms tight to his sides, arms bent, in a tight defensive position. This gives little opportunity to attack. In a street fight this would not be a problem—a few punches would soon open the opponent up. Here, however, a different approach is called for. Renzo pulls up on the elbow of the arm he wishes to attack. As he does so, he wedges his knee on the same side up under the armpit of that same arm. This has the effect of trapping Royler's arm in a vulnerable position. Now Renzo will enter into the move.

2

Renzo reaches across and grabs the wrist of the arm he wishes to attack. If you wish to attack your opponent's right arm, grab his right wrist with your right hand. If you wish to attack his left, grab it with your left. Note that Renzo grips without using his thumb and that his hand position is such that his palm is down.

3

Renzo pushes Royler's wrist to the floor. He does this not by merely pushing with the strength of his arm. That may not be successful on a stronger opponent; rather, he comes down with the weight of his entire upper body. Renzo places the elbow of his own arm (the one with which he is gripping his opponent's wrist) on the floor right next to his opponent's ear. Renzo is sure to keep Royler's arm bent at ninety degrees.

4

Now Renzo brings his other arm under his opponent's tricep and grabs his own wrist (again, holding without the use of the thumb).

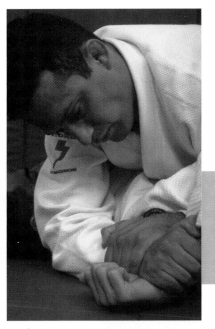

Note the hand and arm positions. Renzo grips across, his right hand to Royler's right wrist, or his left hand to Royler's left wrist. Renzo grips palm down without using the thumb—this makes for a stronger grip and lessens the risk of spraining your thumb should your opponent twist to escape.

5

To apply the lock, Renzo drags Royler's wrist down toward his own hips and simultaneously brings Royler's elbow up toward the ceiling. He is sure to never allow Royler's wrist to leave the floor. This dual action of dragging and lifting quickly puts tremendous pressure on the elbow and shoulder. To avoid injury, Royler must tap. In a real fight there is some danger of the opponent trying to bite you or scratch at your eyes. A simple counter to this threat is to bury your face in the crook of your own elbow as you perform the move.

Arm bar from the mounted position

The mounted position is generally regarded as the best one to attain in a real fight. It allows the mounted fighter to strike with near impunity upon his opponent. In addition to strikes, there are many highly effective submission holds that can be employed from the mounted position. One of the best is the basic arm bar.

1

Royler is mounted on Renzo. In a real fight, as soon as the top man begins punching a very common reaction for the man underneath is to reach up to try to stop the punches. Some people try desperately to push the man off their chest as though performing a bench press. In both cases, the man on the bottom commits the grave error of extending his arms. Renzo pushes on Royler's chest in the manner of inexperienced ground fighters, presenting Royler with a great opportunity to attack with the arm bar.

2

Royler quickly places both his hands on Renzo's chest and leans his weight forward. Note that Royler has come around Renzo's extended arm with his own arm, effectively trapping it in place.

3

Royler wants to rotate around that trapped arm. To do this, he first pops up lightly on his toes. He bears his weight entirely on his two hands at this point, squatting very low over his opponent's chest. He then steps his foot up to his opponent's head. In the photo sequence shown here, Royler is demonstrating how a beginner might first attempt this arm-bar attack. At first it can be a little difficult to spin straight into the arm-bar position, so Royler is breaking it down into easy stages.

4

Royler continues the turning motion by stepping over Renzo's head. Note that Renzo's arm is between Royler's legs. Royler is sitting on Renzo's shoulder, ready to fall back into the arm bar. In a genuine combat application of this move, Royler would jump and spin straight from the mount to this position. Since he is demonstrating how the move might be learned by a beginner, he added the extra step seen in the previous photograph.

5

Royler falls straight back, holding the wrist of Renzo's trapped arm. This motion extends Renzo's arm out straight. Royler applies the arm bar by pushing his hips up to the ceiling.

Note the position of the arm bar. Initially Royler holds on tightly with both hands to Renzo's extended arm. One hand holds Renzo's wrist, the other Renzo's elbow. *It is crucial that Royler squeezes his knees together as he applies the arm bar.* This makes escape much more difficult and also tightens the lock considerably. Renzo must now submit or risk serious injury to his elbow joint. To hyperextend the arm, Royler need only squeeze his knees together and push his hips up to the ceiling.

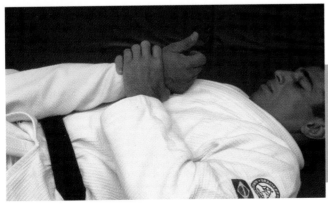

The arm bar can be made much more efficient by holding the opponent's thumb up to the ceiling. Slide both your hands down to the opponent's wrist and turn the thumb to the ceiling. Then straighten the arm and push your hips up.

Defense against a guillotine choke

Learning to defend against the sequence of moves shown here—a snap-down into a guillotine choke is of paramount importance. The reason is simple: pulling an opponent's head down and locking the neck is a very common move, both among seasoned grapplers and street fighters. It is a very simple, yet highly effective move. Even experienced grapplers can fall victim to it if it is well applied. It can be used very effectively in a wide array of situations and will quickly result in unconsciousness if applied well.

1

Renzo reaches out with his left hand and grabs Royler behind the neck. This can be a very dominating grip. Many good grapplers use this grip to "snap down" their opponent's head into a guillotine choke or front headlock. Used well, it is very difficult to resist. In the context of a street fight, it is often used by tall, strong men to dominate smaller opponents.

2

Renzo snaps down Royler's head and begins to bring his right arm over to entrap Royler in a guillotine choke.

3

Renzo locks the guillotine choke by grabbing his right wrist with his left hand. There is real danger now for Royler; if he does not react, he can be choked very effectively. Royler immediately places his hands on the front of Renzo's thighs just above the knees.

4

Royler steps in deeply between Renzo's legs with his right leg. A deep penetration step is vital here.

5

Royler sits down on his buttocks and pushes up with both hands. He has penetrated so far under Renzo that when he sits he effectively places a fulcrum under Renzo's feet over which Renzo has no choice but to rotate. Royler's arms pushing upon Renzo's thighs add to the effect. The result is that Renzo is easily tossed over Royler's head.

6

Royler has removed the danger in a spectacular and potentially punishing way. He is now free to get up and escape or quickly take a top position and continue the fight.

Standing guard pass

Learning how to cope with and pass the guard is one of the major elements of Brazilian jiu-jitsu. Earlier we saw a basic method of guard passing that was really more of a drill to teach the crucial skill of stacking an opponent in order to pass his guard. Here we look at a combat-effective means of passing the guard. It involves standing up inside your opponent's guard in order to pass. The advantage of this approach is that your opponent cannot punch you in the face as you attempt to pass, as would be the case if you pass while down on your knees. Moreover, the standing position makes it more difficult for him to successfully apply arm bars and triangles on you as you pass.

1

Royler is held inside Renzo's closed guard.

2

Placing both hands on Renzo's upper chest (or biceps), Royler stands up.

3

Bringing one arm back, Royler grips Renzo's belt. He places the elbow of that same arm on Renzo's inner thigh. If Renzo were not wearing a gi and belt, Royler would simply place his elbow on Renzo's inner thigh.

4

This standing position makes it very difficult for Renzo to keep his feet locked together. Royler presses down with his elbow into Renzo's inner thigh, breaking Renzo's feet apart and opening the guard.

5

Utilizing his free hand, Royler reaches under Renzo's leg at the thigh and pulls it upward.

(!) Here you can see Royler's hand and arm position. His hand on the belt controls Renzo's hips, pushing down to make triangle and arm-bar attacks very difficult. His other arm pulls up to lift Renzo's thigh to his shoulder.

6

Placing the back of the thigh that he has just pulled upward on his shoulder, Royler reaches across to the opposite side of the collar and grips it, thumb inside the collar, fingers outside. If Renzo were not wearing a gi, Royler would grip the trapezius muscle.

7

Leaning his bodyweight forward, Royler stacks Renzo. The idea is to bring your opponent's knee up to his nose. This can be a slow, controlled movement. Speed is not essential. As Royler stacks Renzo and brings Renzo's knee to his nose, he walks around the stacked leg, still driving his weight down on Renzo's legs. Coming around the stacked leg, Royler puts his lead arm around Renzo's head to trap it and make it very difficult for Renzo to escape.

8

The result is total control and a clean guard pass into a dominating position across Renzo's side. Royler switches arm position into a classic across-side hold-down. One arm over Renzo's head, the other on the floor at Renzo's hips to prevent Renzo putting him back in guard.

023 The double ankle grab sweep

It is quite common for your opponent to stand up in your guard. This is true of both experienced grapplers and un-skilled street fighters. A skilled grappler might stand up in your guard in order to initiate a passing move. A street brawler might do it in order to be able to punch you more easily, or even to pick you up and slam you down on the floor. Either way, the double ankle grab sweep is an excellent and simple counter to an opponent who is standing up in your guard.

1

Royler stands up in Renzo's closed guard. This puts Royler in good position to begin passing the guard, or perhaps to strike or slam Renzo.

2

Recognizing the danger, Renzo quickly grabs both of Royler's ankles from the outside and uncrosses his feet. By uncrossing his feet, Renzo lets his buttocks drop to the floor. Royler can no longer pick Renzo up to slam him. Renzo brings his knees together on Royler's stomach. His knees form a useful barrier to punches.

ⓘ Note the way that Renzo pinches his knees together. His feet are turned in as a result. His knees are almost touching in the middle of Royler's stomach. If the knees are too far apart, the move will be far less effective.

3

Renzo explosively pushes up toward the ceiling with both knees as he grips and pulls on Roylers ankles. The key here is to push *up*, not back, with both knees. Since his legs are blocked at the ankles, Royler cannot retreat to regain his balance. He falls backward.

4

Renzo maintains his grip on Royler's ankles until Royler is all the way down to the floor. Renzo is already sitting up as Royler goes down. If you delay sitting up too long, your opponent will have a good chance to sit up and recover, or even attempt a footlock as a counter.

5

Wasting no time, Renzo sits up to one side, in this case, his left side. Renzo posts out his left hand to push off and reaches across with his right hand to grab Royler's right elbow.

(!) A key point here is that Renzo does not sit up straight toward Royler, rather, he twists his trunk to one side (in this case, his left side). This greatly facilitates the act of sitting up. If you sit up straight toward your opponent you will inevitably get stuck at a certain point and be unable to get on top of your opponent.

6

Since Renzo has twisted his trunk to his left side, he can push off the left hand that he posted on the floor and pull with the right that he has used to grip Royler's right elbow. When Renzo comes up to take the mounted position *he throws his hips forward*, over Royler's hips, pulling with his right arm as he does so. Doing this makes it much easier to come up and over to a full mounted position. Royler's legs form a partial barrier to Renzo's attempt to get mounted. By raising his hips over Royler's legs, Renzo ensures he will attain the mounted position.

7

As soon as Renzo gets the mounted position he bases both hands out wide to stabilize his position. This ensures that his opponent will not bridge and roll him off as soon as he comes up mounted.

A common counter to the double ankle grab sweep

In the previous series of moves we saw a highly effective sweep that involved grabbing both the opponent's ankles as he stands up in your guard and knocking him backward with your knees. Here we take the same move and show a common counter. The counter that is shown has definite technical limitations that will soon be made obvious. Better counters exist; however, this counter is so common and natural that it merits discussion. In addition, the course of this discussion will reveal some important themes of Brazilian jiu-jitsu.

1

Royler stands up in Renzo's closed guard. This can be dangerous for Renzo in a street fight. In a tournament it usually signals the beginning of a guard passing attempt. Renzo elects to go on the offensive and attempt the sweep.

2

Renzo quickly goes for the sweep by grabbing Royler's ankles, uncrossing his feet, and bringing his knees together. He drops his butt to the ground, then punches his feet forward and down toward the ground, easily knocking Royler backward.

3

Royler goes down. Even as he falls, however, he is beginning to counter. Most people, even those without training, recognize the danger of being swept over and conceding a top position to the opponent. In response to the danger they resist the sweep by trying to get back up. Royler posts his right arm back as he falls.

4

Renzo tries to mount as in the previous series of moves, but Royler is aware of the danger. In response, Royler sits up and posts his left hand on Renzo's chest, thus preventing Renzo from coming up and getting mounted.

5

Having prevented Renzo from mounting, Royler now concentrates on righting himself and regaining his position. He sits forward and comes up inside Renzo's guard.

6

Once inside Renzo's guard, Royler can begin again. He has been knocked down, but he prevented Renzo from taking advantage of this. This counter to the sweep is seen very often. It is a very natural reaction to the sweep since it relies on the simple method of pushing on the chest to prevent the opponent from coming forward. The sheer frequency of this counter makes it worthy of study, in spite of its technical imperfections (to be seen soon). An instinctive fighter would probably react in this manner. He can instinctively recognize the danger of being knocked down and the opportunity this presents to his opponent to take a dominating position.

Double leg sweep to arm bar

We have been studying the two-handed sweep as a response to your opponent standing up in the guard. When you sweep your opponent backward a common reaction on the part of your opponent that we saw in the previous section is for him to post his hand on your chest and push you down, thus preventing you from sitting up and taking the mounted position.

Thus we have a series of moves that evolves out of our opponent's response to our initial move and our counter to that response. This is an important principle. The idea being that live training requires us to combine attacks fluidly in response to our opponents reactions to our attacks.

1

Royler stands up in Renzo's guard, a sound move on Royler's part as it enables him to strike quite effectively or to begin passing the guard.

2

Renzo immediately responds by attacking with the two-handed sweep, as seen in the previous sections. His intent is to knock Royler down and sit up into the mounted position.

3

As Royler goes down, he realizes the danger of being mounted and thrusts out his left arm, pushing on Renzo's chest, to prevent Renzo coming forward into the mounted position. While this is an effective way of preventing Renzo from mounting, it leaves Royler open to a counter that we shall see now.

4

Realizing that mounting Royler is now impossible, Renzo switches his attention to the source of his trouble—Royler's arm pushing on his chest. Renzo posts his left arm on the floor for balance and grips Royler's outstretched arm at the wrist.

 The key elemt here is that Renzo thrust his hips high into his opponent's chest. If his hips remain low his opponent will be able to pull his threatened arm out of danger. Renzo is pushing up with his left arm to ensure that his hips come up high on Royler's chest.

5

Notice how Renzo has thrust his hips well up off the floor up to Royler's armpit, pushing hard with the arm that is braced on the floor. His whole body is now turned toward his left side as a prelude to the next step.

6

It is now a simple matter for Renzo to throw his right leg over Royler's head to enter into an arm bar. He still has a tight grip on Royler's wrist as he turns his stomach to the floor. Royler's arm is now effectively trapped.

7

To complete the move, Renzo simply holds Royler's arm at the wrist with both his hands, squeezes his knees together, and pushes his hips forward. This hyper-extends his opponent's elbow, causing great pain and injury if the opponent should not immediately submit.

Push sweep

We have been looking at sweeps as our opponent is in our closed guard. Here we look at a useful variation of the previous sweeps. Often you will find your opponent reacts defensively to a sweep attempt, trying hard to maintain his balance. This may well require you to switch to another form of sweep.

1

Renzo is in Royler's closed guard. Royler takes the preferred grip. One hand (his right) in his opponent's opposite collar (a cross grip), the other gripping the opponent's sleeve at the elbow. If Renzo were not wearing a gi, Royler would have his right hand gripping behind Renzo's neck, his left gripping Renzo's right elbow.

2

Renzo initiates an attempt to pass the guard by stepping up with his left leg. This is a common situation when holding someone in the guard. It might signal an attempt to stand up, to begin passing, or to improve balance as a prelude to a flurry of strikes.

3

Royler quickly reacts by opening his guard and turning to his left side. Royler drops his left foot to Renzo's right knee. Royler brings his right knee across Renzo's belt line just as he did for the scissors sweep. Alternatively, Royler could hook his right foot in the bend of Renzo's left knee.

4

Sensing that that scissor sweep will not work in this situation (perhaps Renzo's base is too wide) Royler places his left foot at the front of Renzo's bent right knee (the knee that is on the floor).

5

Royler pushes with his left leg as he pulls with both arms. This has the effect of stretching Renzo and destroying his balance. Renzo has no means of recovering his balance since his limbs on the right side of his body are completely controlled by Royler's simultaneous pulling and pushing action.

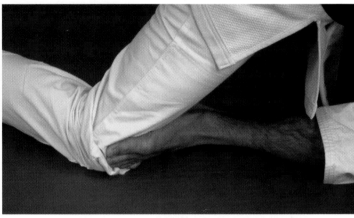

(!) Note how Royler has positioned his left foot at the top of Renzo's bent right knee.

6

It is a simple matter now for Royler to overturn Renzo by extending his right leg, either with a scissoring action across the line of Renzo's belt, or by elevating if he had hooked under Renzo's left knee.

7

Royler comes up into the mounted position. To ensure good control he pulls up strongly on Renzo's right arm as he mounts. Notice how Royler's hand position has not moved throughout the sequence.

027 Elevator sweep

Here we continue the series of sweeps as our opponent puts one leg up while inside our closed guard. Here the slightly different action of the man in our guard necessitates a different sweeping method.

1

Renzo is in Royler's closed guard. Royler immediately takes the preferred grip, right hand across to the opposite side of the collar, left hand on the opponent's right sleeve at the elbow.

2

Renzo steps up with his left leg to begin passing.

3

Renzo gets his left arm under Royler's right leg as a prelude to stacking Royler and passing his guard. If Royler does not react there is a definite danger that Renzo will lift the leg to his shoulder, stack Royler by driving his right knee to his face, and from there, pass Royler's guard. Note that Royler has turned to his left side, as always he is avoiding being flat on his back while working from the guard position. Royler's left leg is in on the ground against Renzo's right knee.

4

Royler knows the danger and immediately hooks his right foot under the bend of Renzo's left knee. This makes it impossible for Renzo to lift Royler's right leg to stack him. This forms a very effective temporary barrier to Renzo's passing attempt.

(!) Look how Royler forms a strong hook by pulling his toes back toward his shins. If his foot was pointed away, the hook would be weak.

5

Royler pulls with both arms and extends his right leg while sweeping with his left leg. This elevates Renzo's left leg and takes him right over. Renzo cannot post out a limb to prevent going over since his right arm is being controlled and his right leg is blocked by Royler's left leg.

6

Royler comes up to take the mounted position. To ensure good control he pulls up on Renzo's left arm. This also helps should Royler decide to immediately attack with arm bars or chokes.

028 Headlock escape 1

The headlock is one of the most common forms of attack, both in a street fight and in grappling training and competition. Most unskilled fighters instinctively grab the head as a means of dominating their opponent, both in a standing position and on the ground. Brazilian jiu-jitsu does not favor the use of the headlock. It presents a skilled opponent with too many opportunities to counter and gain superior position, however, because it is such a common form of attack it is essential that you practice escaping quickly and efficiently. There are several ways in which your opponent can hold you down on the mat with a headlock. Some are more efficient than others; again however, it is important that you familiarize yourself with them all since it is more likely that you will run into one of these variations in a real fight than almost any other grappling move.

1

Royler is holding Renzo in a typical street-attack headlock. Royler has his right arm under Renzo's head and has joined his hands.

2

This kind of headlock is relatively easy to escape from. It can feel intimidating to the inexperienced, but it offers little control over the man underneath for the simple reason that it cannot prevent the bottom man from turning to his side. Renzo capitalizes on this by immediately turning in toward his opponent. He then places his left forearm across Royler's jaw and braces his left wrist with his right hand. This prevents Royler from bringing his head down toward Renzo.

(!) Note how Renzo grips his wrist. His palm is facing Royler and his left arm is bent at ninety degrees. This forms a very strong brace to prevent Royler from bringing his head down.

3

At this point, Renzo scoots his hips away from Royler, still pushing on Royler's face. This creates space between the two opponents and brings Royler's head closer to Renzo's hips.

4

Renzo throws his legs up behind Royler's back, his hips coming off the floor. His left leg is the key element here. It comes around Royler's head and over his face. Royler cannot duck his head under Renzo's left leg because his head is braced by Renzo's arms.

5

Renzo now crosses his ankles and uses the strength of both legs and his hips to push Royler's head back. Royler is forced to roll onto his back.

6

Renzo comes up to his knees to take a top position. Royler is still holding onto Renzo's head but is now doing so from an inferior position. We shall soon see how to make Royler release his hold.

Having attained top position, Renzo hugs himself tightly to Royler. Note how Renzo keeps his hips low to prevent Royler rolling him over again.

Headlock escape 2

It must be stressed that there are several ways for an opponent to hold you down with a headlock and that there is an optimal method of escaping from each. In the previous section we looked at a method that relied upon pushing the opponent's head back. Now we consider an opponent who is wary of this and who therefore keeps his head down, preventing us from utilizing the first escape. This demonstrates again a key element of Brazilian jiu-jitsu, the idea that your responses to an opponent must be flexible and take into account the movements and counters of a live, resisting opponent.

1

Once again Royler has Renzo in a headlock where he has joined his arms around Renzo's head. Renzo's first concern, as always when held in a headlock, is to turn to his side toward his opponent and bring the elbow of the arm on the same side tight into his ribs. Since Royler is not controlling Renzo's right arm this is relatively easy.

2

Royler brings his head down close to Renzo's head. This prevents Renzo from performing the previous escape. In response, Renzo throws his left arm around Royler's back, holding him at the far shoulder. Renzo is moving toward Royler's back.

3

The key element in this move is Renzo throwing his left leg over Royler's left thigh and hooking it at the hip. This powerful hook will enable Renzo to pull himself around to Royler's back with ease.

Note how Renzo is using his left arm and leg to slide himself around to Royler's back. His right hand is on Royler's left bicep, blocking any punches.

4

Renzo utilizes the impressive leverage afforded by his left leg to pull himself to Royler's back.

Royler's arm around Renzo's head is now put at such an angle that it has little strength. Renzo uses his right hand to grasp Royler's right wrist and peel the arm away from his head.

5

It is now a simple matter for Renzo to slip his head out of the headlock and take a very dominant position on Royler's back. Renzo is securely hooked into Royler's hips and from here can attack in many ways.

Renzo retains control of Royler's right wrist to prevent Royler from effectively defending any follow-up attacks such as chokes or strikes.

Elbow escape from bottom of across-side position

We have already seen the elbow escape in the context of escaping the mounted position. The importance of this basic move cannot be stressed enough. It forms the basis of all positional escapes from underneath an opponent. Due to its great mechanical efficiency, it provides the best means of escape against a larger opponent. It can be used in a great many contexts, to escape the mount, the half mount, across-side position, even when your opponent is passing your guard and you are scrambling to recover position. Moreover, it combines so well with many other escapes that it is truly the single most important move from the bottom position. Here we look at it in the context of recovering the guard position against an opponent who has attained the across-side position.

1

Royler is holding Renzo in an across-side pin. This is dangerous for Renzo. From his superior position, Royler can apply a great many submission holds or get mounted on Renzo. In addition, Royler can strike with knees and elbows. The onus is on Renzo to improve his position. The means of escape that Renzo will employ is largely determined by the manner in which Royler is using his arms to hold the across-side position. Note that Royler is holding Renzo with both his arms across Renzo's body. This makes the elbow escape the most appropriate means of escape. Note Renzo's arm positioning. This is very important. There is considerable danger of being struck or arm locked while being held down across-side. Renzo lessens this by good arm positioning. He places the elbow and forearm of the arm closest to his opponent in his opponent's hips, tucked in securely. His forearm goes along the line of his opponent's belt. Renzo's other arm is tucked under his opponent's far armpit, the palm of his hand on his opponent's far latissimus muscle.

2

Renzo's first move is always to bridge his hips up off the floor and scoot his hips out and away from his opponent. This creates space between him and his opponent—space that will be useful when he comes to escape. Also, it allows Renzo to turn in toward his opponent and get to his side. It is a general axiom of bottom position that you do not want to be flat on your back underneath your opponent. This makes it difficult to escape, even to breath in the case of a heavy opponent. Try always to bump up with your hips and turn in toward your opponent. Note how Renzo is pushing on Royler's hips with his elbow, creating space between his hips and Royler's.

3

Renzo brings the knee of the leg closest to his opponent into the gap he has created between his hips and Royler's hips. Renzo is bringing his knee up to his own elbow. Now his knee and shin form a barrier between him and his opponent.

4

Renzo places the foot of that leg on the ground *and scoots his hip out from under his opponent*. The importance of this detail cannot be overstated. It is easy for your leg to get trapped between you and your opponent, making it very difficult to get him back in guard. To prevent this, you must place your foot on the ground and scoot your hips out. This creates sufficient space to enable you to complete the move.

5

Renzo finishes the move by locking his legs around his opponent, putting him back in the guard position. From this position Renzo is able to defend himself much better and even go on the attack. This basic move does not look dramatic but is one of the most useful moves when fighting from underneath. It demonstrates well the theme of escaping from bad positions and getting to better ones from where you can dominate the fight.

031 Defense against the front bear hug

Many people dismiss the bear hug as an unskilled move relying upon strength. In fact a well-applied bear hug is a very effective move for controlling and taking down an opponent. There is considerable danger in allowing an opponent to secure a bear hug. The danger is not from the bear hug itself, rather the danger consists in the control that the bear hug allows your opponent to exert on you. He can use it to maneuver you around as he likes and then take you down, landing in a dominant position. An effective counter is needed to this very dangerous form of attack. The form of bear hug utilized here is one where the opponent goes under both your arms and locks his hands around your lower back. This allows him to pull you in and crunch you over backward, taking you down to the ground and landing on top of you in a very dominant position.

1

Renzo and Royler square off.

2

Renzo lowers his level, steps in, and thrusts his arms under Royler's and locks his hands. Royler is in real danger at this point.

3

Royler reacts immediately to the danger. He quickly sprawls his hips back and drops his level. This prevents him from being crunched back down to the ground. At the same time he places both his hands under Renzo's chin.

4

Royler pushes his arms out. He is using a simple principle here—"where the head goes, the body must follow." By pushing up under the chin, Royler gets his opponent's head to move backward, preventing the forward drive that could take him down, while at the same time breaking his opponent's grip.

5

Royler takes advantage of the space he has created between himself and his opponent to throw a knee into Renzo's midsection or groin.

032 Defense against a standing rear choke

A very common form of street attack is a choke-hold, applied from behind in a standing position. There is considerable danger in such an attack. If your attacker manages to get a good chokehold on you there is a very good chance that you will be rendered unconscious, putting you completely at his mercy. Moreover, as he is behind you, it is very difficult to counter his attack. What is needed is an effective means of removing the stranglehold and of getting your opponent out of his advantageous position behind you.

1

Royler approaches Renzo from behind.

2

Royer begins his attack by reaching up quickly to throw his arm around Renzo's neck.

3

Renzo senses the danger of the stranglehold and immediately begins to defend his neck by grasping Royler's arm. Renzo does not want his opponent to be able to pull him backward and down as this makes escape more difficult. He must react before he is pulled down.

4

As Renzo pulls down on the choking arm, preventing it from strangling him, he lowers his level, bending at the knees. You can see that Renzo's belt is lower than Royler's, clearly showing that Renzo has dropped his center of gravity beneath that of Royler.

(!) Notice the way in which Renzo defends his neck. He grabs the arm that is choking him with both hands and pulls down. He places one hand in the crook of his opponent's elbow, the other at the wrist. Preventing the strangling effect is Renzo's first priority. This grip is his initial defense.

5

Renzo snaps his upper body forward, as though bowing. Since his center of gravity is well below that of his opponent, he sends his opponent flying over his back.

6

Royler lands heavily on the ground. Renzo is in a perfect position to continue attacking, should he wish. He has simultaneously removed the danger of strangulation and taken his opponent from his advantageous position, finishing with a punishing throw and a very dominating position for himself.

Defense against the bear hug (over the arms)

The bear hug is a very common form of attack, both in street fights and in competition. In the hands of a skilled grappler it can be a devastating method of takedown and control. Contrary to popular opinion it can be a very technical move when utilized by an expert. There are three options when attacking with the bear hug. First, you can lock your hands around the waist under both your opponent's arms. This is the preferred method if you wish to crunch your opponent backward and down to the mat. Second, you can lock your hands under one arm and over the other, trapping one of your opponent's arms. This method is very popular with wrestlers as it allows for a range of hip tosses and back-arching throws. Third, you can wrap your arms over both your opponent's arms. This option

tends to be used mostly by the street fighter. In all three cases the basic strategy of a bear hug attack is the same. The person using the bear hug wants to lock his hands around your lower back and pull his hips in close to yours. This gives him great control over you. He can use this control to maneuver you around at will, hitting with knees and head butts. In addition he can bend you over backward to take you down or throw you. Here we see a defense to the bear hug where the opponent wraps his arms over *both* of yours. The same defense also works if he wraps his hands over one arm and under the other (as wrestlers often do). In the case where the opponent goes *under* both your arms we will show another defense that relies upon pushing the opponent's chin away.

1

Royler steps in and locks a bear hug over both of Renzo's arms.

2

The key to a successful bear hug is in getting your hips in tight to those of your opponent by pulling in on his lower back. The key to defending the bear hug is in preventing your opponent from doing this. Accordingly, Renzo places his hands on Royler's hips and pushes. This keeps space between their hips and prevents Royler from getting control. At the same time Renzo sags his hips down and back.

(!) Note Renzo's hand position. Elbows in, fingers turned out, heels of his palms on Royler's hips, thumbs uppermost.

3

Having stopped the attack, Renzo steps around to one side, keeping a tight clinch position.

4

Renzo steps the leg that he had put behind Royler in front of Royler's far foot. This is the classic hip throw position. Note how Renzo's feet are right in front of Royler's, facing the same direction. Renzo slides his hips in front of Royler's and bends his knees to lower his hips under those of Royler.

5

It is a simple matter now for Renzo to straighten his knees to easily lift Royler from the ground. Renzo makes sure to pull on Royler's arm to draw Royler up onto his toes and off balance.

6

Royler goes over Renzo's hip in a high arc. Obviously this could be a very hard fall if Renzo desired.

7

Renzo finishes in a very dominant position. From this point he has many favorable options.

Attack from the guard position, "Kimura"

The "kimura" lock is one of the best submission holds in jiu-jitsu. It puts great pressure on the elbow and shoulder joints and is potentially very damaging. It can be employed from several positions. Here we see a simple application from the guard position. There are many opportunities to use "kimura" from the guard. Any time you are able to sit up to the side you can attempt "kimura." One of the best opportunities is when your opponent sits up inside your closed guard (this gives you the space you need to sit up to the side) and places his hands on the floor or on your hips.

1

Royler is holding Renzo in his closed guard. Renzo has a hand on the floor and sits up, giving Royler the perfect opportunity to attack. Royler immediately grabs the wrist of the arm that he is planing to lock.

2

Royler unlocks his legs and thrusts his other arm (the one that is *not* grabbing his opponent's wrist) up past and over the shoulder of the arm he intends to lock. He sits up quickly to the same side as the arm he is about to lock. Note that Royler twists his trunk to the side rather than sitting straight up. This is a much easier motion than a straight sit up (which is taxing on the stomach muscles) and lessens the danger of being struck in the face by the opponent.

3

Royler brings his free hand over the back of his opponent's arm, then under the crook of the elbow to grab his own wrist. The lock is now in place.

4

Royler scoots his hips out from under his opponent in order to gain more leverage. He places his leg (the one on the same side as the arm lock he is applying) on Renzo's back. This prevents Renzo from rolling forward and escaping the lock. Making sure to keep Renzo's arm bent at ninety degrees, Royler brings Renzo's wrist up toward Renzo's ear. This puts great pressure on Renzo's elbow and shoulder. To avoid injury, Renzo must submit.

Headlock escape 3

We have seen that the method used to escape from a head-lock in a ground-grappling situation is dependent upon just how the opponent is holding us down and how he is reacting to our attempted escape. The previous escape is used when the opponent has his head down but has his rear leg back, allowing us to throw our leg in as a hook to lever us toward his back and escape. Say that now our opponent senses our attempt to throw in the hook and brings his rear leg forward, preventing us from hooking our leg in. Now we shall need a different means of escape. Again we see a central theme of training in Brazilian jiu-jitsu, the idea that in preventing one form of escape the opponent leaves himself open to some other form of escape.

1

Royler is holding Renzo in a tight headlock. Royler has his head down tight so any escape that relies upon pushing the head back is inadvisable; moreover, Royler has brought his left leg forward, making it very difficult for Renzo to hook his leg over Royler's hips as he did in the headlock escape 2. As always, Renzo's first reaction is to turn to his side toward Royler and pull his left elbow in to his ribs. Renzo's left arm comes around Royler's back and grabs the far shoulder.

2

Due to the position Royler has adopted as a means of frustrating the first methods of escape, it is relatively easy for Renzo to simply get to his knees. This is made easier by ensuring that the elbow closest to your opponent is tight to your ribs and by pulling yourself up with the arm around your opponent's back.

3

Renzo has now gotten to his knees.
Royler is still holding on to the headlock.

4

Renzo puts out his right arm as a brace and shuffles away from Royler on his knees. If Royler were to let go of the headlock at this point, Renzo would go straight to his back and look to finish with a choke. However, Royler is persisting with the headlock.

5

Renzo's goal is to pull Royler in a direction where he cannot brace himself, thus overturning Royler. He does this by pulling with the arm that is around Royler's back and pushing off with the hand that is posted on the floor. *Note that Renzo extends his left leg*. This is a crucial part of the move. It takes Royler in a direction where he cannot resist going over.

6

At this point, Renzo looks upward to the ceiling and turns his entire body to his left, easily taking Royler backward. Renzo is pushing with his right arm, pulling with his left.

7

The only way Royler can resist being put on his back would be to release the headlock and brace out with his arms. However, this would allow Renzo to escape and go right to his back. Since Royler has elected to stay with the headlock Renzo simply turns to his left to overturn Royler.

8

Renzo places Royler on his back and takes a dominant position. There are many attacks Renzo can employ at this point.

036 Headlock escape 4

So far we have looked at headlock escapes where the opponent simply grabbed around the head and locked his hands together. This is the type of headlock used by unskilled grapplers. It allows the man on the bottom to easily turn in toward his opponent and pull his elbow in tight to his ribs. From here escape is relatively easy. An experienced grappler, however, utilizes a different kind of headlock. Instead of simply locking around the head, he will pull up on the arm nearest to him. This makes it very difficult for the man on the bottom to escape, since it precludes his two best moves, pulling the arm tight to his ribs and turning to his side. Now the man on top can keep his opponent flat on his back, making breathing difficult and the previous escapes nearly impossible. Against this experienced opponent, a new method is needed.

1

Royler holds Renzo in a headlock that indicates a sound knowledge of grappling skill. Royler is keeping Renzo flat on his back by pulling up on Renzo's right arm. This prevents Renzo from pulling his right arm into his ribs and from getting to his side.

2

Recognizing the danger posed by someone who is clearly an experienced grappler, Renzo locks his hands around his opponent's ribs. This prevents Royler from pushing Renzo's right arm down into a submission hold. Renzo then tries hard to turn in to his opponent and get to his knees. Renzo will not be able to do so as Royler is controlling his right arm well; however, by doing so Royler is forced to react by pulling up on the right arm and leaning into Renzo. This will set up Renzo's escape. Renzo gets his hips close to Royler's.

3

Sensing Royler's effort to prevent him from getting to his knees, Renzo explosively bridges and simultaneously throws both hands (still locked together) over his head. This brings Royler's hips off the ground, making him feel light. It is crucial that the bridging and arm-throwing motion be directly over your head so as to bring your opponent's weight well forward, over your head.

4

Having brought his opponent forward, Renzo then turns to his left to roll Royler over easily. If you begin by turning to the left without first having brought your opponent forward, the move will fail. The opponent should feel light as you turn him over. If he feels heavy, chances are you did not bring him forward far enough with your initial bridging motion.

5

Renzo has turned Royler over and can take a top position. From here he can attack with a number of finishing holds.

037 Defense against the rear hook

When thrown well, the rear hook can be a useful part of a good boxer's arsenal. Inexperienced fighters, however, throw the rear hook in a wide, looping motion that is relatively easy to counter. Due to the fact that this wide, swinging rear hook is so very common in street attacks (it is probably the single most common form of blow thrown in actual street fights), there is a need to practice a powerful and simple defense to it. The defense shown here is based upon the basic hip throw, showing once again the great versatility of this move.

1

Renzo and Royler square off. Renzo draws back his rear fist in the style typical of an unskilled street brawler.

2

Renzo lets fly with a wild swing form of rear hook, so common in street fights. Royler immediately puts up both hands. The idea is to have your hands inside those of your opponent. This is made easier by the wide-open style of punch used by the opponent.

Here you can see clearly how Royler swims his hands inside those of Renzo. Royler's hands are at shoulder height, fingers toward the opponent.

3

Royler steps in as he slaps his hand into the bicep area of the Renzo's punching arm. This is relatively simple to perform, as the bicep moves much more slowly than the fist. By blocking at the bicep, the punch is effectively intercepted and blocked.

4

Royler steps in and has both his hands on both of Renzo's biceps. This simple clinching tactic removes the threat of punches. The whole procedure is based on the idea of "inside control," keeping you hands inside those of your opponent, stepping in and locking up his arms at the biceps, keeping your arms inside his.

5

At this point Royler tightens the clinch by wrapping with the arm of the hand that initially blocked the punch over the punching arm in a strong overhook. At the same time he puts his other arm under Renzo's arm and around Renzo's waist, stepping his leg around behind Renzo. Royler keeps his head buried in Renzo's chest, out of harm's way. This is a very tight, controlling, and safe clinch.

6

From this secure clinch position, Royler can go on the offensive. He steps the leg that was behind Renzo around in front of Renzo. You can see that Royler's feet are directly in front of Renzo's, the same width apart and facing the same direction. This is the position you want your feet to be in. Royler slides his hips across in front of Renzo's hips and lowers his level by bending at the knees.

7

The leverage afforded by this simple hip throw is very impressive. Royler easily picks up Renzo off the floor by straightening his legs.

8

Using the arm around the waist and also pulling hard on the arm that he has grabbed, Royler brings Renzo over. The great control this throw offers allows Royler to dictate just how hard his opponent falls.

9

Royler finishes in a totally dominating position. Now he can determine the course of the fight as he sees fit.

The guillotine choke

The guillotine choke is one of the most fundamental submission holds in Brazilian jiu-jitsu. In mixed martial arts competition this move has brought about more victories than any other. It is relatively simple to apply and can be performed in a great many situations. Here we look at the guillotine as an attack on someone locked in the guard. One can also begin with the guillotine in a standing position, then fall down to the guard position to tighten the hold. There is a common misunderstanding with regard to the guillotine choke. Often it is dismissed as a beginners technique, one that it is easily defended by an experienced grappler and that accordingly it is of little use on anyone save the most inexperienced. This is simply not the case. The guillotine is regularly and successfully employed at the Abu Dhabi grappling competition, where the greatest grapplers in the world meet and duel. Even at the highest level of competition this simple move is a serious threat. In one of Renzo's fights in Japan he had a protracted and difficult battle against the very strong and skillful Sanae Kikuta. The Japanese champion resisted all manner of submission attempts until finally, after nearly an hour of struggle, Renzo secured a guillotine choke, dropped in to the guard, and secured victory. The reason why the guillotine is seen as a beginner's technique is that it is simple to apply for even an absolute beginner. Beginners apply it with little skill. Consequently it is not difficult to escape such poorly applied guillotine chokes. From this people mistakenly infer that *all* guillotine chokes are easy to escape from. Nothing could be further from the truth. A well-applied guillotine can finish anyone, at any level of competition.

1

Royler holds Renzo in his guard. Renzo is sitting up. This gives Royler sufficient room to sit up to the side, just as he did for the "kimura" lock from the guard. ("Kimura" and the guillotine combine together very well. If one fails, you can invariably attack with the other.)

2

Royler takes advantage of that space to quickly sit up to one side and throw his arm over and around Renzo's neck.

3

As Royler's arm comes around Renzo's neck, Royler takes his other hand and grabs his own wrist

Here you can see the method Royler is using to lock the choke. It is a simple matter of holding the wrist of the arm that circles around the opponent's head and neck. Be sure that the forearm of the arm around the head and neck slides under the opponent's chin and into the throat. This creates a painful and effective chokehold. To be sure, there are other methods of locking up a guillotine choke. However, the one shown here is the simplest and works well.

4

Now it is an easy matter for Royler to push away with his legs and at the same time pull up with both hands. This brings Renzo's head down and Royler's forearm into Renzo's throat. Renzo will be rendered unconscious if he does not submit.

Defending the guillotine choke

There is considerable danger in being caught in a guillotine choke. The technique is so simple to apply that even a novice can attack with it. It is important, then, to be able to defend it well. Here we see a defense to a guillotine applied from the guard position.

1

Royler has Renzo locked in a tight guillotine choke from the guard position. If Renzo does not escape in the proper manner, he will be forced to submit.

2

Renzo places his hands on the ground and pushes himself a little more upright. This takes a little pressure off the choke and enables him to go into his defensive counter.

3

The first concern is defending the neck. In a chokehold, seconds count. Renzo quickly grabs the wrist of the arm that is encircling his head and neck and pulls it down from his throat, relieving a lot of pressure. With his other arm, Renzo reaches over Royler's back so that his hand is between Royler's shoulder blades. This helps to prevent Royler from arching back and making the choke stronger.

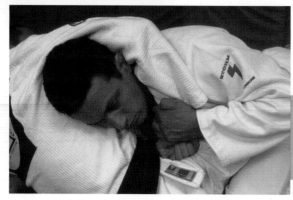

(!) Note how Renzo grabs the wrist of the choking arm. He slips his fingers over the wrist without using his thumb, pulling down on the wrist.

4

Now Renzo bears his weight forward into Royler. He is sure to drive Royler back onto the opposite shoulder of the choking arm encircling Renzo's head and neck. In other words, if Royler is choking with the right arm, Renzo drives him back onto the left shoulder. This destroys the leverage needed for an effective choke.

5

Having taken the danger out of the choke, Renzo can work on extracting his head. Keeping his weight forward, Renzo takes the arm that was thrown over Royler's back and places forearm of that arm on Royler's throat.

! Here you can see how Renzo uses his forearm in Royler's throat to create a painful distraction.

6

Renzo pushes with the forearm in the throat and pulls on Royler's wrist with his other hand. This weakens Royler's grip very dramatically, making it a simple matter for Renzo to slide his head backward and out of the choke. Renzo has escaped the choke and can now sit up to commence passing Royler's guard.

Defense against the shoulder grab

Very often, real fights begin with grabbing attacks as a part of the verbal/psychological prelude to actual violence. One of the most common ways to grab a victim is on the shoulder. Here is a simple and effective counter to such an attack.

1

Royler reaches out and grabs Renzo by the shoulder.

2

Renzo brings his arm inside Royler's and up toward the ceiling.

3

Wrapping his arm all the way over and around Royler's grabbing arm, Renzo then joins his hands palm to palm. This traps Royler's arm very tightly. Renzo clamps the elbow of the arm that he has used to overhook Royler's tight to his own ribs. This keeps Royler's trapped arm bent at ninety degrees. Note the awkward angle at which Royler's arm is trapped. He is caught in a shoulder lock.

4

To apply the lock, Renzo brings both his hands up toward his own throat. This puts great pressure on Royler's shoulder. Royler's natural tendency is to come up on his toes and lean backward in order to relieve the pain in his shoulder. This brings him completely out of balance and makes him very easy to move around and control.

Another defense to the shoulder grab

041

The shoulder grab is so common that it is worth knowing another move as a defense against it. The two moves complement each other well. The first works by bending the opponent's arm at ninety degrees and then going into the shoulder lock. Sometimes, however, the opponent feels the danger and straightens his arm in order to avoid the shoulder lock shown in the previous move. Should this happen, the following move is an excellent alternative.

1

Royler grabs Renzo's shoulder as before.

2

Renzo brings his arm on the same side as the shoulder being grabbed inside and over his opponent's arm.

3

Renzo joins his hands together. If Royler's trapped arm bends, Renzo can perform the previous move. However, this time Royler straightens his arm to prevent the shoulder lock.

4

Stepping in toward Royler, Renzo thrusts his leg across in front of Royler's thighs. He is sure to use the leg on the same side as the arm he is using to overhook Royler's arm. This leg pushes back into Royler's thighs, blocking them from coming forward and escaping the lock. At the same time, Renzo has his forearm of the arm overhooking Royler's trapped arm directly on Royler's elbow, pulling strongly forward, locking Royler's arm very effectively. In this position there are also many opportunities to throw the opponent to the ground.

Defense against the throat grab

Grabbing or pushing the shoulder, throat, lapels, and chest constitute some of the most common forms of aggression in real fights. Often they are used as simple intimidation tactics, other times they are a prelude to more vicious attacks. Either way, you must know how to deal with them in an effective fashion. The move shown here is one of the most versatile responses to such aggression. It is shown here as a counter to a throat grab, but it is equally effective in any kind of upper-body grabbing or pushing situation. If your opponent places his hand on your upper arms, throat, shoulder, lapel, face, or chest you can use this move very effectively.

1

Royler goes to grab Renzo's throat. There is considerable danger with such grabs. Often the opponent will pull, push, and drive you backward, keeping you off-balance and thus unable to stop the rain of blows that you can expect with the other arm.

2

As soon as Royler makes contact, Renzo grips the wrist of Royler's outstretched arm with both hands.

> ⚠ Note the manner in which Renzo grabs Royler's wrist. Both palms are facing the floor, elbows are high. Renzo utilizes the thumbs in this move. Both hands grip with forefingers and thumbs.

3

Renzo swings the elbow of his arm over Royler's arm in a high arc. Note that it is the arm *outside* Royler's arm that goes over. As he does this, Renzo steps across in front of Royler, using the foot on the same side as the elbow going over Royler's arm.

4

Maintaining his tight grip on the wrist, Renzo clamps his elbow tight to his ribs, trapping Royler's arm against his body. Renzo has Royler's elbow right under his armpit. From here, Renzo arches his back, thrusts his hips forward, and pulls Royler's wrist upward. This puts tremendous pressure on Royler's elbow. Renzo has the option of sliding his forward leg down to the floor to finish in a sitting position should he wish to take the fight to the ground.

Side kick

There are relatively few punches and kicks in Brazilian Jiu-Jitsu. In general the jiu-jitsu fighter always looks to throw strikes from a position where his opponent cannot strike back effectively. A good example of this is the mounted position. When both you and your opponent are standing in front of each other, your opponent has the opportunity to trade blows with you on an equal basis. Should your opponent be larger, stronger, and more athletically gifted than you, there is consider-able risk of defeat. This is why Brazilian jiu-jitsu favors a strat-egy of controlling an opponent and placing him in a position where he cannot trade blows with you on an equal level. Nonetheless, there are times when standing strikes are en-tirely appropriate. One of the most effective blows is a side kick to the knee of your opponent. This technique is simple, does not require any athleticism, and does not expose you to many counters.

1

Royler and Renzo square off.

2

Royler draws back his lead leg, chambering his kick. Notice that he keeps his hands high to protect his face.

3

Royler thrusts his foot out straight, aiming for Renzo's knee. The advantage of this move is that it allows you to attack the closest target your opponent offers (his lead knee) with your longest ranged weapon (your lead leg). Also it often sneaks in under your opponent's vision, especially if you fake high with your hands as a prelude to the kick. It can be used as a direct attack in itself, or as a distraction that enables you to shoot in on your opponent and enter into a clinch or a takedown.

Defending the guillotine choke

044

The ease with which even an inexperienced opponent can slip a guillotine choke around your neck in the course of a real fight and the speed with which this devastating choke takes effect make it essential that you know how to effectively counter the guillotine.

1

Royler shoots in on Renzo in an attempt to take him down.

2

As Royler makes contact, Renzo throws his arm around Royler's neck and throat in a classic guillotine. The move is so natural that even people with no grappling experience will often go for the move instinctively. An experienced opponent will actively look for the move.

3

Royler's first move is to defend his neck. The guillotine can render you unconscious very quickly if well applied so quick defense is essential. Royler slips his fingers around the choking arm to pull the choking arm down and away from his throat. Royler throws his other arm over Renzo's back to prevent Renzo from arching back and adding strength to the choke.

(!) Here you can see clearly Royler's defensive handwork. The arm over Renzo's back is placed right in the middle of the upper back, the other hand grips the choking arm at the wrist.

(!) Here we see very clearly the manner in which Royler defends his neck. He grips Renzo's choking arm at the wrist gripping from underneath. Note that the thumb is not used in the grip. Royler pulls the choking arm down, away from his throat.

4

Having defended his neck, Royler steps to the side and past Renzo with the leg on the same side as the arm he has thrown over Renzo's back. You can see that Royler has advanced his foot past Renzo's and it is now behind Renzo's foot.

5

Using the leg that he has placed behind Renzo's leg, Royler presses his knee into the back of Renzo's knee, bending Renzo's leg and breaking his balance.

> (!) Note the knee-pressing action. Royler presses his knee into the back of Renzo's knee to topple him backward.

6

Royler takes Renzo over backward. Note that Royler can control the speed of Renzo's fall using the hand over Renzo's back.

7

Landing across Renzo's side, Royler now works to free his head. At this point the choke is ineffective, so Royler can take his time. He places his hand on Renzo's far shoulder, his forearm across Renzo's throat.

8

Driving his forearm down into Renzo's throat creates a lot of uncomfortable pressure. At the same time, Royler pulls on Renzo's wrist. Royler then extracts his head, finishing in a very dominating position.

Elbow strikes

Brazilian jiu-jitsu does not generally encourage pugilistic skills. It is risky to trade blows with a powerful opponent when you each have the same opportunity to strike each other. Another problem in a real fight is that contrary to Hollywood movies, the human hand, even when well conditioned, is very likely to be severely injured in a bare-knuckle fight. In the early mixed martial arts events, few competitors wore gloves and many of them were forced to withdraw with broken bones in the hands as a result of landing heavy blows on their opponents. A good alternative is the elbow strike. The elbow and forearm are much sturdier than the hand and in addition can severely cut your opponent. Moreover, the elbow is a great weapon for the grappler, since it can be readily employed from the clinch. Here we see Royler practice a drill for elbow strikes that develops the loose hip and shoulder movement that generates great power.

1

Royler stands in front of Renzo and grips his own lapels at chest height.

2

Royler twists his trunk back.

3

Note the great rotation of hips and upper body as Royler swings back in a relaxed manner, generating tremendous force without any danger of harming himself as would be the case if striking with the hands. This is really more of a drill to develop power.

046

The rear naked choke, "Mata Leão"

"Mata leão" is one of the classic submission holds of Brazilian Jiu-Jitsu. In a real fight it represents one of the safest and most effective means of controlling and subduing a powerful attacker. In the heat of real combat a strong-willed or intoxicated attacker can endure tremendous pain and still press home his attack. However, no matter how strong-willed or intoxicated he is, if a "mata leão" is well applied, the fight is over. The rear naked choke is a highly effective strangle that cuts off the supply of blood to the brain. This results in unconsciousness in a matter of seconds, irrespective of strength, size, or ferocity. Moreover, because you are behind the opponent as you apply the strangle, it is very difficult for him to strike, gouge, or bite you. You are attacking him with a highly efficient submission hold that requires very little strength, from a position where he can do little to harm you—that is the essence of Brazilian jiu-jitsu strategy. This is the reason why "mata leão" is the classic expression of Brazilian jiu-jitsu in action.

There is some danger associated with strangleholds. If held too long they can be injurious or even fatal to the victim.

Unconsciousness usually results in about ten seconds if the hold is well applied. *Be sure to release the hold as soon as your training partner taps to signal submission.* In a real fight where tapping out is not an option you may well have to render your opponent unconscious. Be aware that choke or strangle holds are illegal in some areas. You may want to check what the law is in your area before using it in a street situation. Should you render an attacker unconscious, release the hold and lay him down on his side. He will come back to consciousness by himself. There are some traditional jiu-jitsu methods of reviving a person rendered unconscious, but it is unclear whether they are any more effective than merely laying the person on his side. How you choose to handle your unconscious attacker is obviously determined by the individual circumstances in which you find yourself.

"Mata leão" is here demonstrated in a way that enables a beginner to learn the choke in a safe manner. This is not the way the technique is applied in a combat situation.

1

Renzo kneels behind Royler.

2

Sliding his thumb down the side of Royler's neck, Renzo brings his arm around Royler's throat until his elbow reaches Royler's Adam's apple. This is an important detail. By having the crook of your elbow directly in front of the Adam's apple, you ensure that the opponent will not sustain damage to his trachea. The blood flow in the carotid arteries running to the brain will be cut off (a strangling effect) rather than cutting off air to the lungs (a choking effect). It is crucial that Renzo's choking arm be under Royler's chin. If Royler can lower his chin into Renzo's arm the strangling effect will be greatly diminished.

3

Renzo places the hand of the choking arm palm down on the biceps of his other arm.

3

The full "mata leão" armwork consists in placing the hand of the nonchoking arm on the back of the opponent's head. Renzo is now ready to apply the strangle.

4

To strangle your opponent, bring your elbows together.

 Note the hand positions for "mata leão." The hand on the back of the head cannot be too high on the head or your opponent will simply reach up and peel it off.

Defense against double-lapel grab

We have been stressing that grabbing and pushing are very common in a street fight. Another common form of grabbing and shoving is done with two hands. The aggressor grips both your lapels at chest level and uses them to pull or push you around. This grip can be very intimidating. It gives your opponent considerable control over your upper body. Moreover, it gives him an excellent grip to throw you to either side with a wide range of throws and takedowns. It is important then, to have a strong counter to this dominating grip.

1

Royler grabs both of Renzo's lapels and pulls up to off-balance Renzo. This is a dangerous situation, both in a street fight and in a sport match. This double-lapel grip combined with the off-balancing allows Royler to enter into a number of very powerful throws to either side (the grip allows for ambidextrous throwing). In a street fight there is great danger from head-butting attacks and knee stikes.

2

Renzo immediately steps in and lowers his base to regain his balance and brings both arms up inside Royler's arms.

3

Wrapping both his arms over and around Royler's arms, Renzo attains a strong double overhook position. Note that Renzo stays side-on to Royler by keeping one foot forward. If Renzo were square-on to his opponent, it would be easy for Royler to lock a bear hug under both arms and crunch Renzo backward to the mat.

4

Renzo bends down a little and brings his head to the same side to which he wants to throw Royler.

5

Renzo's entry into the throw is a back-step. He steps back with his rear leg a little outside and in front of Royler's foot (the one on the opposite side that Renzo will throw Royler). Renzo then places his other foot across in front Royler's other foot and pulls strongly with his arms. Be sure that this is *not* a hip throw. Renzo's hips do not come across in front of Royler's as they would for the basic hip throw. Rather, Renzo's hips are shallow. It is Renzo's outstretched *leg* that blocks Royler's movement, not his hips. Note that Renzo's outstretched leg is bent and on its toes.

6

Pulling strongly on the arm on the same side toward which he is throwing Royler, Renzo straightens his outstretched leg, snapping Royler's legs up into the air for a strong and fast throw.

7

Renzo finishes in a very dominant position from which he can attack with numerous submission holds or pins.

048 The triangle choke

Of all the many submission holds in Brazilian Jiu-Jitsu, the triangle choke is one of the most efficient and versatile. It can be used from the guard position, the mounted position, across-side (both top and bottom), and when your opponent is on his knees. In addition, there are many ways to apply it. There are front triangles, rear triangles, reverse triangle, and side triangles. The common element in all triangle attacks is that the attacker's legs are locked in a triangular, figure-four pattern around the head and one arm of the opponent. This produces a very efficient strangling effect by utilizing the attacker's legs and the opponent's own shoulder to cut off the carotid artery blood flow. It combines well with many other forms of attack and is not easy to defend. Here we look at one of the most basic forms of the triangle, from the front, while the opponent is trying to pass the guard. This is a simple way to introduce a very sophisticated form of attack.

1

Renzo is locked in Royler's closed guard.

2

Seeking to pass Royler's guard, Renzo posts his leg out wide and reaches under Royler's thigh, hoping to stack Royler and get around his legs.

3

Royler immediately sees a classic opportunity for a front triangle choke. He throws his leg up onto Renzo's neck and pulls on the arm that is now caught between his legs. This is the key to any triangle choke. The opponent's head and one arm are caught between the attacker's legs.

4

Royler pulls the trapped arm across his stomach. Control of this trapped arm is vital. Should the arm slip out from between Royler's legs, the triangle choke is lost. Royler brings the calf of the leg encircling Renzo's throat and neck toward the back of Renzo's neck.

5

To tighten the stranglehold, Royler pulls the foot or shin of the strangling leg toward himself. Now his calf runs along the line of the back of Renzo's neck and the foot of the strangling leg fits neatly into the cook of his other leg's knee. This all sounds complicated, but with a little practice the movements can be done quickly and smoothly. The front triangle choke is regularly performed in no-rules fights, even when the opponent is punching and head butting.

Here you can see clearly the figure-four triangle of the legs. See how the strangling leg goes along the line of Renzo's neck and how the foot of the strangling leg goes into the bend of the opposite knee.

6

Having locked the triangle, Royler puts both his hands on the crown of the opponent's head and pulls down strongly. This greatly increases the strength of the choke and makes escape by standing up much more difficult.

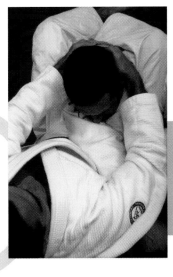

The close-up reveals the hand position on the head. You can clearly see how Renzo is being strangled by a combination of his own shoulder and Royler's inner thigh. The power of this strangle is very impressive.

The elbow escape drill

When most people come to study Brazilian jiu-jitsu they are most interested in the submission holds, fast and spectacular guard passes, and high-flying throws. However, the most useful movements are usually not very glamorous. Probably the most useful movement for the man on the bottom is the sliding hip movements associated with the elbow escape. This simple sequence of movements is utilized more than any other in actual combat and sparring. It allows a smaller person to escape the pins of a much larger person. It is used to escape the mount, the half mount, the across-side position, and to prevent an opponent from passing your guard. You can never drill this simple movement too much. It is an excellent way to warm up before engaging in hard grappling training and it will save you from more dangerous situations than all the fancy moves put together. When you perform the drill, use your imagination. Try to imagine an opponent mounted on you and you using the movement to escape. Think of a determined opponent coming around your legs to pass your guard and you sliding your hips out to create the space you need to put him back in your guard.

1 Royler begins the drill flat on his back. His arms are at his sides. He draws up one leg, bringing the foot close to his buttocks. The other leg remains extended.

2 Pushing off with the foot of the drawn-up leg, Royler scoots his hips out and turns his body to the opposite side of that leg. His hands mimic the action of pushing someone away. In a real elbow escape against a live opponent he would be pushing on the opponent's knee, hips, or shoulders, depending on the situation.

3 Royler draws up the extended leg, bringing his knee up to his hands. In a live situation the knee is brought inside the gap that is opened between you and your opponent as a result of the hip action.

4

Having brought up the knee, Royler places the foot of that leg on the ground and extends his other leg. He turns his body over to the other side, preparing to repeat the hip movement on the opposite side.

5

Royler lifts his hips off the ground and scoots his hips out to the other side. Once again he pushes with his hands in the opposite direction of the hip movement.

6

Royler finishes in the starting position. In a live situation he would finish by putting the opponent back in the guard position. You can keep going with the drill, working your way up and down the training hall. This will give you great endurance on the mat. You will find that correct form results in a snakelike pattern of movement in your hips. Your hips scoot out one way, then the other, and you move backward.

050 The elbow escape from the mounted position

The elbow escape is perhaps the single most important move for the man on the bottom in Brazilian jiu-jitsu. Due to the highly efficient use of leverage embodied in the technique, size is irrelevant—without a doubt it represents the best hope for a smaller fighter to escape from the controlling pins of a larger and stronger opponent. Since the elbow escape can be used when mounted, when underneath across-side, to prevent the opponent from passing your guard and while defending the half guard, it is constantly being used in every conceivable situation by the player on the bottom. Here we see the elbow escape being used to escape from the mounted position, the classic application of the technique. It is being used in conjunction with another classic escape from the mount (demonstrated elsewhere in this book), the "upa" escape.

1

Royler is mounted on Renzo and gripping the collar in preparation for a strangle. Renzo grabs the wrist and elbow of the arm gripping the collar.

2

Renzo bridges hard over to the side of the arm he is gripping in a strong attempt to roll Royler over with the classic "upa" escape from the mounted position. Royler defeats this escape attempt by posting his leg out wide, preventing the roll.

3

Royler may have defeated the "upa" escape by posting his leg out wide, but he has presented Renzo with a golden opportunity to switch into an elbow escape. There is a lot of room under the posted leg. Renzo quickly slides his knee flush with the floor under Royler's posted leg, bringing his knee up to his elbow. Renzo's elbow pushes up and out on the inner thigh of Royler's posted leg, creating yet more room for Renzo to bring his knee inside and under Royler's posted leg.

(!)

Note how Renzo pushes with the elbow under his opponent's inner thigh (close to the knee). Many people push with the hand at this point, but this is easy to peel off and can set you up for some unpleasant submission holds. Make a habit of pushing not with the hand, but with the elbow. Note also how Renzo's leg is turned outward and is flush with the ground. This makes the task of joining knee and elbow much easier. It is crucial that you turn to the side to which you are joining knee and elbow. The move is difficult to accomplish if you are flat on your back.

4

As Renzo brings his knee and elbow together inside and under his opponent's thigh, he places the foot of that leg on the ground and scoots his hips out wide. This hip-scooting movement is vital to the success of the move. It pushes the opponent's hips back and greatly facilitates your attempt to extract your feet from under your opponent's thighs. Without this hip scooting movement there is a strong possibility that you will be unable to extract your legs fully and get them around your opponent's waist.

5

After getting his hips out to the side and extracting his foot from under Royler's thigh, Renzo hooks around Royler's leg to prevent Royler from remounting. At this point Renzo is halfway out. He has successfully wrapped one of his legs around one of Royler's. Royler still has a half-mount position, so Renzo must carry on.

6

Focusing his attention to his other leg, Renzo turns over to the other side and places his other elbow inside his opponent's thigh, pushing up and out. Once again, Renzo brings his knee and elbow together, just as he did on the other side.

7

Renzo brings his knee inside Royler's thigh and places his foot on the ground. Just as he did on the intial side, Renzo scoots his hips out wide to ease the task of extracting his leg from under his opponent's thigh.

8

This makes it easy for Renzo to wrap his legs around his opponent's stomach and lock a full guard. Using a simple yet highly efficient set of movements, Renzo has gone from being mounted to holding his opponent in his guard. The key to understanding the elbow escape is to realize that it is one movement performed twice—once on each side. You must become very adept at this simple move if you are to progress in Brazilian jiu-jitsu. It can be done as a solo drill to warm up before class and repetitively drilled with a partner. The time invested will be well spent.

Arm bar from the guard position

The basic arm bar is an extremely versatile submission hold. It can be used from the mounted position, across-side, knee-on-stomach, and half guard. Here we see it used from the guard position. It is worth spending the time to perfect this move. In mixed martial arts competition and grappling tour- naments the arm bar is probably the single most successful finishing hold (only the guillotine choke comes close). In addition the arm bar combines very well with other moves such as the triangle choke, all the collar chokes, and the knee bar.

1

Royler is in Renzo's closed guard. The best time to attack with the arm bar is when your opponent extends his arms. Should he have his hands on your chest, arms, neck, or face you can go for the arm bar. Here Royler has his hands on Renzo's chest, his arms straight, presenting a perfect opportunity.

2

Renzo chooses an arm to attack. The key here is to get a strong grip on the arm to be attacked. If the opponent can pull his arm out, the move is lost (though there are other follow-up moves you can flow into should your opponent successfully pull his arm out). The most efficient grip is to grip the opponent's wrist (if you are attacking his right arm, your left hand grabs the wrist) and hold it to your chest. By simply holding his wrist to your chest you make it much tougher for him to pull his arm back. Renzo reaches across with his other hand and passes it *under* the opponent's other arm (the one that is *not* being locked). If you go *over*, it is much easier for your opponent to pull his arm out. He grabs the arm that is to be locked at the crook of the elbow.

3

Renzo puts his foot on Royler's hip (on the same side as the arm that he is attacking). He uses it to push his hips out to the same side as the arm that is to be locked. This push is critical to the success of the move. It puts you at a right angle to your opponent. The move is difficult to perform if you are directly in front of your opponent. By pushing on his hip with your foot you put yourself out to the side in good attacking position. A simple test to see if you have done this is after pushing yourself out to the side you should be looking into your opponent's ear. Be sure that you push off the foot on your opponent's hip so that your hips and buttocks come completely off the floor. Your pelvis should be driving up into your opponent's arm. If you are lazy with your hips and allow them to drop low or stay on the floor, it is much easier for your opponent to pull his arm out and escape. Renzo's other leg comes up high on Royler's back, up into the back of the arm that is *not* being attacked. It is used as a hook that keeps your opponent's upper body down and bent forward, making the move much easier. Also it can help to keep your hips up.

(!) Here you can see clearly how the leg is used high on the opponent's back, almost up to the back of the opponent's neck. It then hooks down hard on the opponent's upper back.

(!) Here is a detail of the hip position on the other side. Note how high Renzo's hips come up off the ground. This enables Renzo to prevent even the strongest opponent from pulling his arm out of the lock and escaping. By driving his hips up, Renzo traps Royler's arm with his hips and leg. It is Renzo's hips and legs that prevent the arm from slipping out. Renzo's arms merely hold the opponent's arm down and in position.

4

Having done all this, it is a simple matter for Renzo to take his foot off Royler's hip and swing it over Royler's face and head. Renzo now grips Royler's wrist with both hands, squeezes his knees together, and brings both his feet toward the floor, keeping Royler's head down. Finally he pushes his hips up toward the ceiling to hyperextend his opponent's elbow. Royler must tap his submission or invite serious injury to his elbow. A common error at this point is to cross your feet. Keep them uncrossed and driving down to the floor.

Underarm collar choke

Some of the most effective strangleholds require the opponent to be wearing a suitable collar. The gi is designed to provide a very good strangling effect if used properly. Some forms of streetclothes replicate the gi collar closely enough to provide very good strangling possibilities in a real fight. One very effective and simple strangle utilizing the collar involves reaching under one of your opponent's arms. It can be done from a number of positions. Here we see it done from the guard position. The beauty of such collar strangles is their rapid effect and surprise value. Unless your opponent is familiar with these moves he will most likely not see any danger until it is too late to do anything about it.

1

Royler is holding Renzo in his closed guard. To begin the move, Royler reaches up to grasp Renzo's collar, pulling it out wide to open it up.

2

Pulling down with his collar grip, Royler brings his free hand under and inside Renzo's arm.

3

Royler is now in a perfect position to wrap his free arm around Renzo's arm in a hooking motion, effectively trapping Renzo's arm. Royler is sure to keep pulling Renzo down with the hand holding Renzo's collar. From here, Royler reaches across with the hand of his hooking arm and grips inside Renzo's opposite lapel. This is made easy by the fact that Royler had previously opened up Renzo's collar with his other hand. The grip should be at upper-chest level.

Note how Royler uses one hand to open Renzo's collar so that the other hand can slide in more easily. Note also the level at which he grips.

4

Having secured his overhook around Renzo's arm and secured a tight grip on the opposite lapel with that arm, Royler releases his other hand's grip on Renzo's collar and reaches with that hand over to the other side of Renzo's head.

(!) Here you can see clearly the details of Royler's grip. His hooking arm is wrapped around Renzo's arm and gripping the opposite lapel at upper-chest level. Royler's other hand comes over to the other side of the collar. Royler grips the collar using his thumb on the inside, fingers outside, next to Renzo's ear.

5

This grip allows Royler to place the blade of his hand directly on the side of Renzo's neck, cutting off that carotid artery to the brain. The other carotid artery is cut off by the other hand pulling on Renzo's opposite lapel.

6

Now Royler can apply the stranglehold. To do so he brings his head up to Renzo's face and moves both his elbows down and out.

Sliding collar choke (strangle)

When you have attained a dominant position behind your opponent, "mata leão" is the most common form of attack, especially in a real fight. If the oponent is wearing a gi or collared jacket, the sliding collar choke is extremely efficient and can be combined with many more strangles than "mata leão." Here the basic choke is shown. The combat application of this choke is different and will be shown elsewhere.

1

Renzo kneels behind Royler.

2

Renzo reaches under one of Royler's arms, grips the collar on the same side at about midchest level, and pulls it out to open it up. At the same time his other arm circles Royler's throat.

3

Taking advantage of the open collar, Renzo slides the thumb of his choking hand inside Royler's collar (thumb inside, fingers outside). Renzo grips high on the collar, reaching around as far as he can. The deeper his choking arm goes around and into Royler's collar, the more efficient his choke will be.

4

Now Renzo takes his other hand and grips the opposite collar at midchest level, thumb inside, fingers outside.

5

To apply the strangle, Renzo pulls straight down with the nonchoking hand (gripping at midchest level). This has the effect of removing all the slack from the gi collar, making the gi like a noose. With the choking hand, Renzo pulls across and around the throat, as though he were cutting Royler's throat with a knife. This produces an immediate strangling effect. In one fight, Renzo used this strangle to put a formidable opponent into unconsciousness in a matter of seconds.

The transition from the mounted position to the rear-mounted position

054

When one watches truly high-level Brazilian jiu-jitsu players in action, one can hardly fail to notice the ease and fluidity with which they move from one position to another. No matter where their opponent goes, they always seem to effortlessly follow and flow into some new position from where the opponent has to face a new set of attacks. One of the most common and effective positional transitions is that between the mounted position and the rear-mounted position. Very few people can take the pressure of the mounted position. As you launch into a barrage of punches from the mount in a street fight, opponents almost invariably turn their backs to protect their faces. Even in a pure grappling situation without punches the pressure of repeated submission attempts often makes an opponent turn his back to you in a desperate effort to escape. Here we look at such a situation. You are mounted upon an opponent who attempts to escape by strongly bridging and twisting underneath you. This gives you a perfect opportunity to make the transition to the rear-mounted position.

1

Royler is mounted upon Renzo.

2

Desperate to escape (imagine in a real fight that he is being struck hard in the face with punches or being strangled), Renzo bridges hard and turns away from Royler. Royler braces his two arms out for support and widens his legs apart. This is an important detail. You must give your opponent room to roll so that you can easily get to his back. If you keep your legs tightly clamped around your opponent's body he either will not be able to turn, or, he will turn and you will be rolled underneath him.

3

Having given his opponent room to roll by opening his legs, Royler sits on top of his opponent who is now face down on the floor. At this point, if your opponent does not move, you may begin striking or strangling right from here. However, it is very likely that your opponent will not stay in this vulnerable position but instead will attempt to get up and escape. Anticipating this, Royler pushes his toes against the outside of Renzo's thighs just above the knees and supports himself on both hands.

Here you can see how Royler pushes his feet against the outside of Renzo's thighs, ready to slide them under Renzo's thighs the moment Renzo attempts to get up.

4

As expected, the opponent tries to get out of what is obviously a bad position. However, Royler's good leg position (both feet pressing against Renzo's outer thighs) allows him to immediately slip both feet under Renzo's thighs into his hips the moment Renzo attempts to get up.

5

Royler's feet slide in all the way. They serve as hooks to lock Royler to Renzo's body. Now Royler will stay clamped to Renzo's back no matter which way Renzo moves or thrashes about. Failure to lock in these hooks makes the likelihood of your opponent escaping very high.

6

Renzo, desperate to escape, throws himself about, falling to one side. However, Royler's feet, both hooking into Renzo's hips, keep him securely in place. Royler holds Renzo with both hands around the neck, ready to go straight into a stranglehold.

7

In this close-up you can clearly see how Royler's feet serve as hooks in Renzo's hips. Note that Royler never crosses his feet in this position. The feet stay apart at all times.

055 Double leg takedown, "Baiana"

A truly crucial skill in a real fight is that of closing the distance on your opponent and taking him down to the ground. If you can successfully get your opponent down and land in good position then you have a massive advantage. Once you have an opponent down in a dominant position, you negate most of his offense and set him up for a finishing hold or strikes from a position that prevents him from effectively striking back. "Baiana," the double leg takedown, is one of the very best means of doing this. It involves you "shooting" in on your opponent and tackling his legs, forcing him to the ground with you in the top position.

1

Renzo and Royler square off. Renzo's intention is to get Royler down on the ground. The problem is that Royler can strike and grapple with Renzo as he attempts this. The solution is to feint high with your hands, then to quickly lower your level and tackle your opponent at the legs, going under his arms fast and low to quickly penetrate his defense without taking any significant damage.

2

Here you can see the entry to the tackle. Renzo lowers his level. This is done by bending at the knees. Try to maintain as upright a position as you can as you shoot in. Wrestlers often shoot in by dropping to a knee. This greatly helps in maintaining an upright posture as you shoot. Brazilian jiu-jitsu generally advocates not going down to the knees as you shoot. You may well be fighting on cement, in which case bouncing off your knees as you shoot in can be injurious. The result is that the shoot in Brazilian jiu-jitsu is typically not as upright as those seen in wrestling. *Always shoot with your head going to the same side as your opponent's lead hand.* You want to stay away from his power hand (the rear hand). *Step in with your lead foot between your opponent's legs.* This is your penetration step. It takes you into your opponent's space. Imagine there is a string tying your opponent's feet together. You want to land your foot on that string with your penetration step. *Do not reach out wide with your arms.* This will make it easy for your opponent to underhook your arms and either block your shot or even turn you over and throw *you* to the ground.

3

Contact! Renzo rams his shoulder into Royler's stomach. This knocks Royler off balance. At the same time Renzo's hands go to the back of Royler's knees. *As soon as Renzo makes contact with his opponent, he steps forward with his rear leg, bringing it up past his initial penetration step.* This is crucial. By bringing up his rear leg, Renzo can go into a lift, continue driving into his opponent to take him down, or "turn the corner" and come around behind his opponent.

(!) Here is a close-up of the ideal contact position. Renzo is fairly upright, in good posture. His knees are bent and he has stepped forward with his rear foot. His head is tight to Royler's side.

4

Renzo prefers the lift. Any time you lift your opponent clear off the floor you make it virtually impossible for him to defend the takedown. Since your opponent can no longer push off the floor, he can no longer generate any power, support himself, or regain his balance. To lift your opponent easily you must step both feet in close to your opponent and lower your hips under your opponent's hips. Then push your hips in toward your opponent and drive up with your legs.

5

Unlike most grappling styles, where the goal is simply to land your opponent on his back, Brazilian jiu-jitsu emphasizes landing in a dominant position. Rather than being satisfied with simply getting your opponent down, *you want to clear his legs as you take him down*, ensuring that you do not end up locked in his guard, where you do not have any great positional advantage. To do this, Renzo swings Royler's legs to the side and drives Royler over by using his head in Royler's side.

6

The result is that Royler never gets a chance to lock his legs around Renzo's body and put him in guard. Royler lands heavily with Renzo already around his legs, ready to take a dominant across-side position.

7

The completed takedown. Renzo has not only taken Royler down to the floor, but has done so in a fashion that allows him to begin in a great position. From here Renzo can go directly to a finishing hold or the mounted position.

Purple Belt

Renzo Gracie faces off against Jean Jacques Machado in the final of the 2000 Abu Dhabi Submission Wrestling World Championship, March 2000.

056

Moving from across-side position into the mounted position · The hip-switching method

A crucial theme of Brazilian jiu-jitsu is that of constantly fighting for better position on your opponent. Attaining a dominant position from where you can strike with complete ascendancy and move freely into submission holds is a huge part of ground fighting. As you grapple you must constantly be working toward two goals: attaining a better position and finishing your opponent. These two goals are closely linked, since most of the submission holds can only be safely applied from a superior position. Your game must be infused with this spirit of constant forward progress toward the final goal of finishing the fight in an efficient manner – that is an essential part of good Brazilian jiu-jitsu. A great part of that constant forward progress is working your way up through the hierar-

chy of positions as you grapple. Here we see the transition from one very good position, across your opponent's side, to what is probably the very best position in a real fight, the mounted position. Moving from one position to another is a real skill, one that is just as important as learning submission holds. Whenever you are in transition between positions the movement required enables your opponent to attempt various forms of escape. To maintain control of your opponent as you move to a new position requires the precise application of good technique. There are many ways to attain the mounted position. The hip-switching method is one of the best. It offers good control of the opponent throughout the movement and is very quick.

1

Royler is lying across Renzo's side. This is itself a very good position. Royler could attempt submission holds from there. However, Royler seeks to further improve his chances by moving into the mounted position. Note the initial position of Royler's arms: they are on the far side of Renzo's body, elbows on the floor.

2

Royler raises his hips by straightening both his legs and coming up on his toes. He then switches his hip position by turning his hips toward Renzo's legs and sitting down on the hip that is closest to Renzo. Royler is sure to place his leg parallel to Renzo. His other leg is placed far back to widen his base and prevent him from being rolled backward should Renzo quickly bridge and turn into him. Note that Royler places the hand of the arm that was closest to Renzo's hips upon the upper-thigh/hip of Renzo's near leg.

ⓘ Here you can see the hip-switch position from another angle. You can see how Royler has brought his hips to face Renzo's hips. His leg is alongside Renzo's body, the other leg posted far back for stability. Royler's hand is posted on Renzo's near thigh to control it.

Here we see the hip-switch position from another angle. Note the tightness of the position. Royler has kept his elbow on the floor tight to Renzo's head (at the ear). This gives great control of Renzo's head movement and, consequently, of the movement of Renzo's whole body. It also prevents Renzo from seeing what Royler is up to. Note also that Royler's hip position has pushed Renzo's near arm out, making escape very difficult for Renzo.

3

It is very easy now for Royler to simply throw the leg that was positioned well back away from Renzo (in order to provide good base) high over Renzo's legs to the floor on the other side of Renzo's body. Royler can use the hand on Renzo's near thigh to push Renzo's legs and hips down to make the act of clearing Renzo's legs easier.

4

Now Royler brings his hips forward into the mounted position. He then puts his hands on the floor out wide in order to gain a wide base and prevent Renzo from rolling his as soon as he mounts.

057 The handstand sweep

Most attacks from the guard position require you to first open your guard by uncrossing your feet and then using your legs to help either sweep or submit your opponent. There are some sweeps, however, that can be done from a closed guard. The handstand sweep is one such example. It is performed upon an opponent who has stood up in your closed guard. In general it is not a good idea to maintain a closed guard on an opponent standing in your guard in a real fight. It is too easy for him to strike you or pick you up and slam you on the ground. Unless you are very confident of your ability it is usu-

ally safer to open your guard and place at least one foot on your opponent's hips to keep him away, preventing him from picking you up and to allow you more attacking options. However, intelligent use of the handstand sweep can allow you to safely maintain a closed guard on a standing opponent, even in a real fight. This is because you can use the sweep to keep your opponent completely off-balance, making it extremely difficult for him to hit you effectively. Indeed, all his attention will be taken up with simply staying on his feet – hitting you or picking you up will not be an option if you use the sweep well.

1

Renzo stands up in Royler's closed guard. It does not matter if Renzo stands up with one foot forward or both feet square, the sweep can be done in either case.

2

Knowing that it can be dangerous to passively hold a closed guard on a standing opponent (it is easy for Renzo to open the guard and begin passing from a standing position; Renzo can punch effectively when he stands over Royler), Royler quickly enters into the handstand sweep. He brings one arm inside one of Renzo's legs and grasps it as shown. To increase his leverage, Royler pulls his head close to the foot of the leg that he has seized. Royler places his other hand palm down on the floor close to his own ear as though he were about to perform a handstand.

3

To sweep Renzo over to his back, Royler pulls on Renzo's trapped foot, pushes hard with the hand on the floor, *and drives up with his hips into and over the inner thigh of Renzo's trapped leg.* This strong upward drive of the hips is the key to success. *You want to open your opponent's thigh outward.* This makes it *very* difficult for your opponent to resist the sweep. It is quite likely that your guard will open at this point. This is not a problem.

ⓘ You can see here how Royler drives his hips up into Renzo's thigh, turning it out and taking Renzo down very easily. Note how low Royler's grip on the trapped leg is. You do not want your arm to slide up the trapped leg as this lessens the leverage.

4

As Royler continues to drive, Renzo goes down. If the sweep is done with conviction it is very difficult to resist. Sometimes however, your opponent regains his balance before he goes down. In this case, simply try again. Persistence often pays off with the handstand sweep. As you keep trying your opponent will be so fixated on keeping his balance that offense will be the last thing on his mind.

5

As soon as Renzo falls to his back, Royler quickly surges forward and reaches across with the hand that pushed up off the floor. Royler grabs the sleeve or wrist of his opponent. If Royler uses the left hand to reach across, he will grip his opponent's left wrist and vice versa. Royler will use this grip to help pull himself forward into a mounted position.

(!) In this close-up you can see the grip Royler uses on the gi sleeve. A crucial point to note here is that Royler does not simply sit up. This would make it easy for his opponent to shove him back down. Rather, he turns his upper body in the direction of the forward arm that grips his opponent's sleeve. *Most important of all, Royler picks his hips up and throws them forward in an exaggerated motion to clear his opponent's hips and take him easily over into the mounted position.* It is as though you are throwing your hips over your opponent's. Failure to do so often results in a failure to get mounted.

6

Still pulling up on his opponent's sleeve for control (and to make escape difficult for his opponent), Royler attains the mounted position.

058 The Achilles' ankle lock

The Achilles' ankle lock is a relatively simple, yet highly effective submission hold. It can be attained from many positions and is also a good move to go for when both grapplers are in a scramble – where neither one has a positional advantage and both move very rapidly to attain a superior position. Unlike some other leg locks there is very little risk of accidental injury when using the Achilles' lock in hard training, so it can safely be made part of daily workouts. Often the Achilles' lock is used as a direct form of attack. In this sequence we look at a different setup. Here the Achilles' lock is used as a counter to a sweep. Your opponent sweeps you backward as you attempt to pass his guard. Rather than regaining your position and trying to resume passing his guard, you go on the offensive and attempt the ankle lock. This is a good, attacking style of jiu-jitsu, taking the fight to the opponent and seeking a quick finish to the fight.

1

Royler stands up in Renzo's closed guard as a prelude to a passing attempt.

2

Renzo quickly opens his guard and attempts the two-handed sweep (shown in detail elsewhere in the book), grabbing both of Royler's ankles and pinching his knees together.

3

Renzo punches his knee up toward the ceiling, knocking Royler cleanly over. Renzo can easily get mounted if Royler does not react. Note, however, that for a short time Renzo's legs are straight and his feet are under Royler's armpits. This gives a great opportunity for Royler to employ the Achilles' lock.

4

Royler immediately brings one of his knees up between Renzo's legs. He places the foot of his other leg on Renzo's hip/stomach area. This traps Renzo's leg between both his legs. It is a general rule with most of the basic leg locks that you must trap one of your opponent's legs with both of yours. Note that the foot Royler has placed on Renzo's hip is *turned out*. This is important. Failure to turn the foot out can result in your opponent performing an ankle lock on *you* – then it might be *your* turn to tap in submission! The positioning of Royler's legs in this manner forms an effective barrier between himself and Renzo. This prevents Renzo from sitting up into the mounted position. Royler begins to wrap his arm around Renzo's trapped foot.

5

Now Royler encircles Renzo's trapped leg at the Achilles' tendon. The key here is to wrap your arm as low on the leg as possible. Having wrapped your arm around your opponent's leg, slide your arm down his shin until his foot prevents you going any farther. This will put you in good position to inflict a very effective lock on your opponent. Royler places the hand (palm down) of his other arm on the front of Renzo's shin.

Note the hand position used by Royler. (There are other methods for this particular lock, but the one shown is simple and very effective). To implement the submission hold, Royler places the hand of the arm encircling Renzo's trapped leg on the wrist of his other arm (which is now placed on Renzo's shin). Note also how Royler has slid his arm all the way down Renzo's shin to the foot before applying the lock.

6

Royler squeezes his legs together to prevent Renzo from twisting around and clamps the elbow of the arm wrapped around Renzo's leg against his own ribs. He then arches back to place tremendous pressure on the ankle and Achilles' tendon, creating a very painful lock.

Moving from across-side to the mounted position · The knee-drive method

Here we look at another means of attaining the mounted position when across your opponent's side. The knee-drive method is a very tight, powerful means of getting mounted. Done well, it is an intimidating experience for your opponent as he feels a lot of pressure as you work through the move. While the hip-switching method relies mainly upon speed, surprise, and timing, the knee-driving method is a more relentless, deliberate method.

1

Renzo is lying across Royler's side. Note Renzo's arm position. He has an arm under Royler's head, giving excellent head control as he drives his shoulder into Royler's jaw. Royler has his leg that is closest to Renzo up high, making it difficult for Renzo to throw his leg over into the mounted position as would be done in the hip-switching method. A different approach is called for.

2

While controlling Royler's head with one arm, Renzo takes his other arm and places the elbow/forearm on the front of Royler's thigh.

3

Renzo then places the hand of that same arm on Royler's hip.

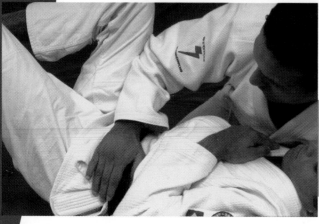

(!) Here you can see Renzo's hand and arm position. The hand is on Royler's far hip, the elbow on the front of Royler's near thigh. This allows Renzo to control Royler's hips and legs very effectively.

4

Now Renzo raises his elbow, clearing Royler's near thigh and giving him the room to begin driving his knee across Royler's stomach. Renzo passes his knee under his own elbow to begin the knee drive. Note that Renzo keeps his head low throughout the movement. It is crucial that you remain tight on your opponent as you move.

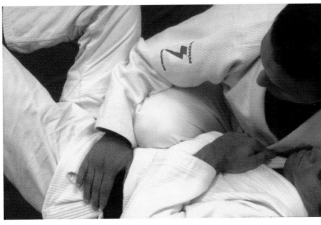

Here you can see clearly the raising of the elbow. Renzo's knee fits neatly into the space that this movement creates and begins to slide along the line of Renzo's belt.

5

Once Renzo's knee is halfway across Royler's stomach there are two key elements. The first is the act of driving his knee all the way to the floor on the far side of Royler's body. The other is to bring his head up to Royler's. This puts you into a very tight mounted position.

6

Having gotten into the mounted position, Renzo maintains his grip around Royler's head with one arm. With the other he controls Royler's arm, driving Royler's elbow out wide, making escape and defense very difficult.

060 Defense against hand on chest

A very common occurrence during the escalation of violence that leads up to street fights is the use of the hand on the chest. This is often used as a means of intimidation, sometimes as a means to shove the victim. The great frequency with which this is seen in real fights and the potential danger in its use means that you must have some quick response to it.

1

Renzo approaches Royler with his arm out, palm open.

2

Renzo's hand makes contact with Royler's chest. This might be part of the process of intimidation (usually accompanied by verbal attack), or it might be a prelude to physical violence. The hand on the chest can be used to shove the victim around and to control his movements. Royler does not hesitate. He places the palm of his hand over the hand on his chest, effectively trapping his antagonist's hand to his chest. With his other hand, Royler grips just above the elbow of his attacker's out-thrust arm. If your opponent has used his right hand to push on your chest, you will trap his hand with your right hand and grasp above the elbow with your left (vice versa if he pushes you with his left hand).

3

Having attained his grip, Royler leans forward into his antagonist.

You can see here how Royler begins to put pressure on the wrist of his attacker. He is sure to pull in tightly with the arm with which he is holding Renzo's triceps.

4

Now Royler takes his hand off Renzo's hand and puts it over his own hand on Renzo's triceps. This allows Royler to pull in with the strength of both arms as he leans in to his attacker.

The close-up reveals the shift in Royler's hand position. Both his hands are gripping Renzo's out-thrust arm just above the elbow. Royler pulls in as he leans forward.

5

This action puts great pressure on Renzo's wrist, putting him in a totally defensive position, allowing Royler to control the situation.

061 How to stand up properly in a street fight

A truly crucial yet commonly overlooked part of a real fight is the ability to stand back up on your feet while in the face of a threatening opponent who is standing over you. As has been constantly stressed throughout this book—MOST FIGHTS END UP WITH ONE OR BOTH COMBATANTS ON THE GROUND! A very common situation is one where one of the combatants is knocked down, while the other remains standing. This is potentially a VERY dangerous situation. The standing fighter has the advantage of being able to kick the man on the ground and pummel him as he attempts to get up. If you do not employ the correct method of standing up, there is an excellent chance you will end up back on the ground – only this time you will be unconscious! This scenario arises most frequently as a result of a powerful strike by one fighter. Often a powerful punch or kick by a skilled striker will knock you right down while leaving your opponent standing. Other times this scenario arises because you shot in on your opponent but failed to take him down. His counter to your takedown attempt left you on the ground and him standing. Another possibility is that your opponent threw you and remained on his feet, or that he is uncomfortable fighting on the ground and stood up. However the scenario arose, it is vital that you know how to get back up safely and quickly.

1

Renzo finds himself on the ground while his opponent is still standing, a very common and potentially very dangerous situation in real fights. Renzo's first concern is to adopt the correct posture. He sits up, rear arm braced back on the floor for support. His forward arm protects his head and face. His forward leg is drawn up to protect his ribs and groin. The foot of his rear leg is placed just in front of his opponent's forward foot. This is a sound protective position. If Royler should rush in with a barrage of kicks or punches, Renzo has the option of falling down to his back with his feet drawn up in defense, ready to kick back, then returning to this position when Royler backs off.

2

To begin the act of standing up, Renzo wants to make Royler retreat a little so that he get to his feet more safely. To force Royler to back up, Renzo thrusts out a kick with the foot that was closest to Royler's front leg. The target is Royler's lead knee. Note that Renzo keeps his lead hand and arm high to protect his head.

3

Having made Royler retreat a little, Renzo seizes his opportunity to stand up. Using his rear hand and nonkicking leg as his base of support, Renzo raises his hips and buttocks off the ground and begins to retract his kicking leg.

4

Renzo brings his kicking leg all the way back in one smooth motion until it is behind his rear hand. Note that Renzo's forward arm is still up for protection.

5

Now Renzo straightens up and returns to a standing fighting stance. The whole move is done very quickly. It is crucial to practice this vital skill since it is required so frequently and the consequences of failure can be very serious indeed. You can drill the move solo by imagining an opponent standing in front of you as you stand in this fashion.

062 Defense against the standing rear choke

A very common form of attack involves attacking a victim from behind with a chokehold while in a standing position. An inexperienced fighter will perform this move while standing up straight. This allows you to counter the attack very easily by throwing him over your shoulder (demonstrated elsewhere in the book). An experienced fighter, however, will break your balance backward while attacking with the chokehold. This makes escape much more difficult. There is no chance of simply throwing your opponent over your shoulder as before since you are being pulled backward. At the same time you are being choked and in immediate danger of passing out.

1

Renzo approaches Royler from behind and throws his arm around Royler's neck to begin the strangle. Note Renzo's stance. He has his body side-on to Royler, the leg of his choking arm is forward, between Royler's legs. This is the stance of an experienced fighter. It will allow Renzo to not merely apply the chokehold but also to pull Royler backward.

2

Renzo locks the choke and breaks Royler's balance to the rear. Royler's first reaction is to defend his neck. The initial danger is in being rendered unconscious. Placing one hand on the wrist and the other on the crook of the elbow of the choking arm, Royler pulls straight down, relieving some of the pressure.

3

Royler lowers his level by stepping back with the leg on the same side as Renzo's choking arm. He steps back and outside Renzo's lead foot. Note that he is still defending his neck from the choke. At the same time, Royler steps his other leg forward a little.

4

Turning *into* the choke, Royler steps his forward leg as far around as it will go while sliding his other leg behind Renzo's forward leg. What Royler is doing here is moving with Renzo's pulling strength.

(!) Here you can see clearly Royler's leg position as he turns into Renzo's chokehold. He wants to finish with his leg behind Renzo's forward leg, trapping it.

5

Using the leg behind Renzo's forward leg as a hook, Royler continues to step around behind Renzo. Now it is Renzo's turn to be off-balance to the rear. Throughout all this movement, Royler has maintained a strong grip on Renzo's choking arm. Even if Renzo should release his chokehold now in an effort to escape the impending danger, he could not, since Royler has trapped his arm with his grip.

6

Royler pulls down sharply with both arms on Renzo's choking arm as he strongly sweeps back with the leg behind Renzo's forward leg. Renzo is easily taken down.

7

This allows Royler to finish in a very dominating position in which he can easily determine the future course of the confrontation.

Defense against the front-thrusting kick

Brazilian jiu-jitsu is very much a grappling art. However, there are strikes in Brazilian Jiu Jistu. Most often these are utilized from grappling positions where the opponent cannot hit back effectively. Good examples of this are the mounted position and the knee-on-stomach position. In addition there is often a good deal of striking from the clinch position while standing. Here you are holding and controlling the opponent with one or both arms while punching, elbowing, head butting, or kneeing him. There are times, however, when the jiu-jitsu fighter launches into strikes without holding on to the opponent in any way, just as a practitioner of the striking arts would. With regard these strikes, Brazilian jiu-jitsu favors the use of the elbows and knees for striking. These are close-range weapons. Consequently they allow the grappler to easily revert back into the grappling mode. Moreover, unlike the fist and feet, they are not delicate at all but can be hammered into the opponent with little fear of self-harm. Here we see an elbow strike used as a counter to a front-thrusting kick.

1

Royler and Renzo square off.

2

Chambering his rear leg, Royler prepares to launch into a front-thrusting kick. This can be a very powerful attack when used by an expert.

3

Renzo steps back with this right foot and brings his forward arm under Royler's kicking leg, brushing the kick off to the side.

4

As Royler's kicking leg comes down to the floor, Renzo is very close to him. It would be easy for Renzo to enter into a clinch and begin grappling. However, Renzo elects to strike instead. Due to the short range the elbow strike is the perfect weapon.

5

Renzo hammers his elbow into Royler's chin. This is a very powerful blow. The elbow often cuts your opponent's face and allows you to rapidly switch into grappling range.

Shoulder lock using the legs, "Omoplata"

"Omoplata," the shoulder lock using the legs, is one of the more exotic-looking submission holds. It looks complicated but is ac- tually quite simple to use. It is almost always used from the guard position, though there are variations from other positions.

1

Royler is holding Renzo in his closed guard.

2

As he opens his guard, Royler places his hands on Renzo's biceps, controlling Renzo's arms. This both prevents Renzo from punching and also sets up the entry into "Omoplata."

3

Royler pushes off his foot that is on the floor in order to turn his body out to the side. He brings his other leg high up on Renzo's back, controlling the elbow of the arm on the same side.

4

Continuing the turn, Royler brings himself around so that he is almost parallel to Renzo. If Renzo should resist the movement, Royler can simply straighten his leg forward to bring Renzo's head down and continue the move.

In this detail you can see how Royler controls the arm. His leg hooks around the back of the arm until his foot comes down over Renzo's collarbone.

5

At this point, Royler sits up and grips Renzo's belt at the lower back. If Renzo is not wearing a gi, Royler simply wraps his arm around the lower back. This is an important detail. Failure to do this allows an experienced opponent to simply roll forward out of the lock.

6

To finish the lock, Royler sits forward, bringing the foot of the leg that he is using to wrap around Renzo's arm toward his own hips. As Royler brings his head close to Renzo's, he puts great pressure on Renzo's shoulder, forcing submission.

065 The arm-inside sweep

When your opponent is inside your closed guard there are a number of very effective moves that rely upon you reaching an arm inside his legs and using this arm to lever yourself into very good attacking positions. These moves combine well with each other and open up many possibilities for attack. When using the guard you will find that most attacks from that position rely upon you getting out to one side so that you are no longer directly in front of your opponent. By reaching inside your opponent's legs you make this movement to the side very easy.

1

Renzo has Royler locked in his closed guard.

2

Royler begins to stand in Renzo's guard. This might be because Royler wishes to pass Renzo's guard, or because he wants to strike or slam Renzo. As soon as Royler gets one leg up, Renzo begins his move. You can actually perform this move even when your opponent is down on both knees and refuses to stand, but here it is demonstrated on an opponent who is trying to stand.

3

Renzo reaches his arm deep to the inside of the leg that Royler has begun to stand on. He places the hand of his *other* arm on his opponent's elbow; if his opponent is wearing a gi, he grips the gi sleeve at the elbow. Unlocking his feet, Renzo explosively pulls his head toward the hand that he has reached to the inside of his opponent's leg while throwing his opposite leg out wide. This places him out to Royler's side at right angles to Royler. Renzo brings his leg that is on the same side as the arm he used to grab the inside of Royler's leg high up into the back of Royler's armpit.

Here you can see clearly how Renzo has reached to the inside of Royler's leg and gripped it at the knee. He is also controlling Royler's opposite arm at the elbow. Note how Renzo has pulled his head very close to the hand that has reached to the inside of Royler's leg, putting him at right angles to Royler.

4

To topple Royler over, Renzo sweeps back with the leg he initially threw out wide while bringing the foot of the leg he had brought up into Royler's armpit down to the floor. At the same time he lifts with the arm that he is holding inside Royler's leg. A crucial point here is that Renzo does not sweep Royler directly to the side. Rather, he sweeps Royler to the side *and forward*. By sweeping to Royler's front corner, Renzo prevents Royler from applying his base and resisting the sweep. It is important that you maintain control of your opponent's elbow as you sweep him, otherwise he will base out with his far arm and prevent the sweep.

5

Taking Royler completely over, Renzo maintains his grip on the inside of Royler's leg for control. He is sure to throw his hips up high onto Royler's chest so as to go easily into the mounted position. The sweep finishes with Renzo mounted on Royler, holding a much better position than that which he started with.

The arm-inside arm-bar

We have seen that reaching an arm to the inside of your opponent's leg when he is in your guard makes it very easy to pull yourself into a great attacking position where you are out to your opponent's side. This method was at the heart of the arm-inside sweep. This method can be used in many other ways also. Here we look at the case where our opponent resists the arm-inside sweep but opens himself to an arm-bar submission.

1

Renzo holds Royler in his closed guard.

2

Royler attempts to stand. Renzo reacts just as he did for the arm-inside sweep. He reaches to the inside of Royler's leg and begins to pull his head toward the hand of the arm with which he has reached to the inside.

3

As Renzo opens his guard and goes for the sweep, Royler senses the danger and maintains a very upright stance, foiling the sweep attempt. The arm-inside sweep relies upon you being able to break your opponent's posture forward. By keeping his head up and back straight, Royler can successfully resist the sweep.

4

However, by resisting the sweep in this manner, Royler leaves himself very vulnerable to an arm bar. Renzo seizes the great attacking opportunity that his positioning out to the side offers and throws his hips up high, placing his far leg over Royler's face.

5

Renzo applies the arm bar from underneath. He is sure to hook the foot of the leg that he has put over Royler's face down toward the floor. This makes it very difficult for Royler to stand and escape. Renzo then squeezes his knees together and raises his hips to the ceiling while pulling Royler's arm straight. This puts breaking pressure on Royler's elbow, forcing him to submit or suffer heavy damage to the elbow joint.

(!) You can see clearly the application of the arm bar here. Renzo holds Royler's arm at the wrist with both hands for control. He puts Royler's thumb uppermost to maximize the effect of the lock. To break the elbow he pushes up with his hips as he brings his knees together.

The "Kimura" lock

The "kimura" lock is a punishing submission hold that puts immense pressure on the shoulder and elbow. Taken to an extreme it can result in massive damage to both joints. It is a very versatile lock that can be used from many positions. Elsewhere in this book it is shown from the guard position. More-over, it combines well with other submission holds, making it an essential part of the jiu-jitsu student's arsenal. Here we see it being used from across the opponent's side and from the north-south position.

1

Royler has a good, dominating position on Renzo and looks to apply a submission hold. The position Royler holds, where he is not so much across his opponent's side but rather facing toward Renzo's legs, covering Renzo's face, is often referred to as the "north and south" position. Royler has control of one of Renzo's wrists with one hand and has come under Renzo's arm with his other hand. Sensing the imminent danger of a submission attempt, Renzo grips his belt with the threatened arm. Doing this makes it very difficult for Royler to secure a regular arm bar.

2

It does not, however, protect Renzo from the "kimura" lock. Accordingly, Royler begins to apply kimura. Royler threads the hand that came under Renzo's arm all the way over to his own wrist, which he grabs.

(!)

In the detail you can see exactly how Royler secures the "kimura" lock. One hand grabs the opponent's wrist, the other comes under the opponent's arm and grabs his own wrist. Note that Royler does not employ his thumbs while gripping in order to gain a stronger grip upon the trapped arm. Once locked, it is very difficult for the opponent to free the trapped arm.

3

Maintaining the lock that he has secured, Royler pushes Renzo to his side so that the trapped arm is uppermost. Renzo is still gripping his belt to defend the arm-bar danger.

4

Royler places his knee over Renzo's face to trap Renzo's head. This prevents Renzo from squirming out of the lock. Royler puts the knee of his other leg on Renzo's back, posting his foot up. This position, one knee down on the ground (covering Renzo's face) the other knee up on Renzo's back, affords the best leverage to apply the lock. To break Renzo's grip on his belt, Royler pulls the wrist of Renzo's trapped arm first toward Renzo's face (to break the grip).

Here you can see the position of Royler's knee on Renzo's back. This position provides great leverage. In addition, should Royler opt to switch into a regular arm bar, he can do so by merely throwing his other leg over Renzo's face and falling back.

5

Then he pulls Renzo's arm up toward the ceiling a little, then toward Renzo's back. It is this motion toward Renzo's back that puts great pressure on the shoulder and elbow. Throughout the locking movement, Royler keeps Renzo's trapped arm bent at ninety degrees.

6

Turning Renzo's captured wrist toward his back, Royler applies the Kimura lock. Renzo cannot turn out of the lock because his head is immobilized by Royler's knee over his face (if Renzo's head was not trapped in this fashion he could easily turn out).

Strangle from across-side

Throughout this book the theme of continually improving one's positional dominance over your opponent has been stressed. The across-side position is a very dominating position. Generally when one attains across-side position, the next step is to go up to an even better position—the mount. However, there is another consideration besides positional dominance—*making your opponent submit*. Submission holds can arise from all kinds of positions (though it is fair to say that the best ones arise only after you have gotten to a good position). If the opportunity to take a submission hold arises in the course of your struggle with your opponent you should go after it immediately, even if your position is not the optimal one. So long as your position is good enough that attempting the sub-

mission does put you in danger of stronger counters, go for the submission hold. This spirit of fighting for the decisive win through submission holds is good jiu-jitsu. With experience you will come to be a good judge of how to strike the delicate balance between your twin desires to improve position and your desire to submit your opponent. Here we look at an attack from across-side. This is not the optimal mounted position, but is nonetheless a very good, stable position from which a vast number of submissions can be safely and successfully attempted. Often it makes more sense to immediately attack with submission holds from here than to fight to go on to the mounted position. Here is one such attack.

1

Renzo is holding Royler down in a classic across-side position. Note Renzo's arm position. One hand is on Royler's near hip, the other over Royler's head.

2

Rather than go on to the mounted position, Renzo decides to finish the fight from where he is. His current position, while perhaps not optimal, is certainly good enough to attack with submission holds. Renzo brings the hand that was on Royler's near hip *under* Royler's near arm to grasp Royler's collar at the back.

3

Note how Renzo grips the back of the collar. His fingers go inside, thumb outside. The grip is deep at the side or back of the neck.

In this detail you can see clearly the grip. Note how Renzo's arm goes under Royler's arm. His palm is facing Royler's head, fingers inside the collar.

4

Having secured the grip with the first hand, it is time to get the second hand into position. Renzo brings the hand of the arm that was trapping Royler's head into the collar on the far side of Royler's neck. He grips the collar with only the thumb inside, his fingers are outside.

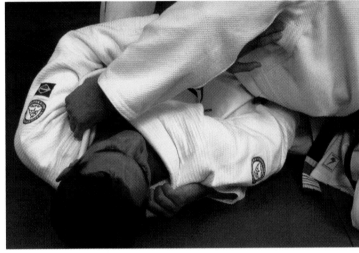

Here you can see the completed grip. Note that Renzo does not grip too far down the far side of Royler's neck. Only the thumb is inside the collar.

5

To apply the stranglehold, Renzo brings his forearm down on Royler's throat, trying to touch the elbow of the strangling arm down to the floor.

6

To maximize strangling power and to hinder any attempt at escape on Royler's part, Renzo thrusts back the leg that is closest to Royler's head, lowering his hips to the floor. As he brings the elbow of his strangling arm down, he also brings it toward Royler's ear, rendering Royler's escape attempts ineffective.

Defending the arm-inside guillotine choke

We have seen the guillotine choke in other parts of this book. It must be said that this choke is one of the most frequently used submission holds. It can be used in a vast number of situations, both standing and on the ground. Used well it is very difficult to defend. Even a beginner can be dangerous with this move if he is strong and persistent. Usually the guillotine choke is performed by locking your arms around your opponent's neck. There is, however, a variation (the arm-inside guillotine) that involves coming around the neck *and one arm as well*. It was this version of the guillotine that Renzo used to defeat a very talented Japanese fighter in one of his professional fights. This version of the guillotine, because it traps one of your arms as well as your neck, makes the escapes to the guillotine shown elsewhere in this book ineffective. Another form of escape is necessary.

1

Royler shoots in on Renzo's legs in order to take Renzo down.

2

However, Renzo defends the shoot by wrapping his arms around Royler's neck and arm. Royler cannot throw his arm over Renzo's back as in the other escapes shown in the book because his arm is trapped. The danger here is that Renzo will arch back and begin choking Royler. To lessen the danger of choking, Royler immediately goes to defend his neck. He takes the hand of his free arm and pulls down on on the wrist of Renzo's choking arm, relieving some of the pressure.

Here you can see the arm-inside guillotine choke. Note how Royler's head *and* arm are trapped.

3

While defending his neck with the free hand, Royler brings his other hand across in front of Renzo's stomach.

4

Using the hand of the trapped arm, Royler grabs the hand of Renzo's choking arm.

5

Royler now takes the hand of his free arm (that was initially defending the chokehold by pulling down on Royler's wrist) and grips Renzo's choking arm just above the elbow.

6

To break the chokehold, Royler uses the hand of his trapped arm to push up on Renzo's hand, bending Renzo's wrist uncomfortably. Once having broken the grip, Royler pushes with both hands and extracts his head from the hold, ready to resume the fight.

(!) In this close-up detail you can see Royler's grip. He breaks Renzo's chokehold by levering up on the hand of Renzo's choking arm. This is a form of wrist lock that forces Renzo to relinquish his grip.

The knee-on-stomach position

Brazilian jiu-jitsu generally extols the mounted position as the most desirable one to attain in a real fight. This is because it is a stable position that allows you to strike your opponent with near impunity while all the time being able to enter into a large number of submission holds. As you become more advanced in your jiu-jitsu skills, however, there is some justification in thinking that another position, the knee-on-stomach position, is on a par with the mounted position in terms of effectiveness. Indeed, there are some aspects in which the knee-on-stomach position is clearly superior to the mounted position. While it may seem unstable to the novice, experts can use it to ride and control even the most wild escape attempts. It offers tremendous mobility, allowing you to move easily in response to your opponent. Like the mounted position, you can strike and submit your opponent with little fear of effective retaliation. An expert can put immense and painful pressure on his opponent through the use of the knee driving into the chest and stomach. This pressure often forces the hapless opponent to expose himself to submission holds or strikes. In a street fight on concrete, the knee-on-stomach position can be used without fear of the usual scrapes and bruises that come from grappling and fighting on cement. Also you can get to your feet more quickly if the situation should demand it. It is essential that you practice attaining and maintaining this punishing position.

1

Renzo is holding across-side position on Royler. This is a good position in itself, but Renzo decides to take it up a level and go to a position that will put more pressure on Royler.

2

Holding the collar and belt, Renzo pops up and places his knee on Royler's stomach.

3

Extending his other leg out as a base of support, Renzo attains the knee-on-stomach position. Note that Renzo's support leg is fairly straight and out wide. To put pressure on his opponent, Renzo can drive his knee down while pulling up with his hands. This places Renzo in great position to begin striking or attempting submission holds.

4

Here we see Renzo switching his hand position. He takes his hand from the belt and goes deep inside Royler's near collar. His other hand takes the gi at the elbow and pulls up toward the ceiling. This is a great grip as it makes it very difficult for Royler to turn into Renzo while at the same time opening up obvious opportunities for strangles and arm-bar submissions.

071 Defense against the knee-on-stomach position

The knee-on-stomach position is one of the most devastating in a real fight. While not quite as stable as the mounted position, it offers far greater mobility with the same potential for punishing strikes and submission holds. For the man on the bottom it can be a nightmarish experience. An experienced grappler can subject you to considerable discomfort by driving his knee into your stomach and chest. If you employ an unsafe method of escape you risk exposing yourself to a number of submission holds. Here we see an effective and safe escape from this potentially punishing position.

1

Renzo has attained the knee-on-stomach position. You can see the obvious danger of strikes from here. Renzo can blast away at Royler's face with punches and also launch into a wide array of submission holds. It is imperative for Royler to escape quickly and safely.

2

Royler places the hand of the arm closest to Renzo upon the knee of Renzo's outstretched leg. He grips the front of Renzo's belt with his other hand. If Renzo was not wearing a gi and belt, he would put his fist or open hand in Renzo's lower stomach.

3

By pushing with both arms and scooting his hips away from Renzo, Royler creates space between him and his opponent—without exposing himself to submission holds. This hip-scooting movement is the same one used in the elbow escape drill shown elsewhere in this book, illustrating once again the extreme importance and versatility of this fundamental form of grappling movement.

4

Taking his hand from the knee of Renzo's outstretched leg, Royler brings his arm back, posting the elbow on the ground as shown. He maintains his grip on Renzo's frontal belt area, pushing his arm into Renzo's stomach. By turning in to Renzo in this way, Royler has safely removed Renzo's knee from his stomach.

5

Still holding Renzo's belt area, Royler gets to his knees in one fluid motion.

6

Royler quickly reaches for Renzo's near ankle for a classic ankle-pick takedown.

7

Pushing with the hand on the belt and pulling with the hand on the ankle, Royler takes Renzo down.

8

Note how Royler pulls up high on the ankle to secure the takedown. Not only has Royler escaped, he has taken Renzo down and obtained a very good position as a result.

072 Arm bar from the knee-on-stomach position

Due to the fact that the knee-on-stomach position puts great pressure on your opponent along with ease of movement on your part, it creates many opportunities for submission holds. Here is one good example.

1

Renzo is holding a strong knee-on-stomach position.

2

In an attempt to relieve the pressure or escape, Royler puts his hand on Renzo's knee, hoping to push it off his stomach. This is a very common reaction and one that opens up an immediate opportunity for attack.

3

Sliding his hand under the crook of Royler's elbow, Renzo begins an attack on the arm that is pushing upon his knee.

(!) Here you can see the fashion in which Renzo begins the attack on the arm. He reaches in palm up at the bend of the elbow.

4

Pulling strongly on the captured arm, Renzo pulls Royler's elbow straight up to his chest. This is crucial. Failure to pull the arm up in this manner greatly diminishes the chances of success.

Note the great control Renzo exerts over the captured arm. The resulting tightness makes escape very unlikely. The idea is to hug your opponent's arm to your chest.

5

Maintaining the tight grip on the arm, Renzo steps with his supporting leg (not the one on Royler's stomach) around and over Royler's head.

Here you can see the step around from another angle. Note how low Renzo keeps his body. This is the result of bending deeply at the knees. It results in a very tight control of your opponent throughout the move.

6

Renzo spins 180 degrees in one easy movement (this might sound difficult but it is really very simple to do) and sits down.

7

Falling to his back, Renzo applies the arm bar. He sits close to Royler. If you sit down too far away from your opponent you may slip past the elbow joint and lose the lock. Renzo squeezes his knees together and pushes his hips up toward the ceiling. Be sure that your opponent's thumb is pointing up to the ceiling to maximize the breaking power of the lock.

Transition from the triangle choke into the arm bar

One of the attributes of a good jiu-jitsu fighter is the ability to rapidly switch from one move to another. Unless your opponent is totally unskilled, it is unlikely that all your submission attempts will succeed on first attempt. Usually a strong or skilled opponent will try very hard to resist the submission hold. In response to your opponent's resistance you must be able to flow into another submission hold. You will soon find that very few opponents can resist a determined attack that comes in combinations. Just as a good boxer does not throw punches in isolation but rather in combinations, a good jiu-jitsu fighter always has a backup move to flow into should his initial move fail to overcome the resistance of his opponent. A good example of the principle is the transition from the triangle choke to the arm bar.

1

Royler attacks Renzo with one of the very best submission holds—the triangle choke.

2

As Royler maneuvers his legs into position, Renzo feels the danger of the stranglehold and begins to pull away. This is a very common reaction. Even a complete novice can feel when he is about to be strangled and instinctively pulls away.

3

Standing, Renzo gets up high enough to prevent Royler from successfully locking his legs into the full triangle choke. There is actually some danger here for Royler. A strong and aggressive opponent can pick you up and slam you very heavily on the floor from this position. Even on padded mats this can be disconcerting, on cement it might well be disastrous. Rather than persist with the triangle, which will be very difficult and potentially hazardous to use at this point, Royler shifts to another move.

4

Uncrossing his legs, Royler brings his left leg over Renzo's face and squeezes his knees together. By pushing up with his hips Royler can break Renzo's elbow with an arm bar from this upside down position. It does not matter if Renzo picks Royler up at this stage, the arm will still break.

5

From another angle you can see clearly the position of Royler's legs. See how he straightens Renzo's arm and raises his hips to bring the lock into effect. Both of Royler's hands control the arm he is attacking at the wrist.

Finger lock

The vast majority of the joint locks in Brazilian jiu-jitsu are applied on the large joints such as the neck, elbow, shoulder, knee, and ankle. Usually the idea is to use your whole body to control the joint to make it very difficult for your opponent to twist out of it. For example, the standard arm bar uses your legs, hips, and arms to control a single arm of your opponent. In addition, most of these locks are applied on the ground, where it is much easier to control your opponent by pinning him to the floor. The fact that you attack a large joint with your whole body while pinning your opponent to the floor is what makes Brazilian jiu-jitsu so effective in a real fight. Very few people can go on fighting after suffering catastrophic damage to a shoulder or knee. Since you can exert great control over your opponent as your attempt these locks, even the strongest, wildest opponent will have a very hard time escaping a well-applied lock. It is much more difficult to apply a lock on a standing opponent since he is much freer to resist and struggle than someone pinned on the floor. In addition, locks to the small digits, such as the fingers, while painful, may not end the fight. A determined opponent may well go on fighting with even a badly broken finger. This is why Brazilian jiu-jitsu (unlike many other grappling styles in traditional martial arts) does not place much emphasis on standing joint locks to the small joints. There are exceptions to this rule, however. Bear in mind that not all acts of aggression are all-out fights or brawls. Violence comes in many forms. Often you can be harassed by an annoying and belligerent drunk, or by someone who wants to simply intimidate (rather than attack) you. In cases such as these, standing locks to the fingers and wrists can be useful. Against a more dangerous opponent it is much safer to get into a clinch and work from there.

1

Renzo has Royler in an intimidating front chokehold.

2

Royler reaches up with both hands and grabs Renzo's fingers. He is trying to isolate and grab a single finger on either hand.

3

Having isolated one finger, Royler wraps his hand around it and begins to bend it back. As soon as Royler isolates a finger on one of his opponent's hands, he brings his other hand over to grip the same wrist for added control.

> ⓘ In the detail photograph you can see clearly Royler beginning to twist Renzo's finger back. Note how Royler's other hand has come across to grip the wrist and help immobilize the trapped finger.

4

Having trapped the finger, Royler can exert considerable control over his opponent. This is an excellent means of taking the initiative in a socially acceptable way against an annoying or belligerent person without getting too aggressive.

075 Stacking the guard position into an ankle lock

Learning to deal with the guard position is a major part of training in Brazilian jiu-jitsu. Newcomers to the sport are constantly amazed (and often dismayed!) at how difficult it is to successfully attack someone while held in the guard position. A good opponent is constantly off-balancing you and controlling your movements, making strikes very difficult to land. Moreover, you are constantly in danger of being submitted by a skilled jiu-jitsu fighter as long as he has you in his guard. In general the best strategy is to get around his legs to a better position where you can control him. However, sometimes opportunities arise to attack your opponent even while he has you inside his guard. If you do not feel confident that you can get around his legs and pass his guard, it can be a good idea to take these opportunities as they arise and go for the attack, even though you have not yet passed his guard. Most such attacks involve going after your opponent's legs, since these are the closest targets. Here we see one such method while inside an opponent's guard position.

1

Royler is held inside Renzo's closed guard. He stands to begin passing the guard.

2

Renzo, however, is a skilled opponent. Rather than pass his guard in the usual manner, which may be very difficult, Royler elects to try a different approach. Placing his hands on the front of Renzo's shoulders for balance and leaning forward, Royler pinches his knees together to break Renzo's feet apart and squeeze Renzo's legs together. Renzo cannot grab Royler's ankles and sweep him backward as is done in the two-handed sweep (demonstrated elsewhere in this book) since Royler is leaning forward.

(!) Here you can see the manner in which Royler's legs pinch together, trapping Renzo's legs.

3

By pulling Royler's arms forward, Renzo off-balances Royler to the front. Royler is in danger of being taken over Renzo's head and mounted.

4

Rather than fight his way back into a stable position, Royler goes along with the forward movement. He places both his hands on the floor to balance himself and scoots forward, stacking Renzo on his head.

5

Royler goes forward all the way, rolling Renzo over his head onto his stomach in a prone position. Royler now finds himself sitting on the back of Renzo's legs, pinning Renzo's legs in a very controlling way.

6

Taking advantage of the vulnerable position of Renzo's ankles and the control he has over Renzo's legs, Royler goes straight for the ankle lock. He selects an ankle, wraps his arm around it and grips his arms just as he does for the other ankle locks demonstrated in this book. The hand of the arm encircling Renzo's ankle is placed on the wrist of his other arm. The hand of his other arm is placed on the front of his opponent's trapped leg at the shin. The only difference is that now he is applying it to an opponent who is lying on his stomach, rather than in a seated position.

7

To apply the ankle lock, Royler sits up straight and arches backward. Due to the fact that he is sitting on his opponent's buttocks, his weight pins his opponent in place, giving him great control.

076 Defense against a rear two-handed grab

Attacks from behind are common in street fights. Violent people often have no moral qualms about attacking you from behind. A very common attack of this sort involves grabbing the victim at the neck with both hands. Here we see an excellent counter to such a threat.

1

Royler grabs Renzo at the neck from behind. This can be a prelude to an attempted stranglehold, takedown, or strike. Renzo must react quickly. The problem is, he cannot see his opponent and must turn in to him to counter.

2

Reaching up with both hands, Renzo grabs Royler's hands close to the thumbs by placing his hands on top of Royler's. Having gotten his grip, Renzo then steps one of his feet behind the other out to the side, then turns to face his adversary.

Here you can see clearly the grip that Renzo employs. Note how his hands cover Royler's and grip close to the thumbs. Note also that Renzo does not use his thumbs to grip.

3

Having turned in toward his attacker, Renzo takes the hand of his opponent that he is turning toward and pulls it off his neck. At this point, Renzo can ignore his attacker's other hand.

4

Bringing his free hand down, Renzo uses it to help grab his opponent's trapped hand at the outside of the hand close to the little finger.

5

It is now a simple matter for Renzo to twist Royler's hand outward, putting great pressure on the muscles and tendons of the wrist. By locking his opponent's wrist in this fashion, Renzo can easily control him and dominate the situation.

(!) Here is the grip shown in detail. Renzo is controlling the hand by gripping on both sides and turning it outward, against the joint. In addition, Renzo pulls the arm straight to further weaken his opponent's ability to resist.

077 Knee-bar attack from inside the guard position

In general students of Brazilian jiu-jitsu are encouraged to go for positional dominance as they fight. The idea is that positional dominance gives a greater likelihood of controlling your opponent in a way that makes it very difficult for him to harm you, while giving you great opportunities to harm him, either with strikes or submission holds. This is high-percentage jiu-jitsu. By securing good position you greatly reduce the risk of being hit or put in a submission hold, while greatly increasing the chance of doing the same to your opponent. Sometimes, however, a good opportunity to apply a submission hold arises when you are not in a dominant position. Other times the great skill of your opponent makes the task of getting to a dominant position so difficult that you seek alternatives. While inside someone's guard you do not have a dominant position. Your opponent can hit you hard and apply submission holds with a good chance of success. Here we look at an alternative strategy that does not involve passing the guard and getting a better position, but rather attempting an attack on your opponent's legs.

1

Royler is holding Renzo in his closed guard.

2

Renzo begins to stand. This might well be part of an attempt to begin passing the guard.

3

As he stands, Renzo torques his body around and presses down on Royler's inner thigh. This breaks Royler's feet apart and opens the guard. Up to this point, there is nothing to distinguish the move from an attempt to stand and pass the guard. However, Renzo senses that his opponent has a good guard. Rather than get into a protracted battle to pass, he will attempt a leg lock.

4

Passing his arm under one of Royler's legs, Renzo pulls up on the leg just below the knee, straightening out the leg he is about to attack.

5

Using his other hand, Renzo pushes out the other leg at the knee. By spreading Royler's legs apart, he gives himself the room he needs to enter easily into the move.

6

Now Renzo passes his knee between Royler's legs straight down to the floor just outside the hip of Royler's trapped leg. Renzo's leg is sharply bent.

7

As Renzo's knee touches the ground he spins to turn his back on Royler. The foot of the leg that he brought between Royler's legs is on Royler's hip. His other foot is on the floor at Royler's buttocks. Hooking his arm around Royler's ankle, Renzo pulls the trapped leg out straight.

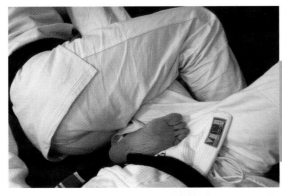

> ⓘ In this detail you can see the position of Renzo's legs. The foot of the leg that Renzo has passed between Royler's legs stays on the hip of Royler's locked leg. Renzo has completely turned his back on his opponent in order to attack the leg.

8

To apply the knee bar, he squeezes his knees together and uses both his arms to straighten Royler's leg. When it is straight, Renzo, pushes his hips forward to hyperextend the knee joint. This can result in catastrophic injury to the knee. Be careful with your training partner! Give him a chance to tap submission.

> ⓘ In this photo you can see the position of Renzo's other foot. It is placed on the floor at Royler's buttocks, making escape by sliding out very difficult for Royler. Note how Renzo's hips are placed just above Royler's trapped knee. They serve as a fulcrum over which Royler's knee will be broken when Renzo pushes forward with his hips.

078 The sweep from the seated open ("butterfly") guard

There are many positions for the open guard. One of the best involves sitting up and placing your feet under your opponent's thighs while holding him with your arms. Since this position involves sitting in a position that resembles the "butterfly" stretching position, it is often referred to as the "butterfly guard." There are several advantages to this approach. Having your feet under your opponent's thighs al-

lows you to easily offset his balance and attempt sweeps to turn him over and attain good position. It also makes it very difficult for your opponent to attack your legs with leg locks. Here we see both the transition from a closed guard to a seated open guard ("butterfly") and a classic sweep from this position.

1

Royler is holding Renzo in a closed guard.

2

Seeking a more aggressive, attacking approach, Royler decides to switch from closed to open guard. He uncrosses his feet and places them on the floor.

3

Scooting his hips out to one side, Royler creates the space he needs to work his way into an open "butterfly" guard.

4

Royler slides the knee on the same side he scooted out across Renzo's stomach, then up to Renzo's shoulder as pictured. The foot of that leg is positioned under Renzo's thigh.

5

It is now a simple matter for Royler to bring his other foot under Renzo's other thigh. Now both of Royler's feet are tucked under both of Renzo's thighs.

6

Royler repositions himself a little more directly in front of Renzo and prepares to sit up.

7

As he sits up, Royler slides one arm under Renzo's arm as an underhook, the other over Renzo's arm as an overhook. If your opponent is wearing a gi, you can use the underhook arm to grasp his belt, if not, simply hold around his back.

8

Here we see the completed position for the sweep. Royler is sitting up into his opponent. Both his feet are securely tucked under both of his opponent's thighs. One arm is under his opponent's arm, the other wrapped over the other arm. Royler is now ready to begin the sweep.

(!) We can note now the most crucial features of the sweeping position from the "butterfly" open guard. Royler is sure to place his head *outside his opponent's head on the same side he is sweeping toward*. This is very important. Your head is a significant percentage of your bodyweight and greatly aids in the sweep's efficiency. *Royler sweeps toward the arm that he has overhooked*. By overhooking the arm, Royler prevents his opponent from posting out with his hand and defending the sweep. Note also that Royler leans toward the side he is sweeping toward, sitting more on the buttock and hip on the same side he intends to sweep his opponent.

(!) Here we see in detail the opposite side. You can see how Royler's arm goes under Renzo's as an underhook. Royler grips the belt.

9

Royler sweeps his opponent *directly to the side that he has overhooked*. This is a crucial detail. Many people make the mistake of falling *back* to attempt the sweep. In fact you want to fall directly to your side. If you fall onto your back it will be very difficult to sweep your opponent over. Royler is sure to elevate his opponent over by lifting with the foot under his opponent's thigh on the opposite side that he sweeps toward. This elevating action off-balances his opponent and makes for an easy sweep. The foot on the same side that the opponent is swept toward pushes off the floor to greatly aid the sweep.

10

The result is a perfect sweep. Renzo is easily rolled onto his back. Without hesitation, Royler rolls on top of him to take the dominant mounted position.

11

Royler finishes in a secure mount. From here he can attack with strikes and submission holds.

The overhead sweep

Anytime your opponent stands in your guard you have a large number of possible sweeps you can use to take him down and come up in a dominant position. Which sweep you choose depends upon your opponent's stance. Here we look at a sweep that is best employed when your opponent is standing in your guard with a wide stance and leaning forward into you. This is common, especially in a real fight, since your opponent wants to reach forward to strike you. Even in a sporting grappling match this is very common. If your opponent has good posture you can *force* him to lean forward by pulling on his arms, or by opening your guard and kicking up with both feet, striking your opponent behind his shoulders and knocking him forward.

1

Renzo stands in Royler's guard.

2

As Renzo comes up to both feet, Royler notes his forward-leaning posture. This signals a great opportunity to use the overhead sweep. Royler grips Renzo's sleeves at the cuffs in order to control his opponent's arms and keep him leaning forward.

3

Opening his guard by uncrossing his feet, Royler deftly places both his feet on Renzo's hips.

4

Once both feet are in place on his opponent's hips, Royler bends his legs sharply and tugs on Renzo's sleeves, breaking his balance forward. It is a common mistake at this point to straighten your legs too early. This merely pushes your opponent away and makes the sweep very difficult. Bring your knees up to your own chest to draw your opponent forward off his feet. You want to have his head directly over your own before you begin to straighten your legs.

5

Once Renzo's head is directly over Royler's, Royler straightens his legs, lifting Renzo easily over his head in a spectacular throw. Good control of your opponents arms is important, otherwise he can place his hands on the ground and resist the sweep.

6

Renzo is carried cleanly over Royler's head. Royler immediately follows up.

7

At the completion of the move, Royler is mounted on Renzo, in total control.

080 Leg-binding sweep

One of the best means to deal with an aggressive opponent who is locked in your guard is to sweep him over and take a dominant position from where you can control the fight. How you sweep your opponent over is largely determined by the manner in which he holds himself in your guard. In this book we look at ways to sweep an opponent who is kneeling down, on one knee, and standing up. In the case of an opponent who is standing in your guard there is a sense of urgency in sweeping him over. A standing opponent is dangerous. In a real fight he can throw a torrent of punches that will be diffi-cult to stop if he is standing over you. In addition a standing opponent is in excellent position to break your guard open and begin passing. Since he is standing the basic submission holds from the guard, triangles, arm bars, and "kimura," are more difficult to apply. Sweeps are thus a very good option. How you choose to sweep a standing opponent depends upon the way in which he stands up. Here we look at a highly effective sweep that is used on an opponent who stands with his legs close together. This is very common. There are thus *many* easy opportunities for the sweep demonstrated below.

1

Royler, locked in Renzo's closed guard, begins to stand.

2

Successfully getting to his feet, Royler is now in good position to begin passing Renzo's guard, or to punch down at Renzo. However, as he stands, Royler makes the mistake of placing his feet slightly too close together, giving Renzo the chance to apply a sweep. Renzo grips Royler's sleeves by the cuffs to gain good control of Royler's arms. If Royler were not wearing a gi, Renzo would grip the wrists.

3

Noticing the error, *Renzo opens his guard by uncrossing his feet, drops his legs quickly to Royler's knees, and quickly recrosses his feet.* This locks his legs around Royler's knees, effectively trapping Royler's legs. The idea is to use your legs like a noose around your opponents knees, tying his legs together in a trap.

(!) Here you can see clearly the sleeve grip that Renzo is employing. Note how Renzo's legs bind around Royler's knees. This brings Royler's knees together, destroying his base and making him very unstable.

 From the other side you can see the fashion in which Renzo's legs trap Royler's legs. The key is to wrap them around the knees, not above or below the knees. Then tightly cross your feet to pin your opponent's legs together.

4

Utilizing the fact that Royler cannot effectively balance himself, Renzo uses both his arms and legs to draw Royler forward over his head.

5

Royler is cleanly thrown over Renzo's head.

6

Renzo is sure to immediately follow Royler over so that he comes up on top of his opponent.

7

The completed move: Renzo is mounted on Royler. From here he is in complete control, ready to begin striking or applying submission holds.

Front lapel stranglehold

Any time your opponent is wearing a jacket, you may use the collar to apply a number of very effective strangleholds. These can be used to force your opponent to submit. Should he refuse to submit he will be rendered unconscious. While training with strangleholds you must be sure to release your training partner IMMEDIATELY when he signals submission tapping. In effect the collar of a jacket is like a noose around the neck. This is especially true of the gi or kimono that is worn in training. Due to the fact that they require very little strength to apply, these strangleholds can be used by a smaller man to easily defeat a larger, stronger man. Here we see a demonstration of one of the most simple, yet effective strangleholds

that utilizes the collar of the jacket. This particular move can be used very easily when you are mounted or have knee-on-stomach or your opponent is in your guard. Here we see an application from the mounted position. Always bear in mind that this front lapel stranglehold combines very well with arm bars. Develop the habit of attacking the neck with the front lapel stranglehold. In order to fend the strangulation attempt, your opponent must use his hands and arms to block your hands and arms. However, doing this will immediately expose him to an arm-bar threat. Combine these two attacks at every opportunity. This basic combination works at all belt levels and when done well is *extremely* difficult to defend against.

1

Renzo is mounted on Royler. He immediately reaches down and pulls open Royler's collar. If he is opening the left side of Royler's collar, he will use his left hand to pull the it open and vice versa. Renzo then reaches across with his other hand and grips with his fingers inside the collar he has just opened up. His thumb is outside the collar. The hand that reaches across is palm up to ceiling as it slides inside Royler's collar.

2

The key here is to *slide the first hand in as deeply as possible*. You want your knuckles to touch the floor if possible.

3

Once he has gotten his first hand in as deep as possible, Renzo immediately looks to work his second hand in to complete the stranglehold. Renzo uses his free hand to reach *over* the arm that is already in place. *This second hand is palm down.* The thumb goes inside the collar, the fingers outside. Note the asymmetry. The first hand goes across into the collar palm up, fingers inside the collar, thumb outside. The other hand goes to the opposite collar palm down, fingers outside, thumb inside.

ⓘ The hand position is made clear in this detail photograph. Note the depth of the first hand inside the collar. By going in deeply with the first hand the stranglehold is far easier.

4

Hands in place, Renzo strangles Royler

5

As he applies the stranglehold, Renzo is sure to lean forward and place his forehead on the floor. By leaning forward in this manner, it is far more difficult to defend the choke. Also, it makes for a wider base.

082 Arm bar from across-side position

Anytime you are lying across your opponent's side you are in a good position to dominate your opponent and attack. This can be done by striking (knees, head butts, and elbows are the best options if you wish to strike, since these allow you to maintain a tight pin on your opponent while you hit him).

Alternatively, you may advance to an even more dominant position (the mounted position, rear-mounted position, or knee-on-belly position) or go directly for a submission hold. It is this last option that we shall look at now.

1

Renzo is holding Royler down in a tight pin from across-side. Royler's far arm is extended out in a very vulnerable position. Sensing the opportunity for attack, Renzo opts to attempt a submission hold on the exposed arm. Wrapping the arm that is over Royler's head around Royler's extended arm, Renzo traps it between his head and shoulder.

2

In order to tighten his entrapment of the extended arm, Renzo brings his hand right up into the armpit of Royler's trapped arm and squeezes it between his shoulder and head.

3

Renzo places his free hand on the floor next to Royler's near hip.

4

Walking around Royler's head will allow Renzo to attack the exposed arm. Since Renzo has placed his free hand on the floor next to Royler's hip, Royler cannot follow him. At this point, Renzo's forearm is tight under the trapped arm at the armpit. Renzo is driving, head down, toward Royler's legs as he turns around Royler's head. This puts a lot of pressure on the opponent, making it difficult to merely breath and almost impossible to extract his endangered arm.

5

Coming all the way around Royler's head to the other side of Royler's body, Renzo places his leg over Royler's head while maintaining the pressure on Royler's arm.

6

To enter into the arm bar, Renzo places the foot of his other leg tight to Royler's back so that he goes into a low squatting position.

Here is the same position seen from the other side. You can see how Renzo is maintaining his entrapment of Royler's arm. Here Renzo is using his free arm to hold Royler's upper body to help hold his low squat position and to slow his fall when he sits back into the arm bar.

In this close-up you can see the details of the low squat position that is the prelude to the arm bar. Note how Renzo's head is down to help balance and keep pressure on Royler. Here Renzo is using his free hand as a support by placing it on the floor. The hand of the arm holding Royler's arm grips his own collar to complete the entrapment.

7

Renzo falls back into a classic arm-bar submission hold. Note how he keeps his knees tight together, making for a very tight lock that is very difficult to escape from. To break his opponent's arm, Renzo straightens the arm and raises his hips. As in any arm bar from this position, Renzo is sure to point the thumb of the trapped arm up to the ceiling.

The arm bar viewed from the opposite side.

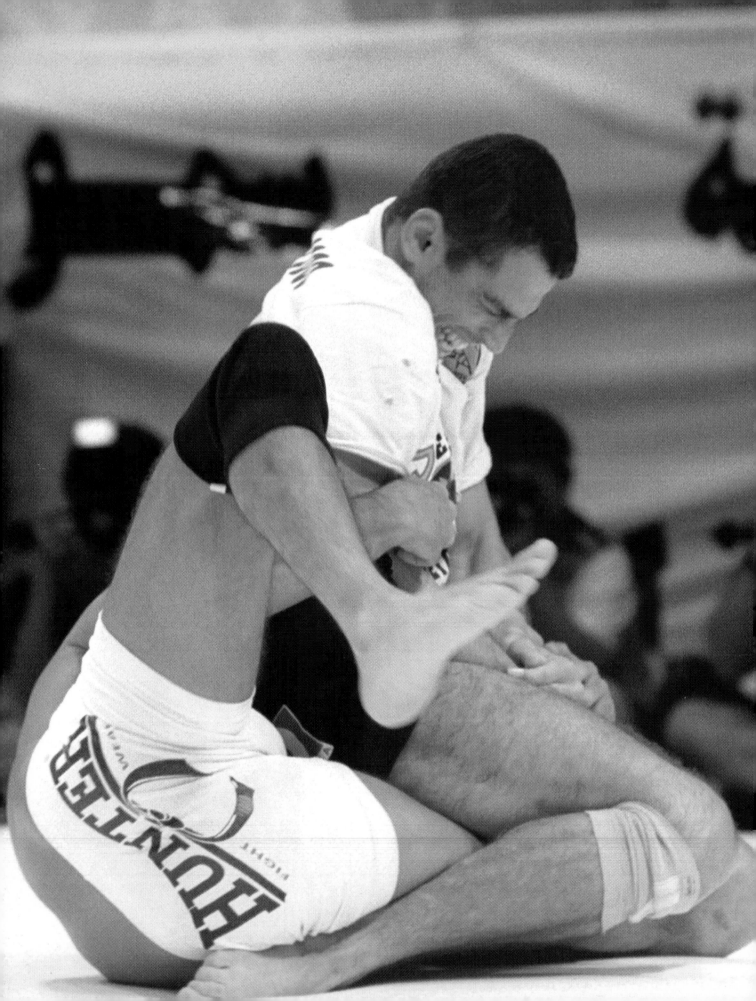

Brown Belt

083 Escape from the common standing headlock

One of the most natural and common attacks in a real fight is the headlock. It is worthwhile investigating the reasons for this, for it furnishes some interesting lessons on fighting. Anytime you control the movements of a person's head, you control the movements of their entire body. This is due to human physiology. The skull is, of course, connected to the spine. Where the head moves, the rest of the body, joined to the head through the spinal column, must follow. When you place someone in a tight headlock you can exert a good deal of control over them, bending them over, throwing them down, moving them at will. Since they are bent over and controlled, it is difficult for them to fight back effectively. The common headlock is uncomfortable and intimidating, especially when used by a very strong opponent. It is simple to attain and hold, even for an inexperienced fighter. In addition, it allows you to strike with the other hand while your opponent, bent over and controlled, cannot effectively punch back. For these reasons, it is very commonly used in real fights. Experienced fighters, however, do not typically employ the common headlock. If they choose to secure the head they do so in more technically sound fashion. The reason for this is that the common headlock is relatively simple to defend against *if you know the means of escape*. Since most people do *not* know the means of escape, it often proves effective in street altercations. A seasoned grappler, however, has little difficulty escaping even a very tight headlock and then securing an advantageous position behind his opponent. Here we look at an effective means of dealing with an opponent who employs the common headlock in a standing position and who is looking to punch you with his free hand.

1

Royler grabs Renzo around the head in the way commonly used to secure a headlock by street brawlers. With his free hand, Royler looks to land some blows. His hope is to use his control of Renzo's head to control Renzo's movements and prevent him from striking back.

2

The first concern is to stop the punches. Renzo quickly reaches with the arm that is closest to his opponent, behind his opponent's back and around the punching arm at the bicep. With his other arm Renzo reaches across in front of Royler and grabs the punching arm at the forearm.

3

Having taken away the immediate threat of punches to the face, Renzo begins his escape. Using the hand of the arm that was reaching across in front of Royler, Renzo grabs the wrist of the arm encircling his neck. Renzo pushes his hips forward and looks up to the ceiling. This motion prevents Royler from bending him over and controlling him. At the same time, Renzo pulls Royler's wrist away from Royler.

Here you can see the grip that Renzo employs upon Royler's wrist. Note that he grips without using the thumb and that he is pulling Royler's wrist toward his own shoulder.

4

At this point the headlock is broken since Royler no longer has any effective control over Renzo's head. Renzo ducks backward under Royler's arm, still controlling it at the wrist. The great weakness of the common headlock is that anytime it fails, your opponent can immediately get behind you to a position of advantage. This is precisely what Renzo has in mind.

5

Renzo completes his duck-under movement while still controlling Royler's wrist.

6

Now Renzo emerges directly behind Royler with his head free. Using his grip on Royler's wrist, Renzo pushes Royler's arm up Royler's back in a painful and immobilizing shoulder lock, forcing Royler up on his toes. It is easy now for Renzo to walk his opponent around at will.

The lock is a variation of the "kimura" lock seen elsewhere in this book. In this application it is secured with one hand while behind the opponent. To apply the lock, simply push your opponent's wrist up toward the back of his neck.

084 Escape from the standing headlock

Several times we have stressed the theme that escapes from the common headlock must be practiced regularly. This is true even though experienced grapplers do not typically use the common headlock, preferring instead to employ more sophisticated and technically sound methods of trapping the head. The fact remains that most street brawlers are not expert grapplers but rather are more instinctive in the way they fight. Grabbing the head as a way of dominating and controlling an opponent is one such instinctive move. It is so common that you must practice defending against it, even though your grappling training partners, who know better than to employ a common headlock, do not often use it. In this case we look at a scenario where your opponent not only grips you in a common headlock, but also succeeds in bending you over and controlling you. This can be a dangerous situation, as he can throw you over his hip or strike you with his free hand.

1

Renzo throws his arm around Royler's neck and enters into a common standing headlock.

2

Locking his arms together around Royler's head, Renzo completes the headlock by bending Royler forward, exerting considerable control over him.

3

Royler reacts quickly to the threat. He places his arm that is closest to Renzo around Renzo's back. He reaches across in front of Renzo with his other arm and places his hand on Renzo's far leg at the knee.

4

Using the leg on the same side as the hand that has been placed on Renzo's knee, Royler steps between Renzo's legs.

5

It is a simple matter now for Royler to sit down and pull with the arm that is around Renzo's back. As Royler pulls with his arm he turns his body in the same direction.

6

There is nowhere for Renzo to go but down.

7

Continuing his turning motion, Royler quickly comes up on top of Renzo, who is still maintaining his headlock. Royler is sure to keep his hips low and arms based out wide so that Renzo cannot roll him over again and take top position. Royler then steps his leg over Renzo's waist to take a mounted position.

8

To release the headlock, Royler places his forearm across Renzo's neck/jaw. His other hand grips the wrist of the arm on Renzo's neck.

9

Pushing down with both hands and straightening his back, Royler escapes the headlock, leaving him mounted on his opponent in great attacking position.

085 **Escape from being pushed up against a wall**

Perhaps the most overlooked element of self-defense training is the role played by the *environment in which you fight*. Most self-defense training is conducted in a training hall with lots of room, soft floors with good traction, lots of space, and good lighting. Real fights, however, occur in all kinds of places, on slippery, beer-covered dance floors, cramped corridors, hard concrete, uneven, broken ground, and so on. One of the most common environmental factors to play a role in real fights is a wall. Often an attacker will pin you against a wall and use it to immobilize and dominate you in the same way you can be pinned and immobilized on the ground. By pushing you against a wall or fence your attacker restricts your shoulder and hip movements, greatly reducing your punching power. It is easy for him to take you down since the wall prevents you from sprawling your hips back. You must know how to deal with this problem. Here we see one effective solution.

1

Royler uses both hands to shove Renzo against the wall.

2

Wasting no time, Renzo grips Royler under both arms at the elbows.

3

Stepping one of his feet closer to and outside Royler's lead foot, Renzo creates the feeling of leaning back away from Royler. Renzo is using the wall to support himself. What Renzo has in mind is to circle his way out, rather than use brute strength to push back at Royler.

4

By stepping out wide to the outside with his lead foot and pushing Royler to the side, Renzo takes himself out of the line of Royler's pushing force and easily escapes the wall pin.

5

Now Renzo is free from the wall and able to move at will. He takes advantage of this to fire a knee into Royler's stomach.

Moving from the north-south position to your opponent's back

086

We have been stressing the theme of positional advance throughout this book. This is the idea, so central to Brazilian jiu-jitsu, that as you grapple with your opponent you must constantly try to improve your position. These positional advances allow you to better control your opponent and place enough pressure on him to open up many opportunities for submission holds. Here we show another instance of this strategy in action. The north-south position is itself an excellent,

dominating position from where you can control and submit your opponent, but an even better position is the rear-mounted position, where you are securely locked behind your opponent's back. From here you can strike with impunity. Your opponent cannot effectively bite or gouge you. Most importantly, you can attack his neck with chokes with little fear of retaliation.

1

Renzo is holding Royler in a tight north-south pin. At this point Renzo has the option of attacking with submission holds from his current position or of seeking a better position. Due to the fact that Royler is defending himself well (he is not exposing his arms and neck at all), Renzo opts to improve position.

2

Sliding both his arms under the point of Royler's elbows, Renzo grips both of Royler's lapels.

3

Renzo pulls Royler's lapels under Royler's upper arms, down to the armpits. Royler's gi jacket is now totally open. This gives Renzo two very strong handles with which to hold and control Royler's upper body. It is as though he has a rope under Royler's arms.

You can see here how Renzo grips the gi. By opening the collar and pulling the lapels under Royler's arms to the armpits it is as though there is a rope that runs from under one armpit, up over the back of Royler's neck, and then down under the other armpit. If you were to grip the ends of such a rope, it would give you great control over your opponent's upper body.

4

In one quick motion, Renzo pops up to his feet.

5

Utilizing his grip on the gi, Renzo pulls Royler's upper body straight up. This does not require great strength since only the upper body is being lifted here. The grip on the gi is very dominating. It opens Royler's arms out wide putting him in a defensively weak position. You can clearly see how Royler's gi is being used like a rope to pull him up.

6

Having gotten Royler into this vulnerable position, it is a simple matter now for Renzo to step his foot inside Royler's hip. This foot will function as a hook, enabling Renzo to lock himself securely to Royler's back.

7

Having gotten one foot inside Royler's hip, Renzo falls back and to the same side as the foot he has placed in as a hook. His grip on Royler's gi ensures that Royler follows him as he falls.

8

To fully stabilize his position, Renzo places his other foot over Royler's hip as a second hook. Now his position is very secure. He can attack Royler with chokes, strangles, arm locks, and strikes with near impunity. Royler can do little but desperately defend.

087 North-south position into toehold

Anytime you are trying to pin your opponent, he will be attempting to escape. Many of the best escapes from pins involve bringing up your knees as a barrier between you and your opponent. Often there is a brief moment where your opponent's foot is exposed to a very quick submission hold called the toehold. Here we see one such example as your opponent attempts to escape from a north-south pin.

1

Royler is holding Renzo in a tight north-south pin.

2

Knowing that he is in a highly disadvantageous position, Renzo immediately tries to escape. One of the best forms of escape from this position begins by pushing with both hands into your opponent's hips in order to create space.

3

Utilizing the space that he has created, Renzo draws his knees up between Royler and himself. His intention is to spin under Royler and recover good position by putting him back in guard.

4

Ordinarily this is an excellent means of escaping the north-south position. However, as Renzo brings his knees up, Royler seizes the opportunity to attack. He selects one foot and immediately puts his hands in position to go right into a toehold.

5

To apply the toehold, Royler uses one hand to grab Renzo's foot at the smallest toe. His other hand circles around Renzo's ankle and grips the wrist of the hand that has gripped Renzo's foot. To apply the lock, Royler pushes Renzo's foot down toward Renzo's buttocks while at the same time, turning Renzo's heel up toward the ceiling. This puts a lot of torque on Renzo's ankle, threatening dislocation and forcing a quick submission.

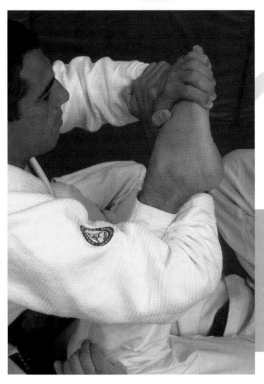

Here you can see clearly the grip used in a standard toehold. The hand on your opponent's foot should grip at the smallest toe for greatest leverage. Note that you do not employ your thumbs when gripping with either hand. When attacking with the standard toehold, if you are attacking his *right* foot, then you grip his toes with your *left* hand and encircle his ankle and grip your own wrist with your *right hand*. Vice versa if you are attacking his left foot.

088 Ankle lock attack from the open guard

A very common perception among grapplers is that one of the best ways to counter the guard position is to attack your opponent's legs with ankle and knee locks. There is very little discussion of the use of ankle and knee locks by the person *using* the guard position. In fact, when your opponent stands in your guard it is often easier to attack his legs than to attack his arms and neck, since the legs are much closer. Here we see one such leg attack option while using the open guard.

1

Renzo is standing in Royler's open guard. Due to the fact that Renzo's posture is upright there is little chance of a successful attack on his arms and neck. The legs are an easier target.

Here we see the same position from the other side. Note Royler's initial position. One foot is on Renzo's lead hip, the other on Renzo's rear leg at the knee.

2

Royler initiates the attack by passing his leg under Renzo's forward leg. The foot of Royler's other leg is placed on the inner thigh of Renzo's rear leg, just above the knee.

3

An initial problem is Renzo's hands on Royler's knees. This enables Renzo to exert control over Royler's legs. Royler accordingly pulls Renzo's lead hand off his knee to make the move easier.

From this angle you can see clearly the action of passing the leg under the opponent's lead leg as a prelude to the attack.

4

Passing his leg under and completely around Renzo's lead leg, Royler places his foot on Renzo's lead hip.

From the opposite angle you can see how Royler has wrapped his leg around Renzo's lead leg, trapping it very effectively. Note how Royler's foot on the lead hip is turned out to prevent any counters on Renzo's part.

5

Now Royler pushes on the knee/inner thigh of Renzo's rear leg, twisting Renzo down to the mat.

In this close-up you can see clearly the pushing action on Renzo's rear knee. This opens Renzo's thigh outward and puts him down.

6

The push on the knee takes Renzo right down to the mat. Renzo's lead leg is still trapped by Royler's leg position.

7

Retaining his foot position, one foot on Renzo's lead hip, the other on Renzo's rear knee, Royler wraps his arm around the ankle of Renzo's trapped leg and then grips the wrist of his other arm. The palm of his other arm is placed upon the shin of Renzo's trapped leg. This grip is very strong. It is the same grip as that used in other demonstrations of ankle locks in this book.

8

To finish the lock, Royler simply arches back, putting tremendous pressure on Renzo's trapped ankle.

089 Knee bar from across-side position

Any time you are on top of your opponent and lying across his side there are many opportunities to attack with submission holds. In general, Brazilian jiu-jitsu favors upper-body submission attacks from this position. This is because there is little danger of losing your good position should an upper-body submission hold fail. If you attempt a stranglehold, neck crank, or arm lock and it fails, it is easy to retain your dominant position. When you attempt a leg lock, however, there is some danger insofar as you may end up in a bad position should the attack fail. Nonetheless, it may be well worthwhile

to attempt a leg lock from across-side under certain circumstances. If your opponent is very good at defending his neck and arms and consequently you do not believe that you can successfully apply a stranglehold, arm lock, or get mounted, you might want to try attacking his legs, since these are often poorly defended. Another good time to try leg attacks from across-side is when your opponent is on the verge of escaping your pin. Since you are about to lose position anyway, there is nothing to lose in attempting a quick leg lock. Here we see an application of the knee-bar leg lock from across-side.

1

Renzo is lying across Royler's side in a tight, controlling pin.

2

Royler's defense is very tight. He is not exposing his arms or neck at all. In addition, he has drawn up his leg in a way that makes it difficult for Renzo to move into the mounted position. Against such a tight defense, Renzo begins to look for alternative targets.

3

Seizing the near leg of his opponent at the bend of the knee, Renzo pops up by standing on the foot of the leg closest to Royler's hips. He is sure to place his foot close to Royler's hips and buttocks.

4

Now Renzo quickly slides the knee of his other leg over Royler's stomach, deep between Royler's legs. He uses his free arm for balance by posting out on the floor.

(!) In this close-up you can see clearly the leg position that Renzo has entered into. Note how tightly he hugs Royler's trapped leg. Renzo pinches his knees together tightly to lock Royler's leg securely in place.

5

Having trapped Royler's near leg between his two legs, Renzo falls back and to his side. Note how the arm that Renzo is using to hold Royler's leg has slid up to Royler's ankle. This makes for a smoother transition into the leg lock. Renzo is sure to pinch his knees together at this point to prevent escape. To finish the hold, Renzo places the foot that was on the floor next to Royler's buttocks on the inner thigh of Royler's far leg. This prevents Royler from escaping the lock. Pinching his knees together, Renzo straightens the trapped leg and pushes his hips forward, hyperextending the knee joint. This causes great pain and injury. Be sure to give your training partner time to signal his submission.

Kimono neck crank submission from across-side position

090

There are a vast number of potential submission holds you can use on an opponent. Each has its own character. Some are difficult to set up, some are easy to escape from. Some require you to take the initiative and force the hold. Others arise when your opponent moves in a certain way – creating the opportunity for you. The move we look at now falls into the last category. Your opponent gives you the opportunity to enter into a submission hold by giving you an opening through some ill-advised movement. In a sense, your opponent is responsible for his own demise. You simply had the knowledge to capitalize on his mistake. This kind of *reactive strategy* (re-active in the sense that you react to your opponent's mistakes) is important in Brazilian jiu-jitsu. A great many opportunities for victory arise out of your opponent's mistakes. You must be ready to capitalize on his errors as soon as they occur. Of course there are many other ways to enter into submission holds that do not make you wait for your opponent to make an error. More often than not you can force the pace and drive your opponent into a submission hold. This kind of *proactive strategy* (proactive in the sense that you take the initiative and make the opponent react to *your* moves) is well represented in other parts of the book.

1

Renzo is holding a tight across-side position on Royler. Royler is in good defensive position.

2

As is so often the case, the bottom man looks up, taking his head off the floor. Many grapplers do this to look for openings to escape from, others do it in reaction to the pressure exerted by the top man, some do it as a prelude to their escape. For whatever reason, Royler has brought his head up off the floor, giving Renzo the opportunity to attack. Wasting no time, Renzo immediately circles his arm around Royler's neck. This would be impossible if Royler had kept his head down. Since his opponent has given him an opportunity, Renzo takes it.

3

Putting his arm all the way around Royler's neck, Renzo grabs the collar of his own kimono or gi.

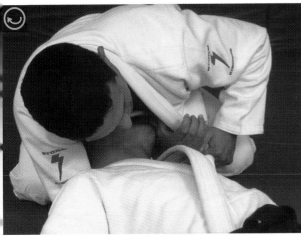

(!) In this detail photograph you can see the grip that Renzo employs. Opening the collar with his free hand, Renzo comes all the way around Royler's neck and grips his own collar as high as possible. His thumb goes inside the collar, his fingers outside.

4

Having gotten his grip, Renzo re-establishes his base.

5

The final preparation is to take the other arm and underhook your opponent's far arm.

6

Renzo now spreads his legs wide apart for base and cranks Royler's head upward with the arm around Royler's head and neck. This puts great pressure on the neck, forcing a quick submission. To maximize the pressure ensure that you keep your opponent flat on his back as you crank his neck and that you turn your hips toward your opponent's head as you crank him.

A stranglehold from the knee-on-stomach position

The knee-on-stomach position is one of the very best attacking positions in Brazilian jiu-jitsu. You can use it to put a lot of pressure upon your opponent, forcing him into costly errors. Here we see a stranglehold applied from this great position.

1

Royler is holding Renzo in a classic knee-on-stomach position. Note that Royler uses the hand of the arm closest to Renzo's head to grip inside Renzo's collar, thumb inside, fingers outside.

2

Without moving the hand already gripping Renzo's collar, Royler slides his other hand palm up into Renzo's far collar. His fingers go inside, his thumb outside the collar.

3

Royler secures his grip. Note that Royler's hands are almost touching behind Renzo's neck.

Here you can see clearly the grip being used for this stranglehold. The palm of the first hand (the one that was initially on the collar) behind Renzo's collar is down, the second hand is palm up. The fingers of the first hand are outside the collar, thumb inside. The fingers of the second hand are inside the collar, thumb outside.

4

As soon as Royler has secured his grip, he spins around Renzo's head into a north-south position, maintaining his grip as he goes. A key point here is that you must try to keep your arms relatively straight as you spin around your opponent and strangle him. Bending the arms weakens the strangle.

5

Here you can see the finishing position. Royler places his head down on Renzo's stomach and strangles Renzo. This is a VERY tight stranglehold.

Pressing arm lock from across-side

We have looked at several ways to lock the arm at the elbow joint. Another possible way to do so involves straightening your opponent's arm, immobilizing his wrist, and then pressing down on his elbow with both hands. This hyperextends the elbow and if your opponent does not quickly submit, can cause serious injury to the elbow. Once understood, this lock can be performed easily and from many positions. Here we look at it being used while across your opponent's side.

1

Royler has trapped Renzo in an across-side pin. Renzo's far arm is in a vulnerable position over Royler's shoulder.

2

Sensing the opportunity to go straight into a submission hold, Royler begins to pull up on Renzo's far arm. In order to make this movement easy, Royler rests his weight on his free hand.

3

To enter into the move, Royler slides his knee on to Renzo's stomach while still pulling up on Renzo's exposed arm.

4

Having gotten his knee on to Renzo's stomach, Royler straightens and pulls Renzo's trapped arm straight. The wrist of the trapped arm is wedged tightly between the side of Royler's neck and shoulder. You can make this trap even stronger by trying to touch your ear to your shoulder on the same side as the trapped arm. Royler slides his forearm up to Renzo's elbow, trapping the arm in place.

5

Renzo's arm is now very effectively trapped. Royler places both his hands on Renzo's elbow and presses inward, against the elbow joint. Since the arm is already straightened, this places great pressure on the elbow, which simply was not designed to bend any farther in that direction.

 Here you can see in detail the workings of this submission hold. Both hands are placed (one over the other) on the elbow of the trapped arm. They press against the back of the elbow. As the arm is already straight this takes the elbow farther than it can go. The result is a quick submission—or injury. Note how Royler presses his neck and shoulder together around Renzo's trapped wrist, making it very tough for Renzo to twist his way out of the lock.

Turning shoulder lock from across-side position

Many of the submission holds from across-side position that we have seen so far depend upon your opponent leaving his arm in an exposed, vulnerable position. Here we see an attack on an opponent who is keeping his arm in tight to his body, leaving little to attack.

1

Renzo is holding Royler down in a tight pin from across-side. Royler has his arms in a good defensive position. His far arm is not drifting out over Renzo's shoulders (where they would be easy to attack with moves shown elsewhere in this book). Rather it is drawn in and kept under Renzo's chin. To attack the far arm, Renzo grasps it at the crook of the elbow with the hand of his arm closest to Royler's head. Note that Renzo grips Royler's arm in such a way that Royler's hand is on his bicep.

2

To enter into the submission hold, Renzo steps the foot of the leg closest to Royler's head over Royler's face and places it on the floor next to Royler's far ear.

3

Now Renzo straightens up and places his other hand on top of the first hand so that they are both on Royler's elbow.

4

Renzo now turns his body toward Royler's legs. To keep the lock tight, Renzo keeps his elbows pressed tightly against his own ribs. Royler's trapped arm is bent and being turned outward. This places great pressure on the shoulder joint.

Here you can see the lock in detail. The key is to keep your opponent's arm bent and to pin his elbow tight to your stomach. Your own elbows should be tight to your ribs. The hand of your opponent's trapped arm should be on your bicep as shown. Turn your upper body toward your opponent's legs to apply the lock.

Getting to your opponent's back from the guard position

094

We have been constantly stressing the theme of improving your position as you grapple with your opponent. One of the easiest and most effective switches in position is that of going from the guard position to your opponent's back. While the guard is a good position from which to fight, it is not nearly so good as being behind your opponent. Attacks from behind your opponent are much easier since you are very close to his neck and arms. Moreover, it is far more difficult for him to defend your attacks from behind than when you are directly in front of him. In addition he cannot strike you nearly as effectively when you are behind him as when you are in front of him. Often you will come across an opponent who has excellent balance. This makes sweeping him over very difficult. In a case like this it makes good sense to get to his back as an alternative to sweeping. *The only thing preventing you from getting to your opponent's back when he is in your guard is his arms. If you can get around either one of his arms you can get to his back.* The key is to clear one of his arms to the side by dragging or pushing it across his chest. This will allow you to climb up around his back and get a very dominant position. Here we see one such example of this strategy.

1

Royler has Renzo locked in his closed guard. Renzo is using a technique very often used by inexperienced ground fighters. He is driving his forearm into Royler's throat. While this might seem an effective tactic to the beginner, it actually sets you up for several easy counters if your opponent is a skilled grappler. It is worth studying here simply because it is so common in real fights.

2

Renzo continues to drive forward with all his weight, trying to crush Royler's throat. Unperturbed by this rather ineffective form of attack, Royler places his hand on the elbow of the forearm on his throat. His other hand goes on the wrist of the same arm, gripping the gi at the cuff. If Renzo were not wearing a gi, Royler would simply grip the wrist.

Here you can see the grip that Royler is using on Renzo's forearm. The hand on the elbow will push Renzo's arm across, the other hand gripping the sleeve cuff will assist by pulling the arm across.

3

Royler pushes Renzo back with his hips. This is crucial. Doing so takes the weight off the choking forearm in your throat and *makes it easy to then push the choking arm across your upper chest.* Royler takes Renzo's arm across his upper body to one side.

4

Having cleared the choking arm out of the way, *there is nothing to prevent Royler from climbing around to Renzo's back.* This is exactly what Royler has in mind. Wasting no time, Royler throws the arm that had previously pushed on Renzo's elbow over Renzo's back and grips the far side of Renzo's back. You will find that the back muscles provide an excellent "handle" to hold on to. Using his grip on Renzo's back for support, Royler works his way out from underneath Renzo, out to the side. Since Royler is hugging Renzo very tightly, Renzo cannot get his arm back in position to prevent Royler getting to his back.

5

Royler has the choice now of climbing up to Renzo's back (if Renzo stays on his knees) or using the arm around Renzo's back to pull Renzo over to his back. Royler takes the latter option. Renzo is easily rolled to his back since he cannot support himself on his trapped arm.

6

Royler locks both his feet on Renzo's hips as hooks. These hooks will keep him securely locked to Renzo's back no matter what direction Renzo moves. From this great offensive position Royler can easily attack with strangleholds and arm bars. There is nothing that Renzo can do but desperately defend.

Foot lock counter to the rear-mounted position

The rear-mounted position is a great place to be in both a real fight and a grappling match. This is because there is very little your opponent can attack you with once you get behind him and place your feet in his hips. Your feet function as hooks, keeping you glued to him no matter how hard he thrashes about to escape. The whole time you can attack his neck and arms with submission holds while he can do little in return. In a real fight your opponent cannot strike you effectively while you can hit him very hard. Nor can he effectively engage in the most common street reactions to grappling holds, eye gouges, biting, and groin grabbing. There is no doubt that the rear-mounted position is one of the very best, if not *the* best place to be in both a real fight and in grappling matches. There is, however, one very important detail that you must be aware of as you utilize this devastating position: *You must never cross your feet while holding the rear mount.* For the beginner it is often tempting to cross your feet just as you do when you use the closed guard—it feels very secure and strong. However, it sets you up for a very simple but painful foot lock that your desperate opponent can easily apply. It is annoying to get all the way to the rear-mounted position and near-certain victory, only to be beaten by a simple foot lock. You can avoid this problem by making sure you do not cross your feet when you get the rear mount. Here we see a demonstration of the foot lock counter to the rear-mounted position.

1

Royler has attained a very dominant position behind Renzo. He looks to secure his position by locking his feet over Renzo's hips as hooks. These hooks will keep him securely locked to Renzo. Here Royler has one hook in place and is looking to secure the other. In addition, Royler is attempting to attack Renzo's neck with chokes.

2

In his haste to secure position, Royler makes a common and potentially disastrous mistake. Rather than simply placing his feet on Renzo's hips, he crosses them. This might feel very secure and strong, but it makes you very vulnerable to a foot lock.

3

Seeing the error, Renzo immediately attacks. He brings the outer shin of one of his legs over both of Royler's crossed feet.

4

He then places the foot of the leg that he brought over Royler's crossed feet under the back of the knee of his other leg. Now Royler's crossed feet are trapped in place. Royler could not uncross them even if he tried to. At this point Renzo pushes down to the floor with both legs. This puts a VERY painful lock on Royler's ankles and feet. Even if Royler is strangling Renzo, he will have to submit before the stranglehold takes effect. The moral is simple: *never cross your feet when holding the rear-mounted position with hooks in!*

Helicopter arm bar

The helicopter arm bar is a spectacular yet surprisingly easy and practical move that combines two moves seen elsewhere in this book, namely, the overhead sweep and the arm bar. While the move may look complex and difficult, it is really quite simple to perform and can be done far more often than most people realize. Anytime your opponent is standing in your guard and is bending forward (either due to his own bad posture, his desire to lean forward and strike you, or because you pulled him down to a bent position) you can attempt a helicopter arm bar.

1

Renzo has Royler locked in his closed guard.

2

As Royler stands, Renzo controls Royler's arms by gripping them at the elbows. This is important. Failure to pull the opponent forward and bend him over makes it easy for him to stand with upright posture, making the move more difficult to perform.

3

As soon as Royler comes up to both feet, Renzo uncrosses his feet and opens his guard.

4

Still pulling on Royler's arms, Renzo places both feet on Royler's hips.

5

Renzo pulls Royler forward until Royler's head is directly over his own. He then pushes with both feet directly up toward the ceiling. This takes Royler up off the floor very easily. Up to this point the move is exactly the same as the overhead sweep described elsewhere in this book. Just as with the overhead sweep, do not make the mistake of pushing away with the feet until you have first brought your opponent forward with his head directly over yours, otherwise you will merely push him away from you.

6

It is at this point that the move deviates from the overhead sweep into the helicopter arm bar. Instead of sweeping your opponent over your head, simply remove one of your feet from your opponent's hips as you are holding him aloft above you. Swing that same leg out wide as though you were going to place it over your opponent's face (which is exactly what you will be doing later). *This will have the immediate effect of making him fall off to the side from which you have removed your foot.* There is nothing difficult about this. Just take your foot (either one) off his hip and open it out to the side so that your opponent falls between your legs.

Here you can see the fall into the arm bar. As soon as Renzo removes his supporting foot from Royler's hip and opens his legs, gravity takes over and Royler falls. Renzo is sure to swing his leg (the same one he has just taken from Royler's hip) over Royler's face as shown.

7

As your opponent falls, swing the leg that you just removed from your opponent's hip over his face. You will find that this places you in a perfect arm-bar position. You have thus switched from an overhead sweep into an arm bar in a fraction of a second merely by taking a foot off your opponent's hips and opening your legs. *Your opponent will spin and fall right into your arm bar!* You must be sure to retain good control of your opponent's arms, especially the one you intend to lock, by pulling on the arms. If you want to assist the turning motion that makes your opponent spin into the arm bar, you can pull on the arm you intend to arm bar and push him with your other arm. You can also give a sharp push with the foot that remains on your opponent's hip to further off-balance and spin him around.

8

Royler falls to the floor on his back in a perfect arm bar. Like any other arm bar, Renzo is sure to squeeze his knees together and straighten Royler's arm. To apply breaking pressure to the elbow he raises his hips off the floor, forcing a quick submission. It all looks rather spectacular. Your opponent is picked up in the air, spun about like a helicopter, and dropped unceremoniously into a perfect arm bar! Underneath the glamour this move is really based on very simple and sound mechanics. You can perfect it in a short time.

The sickle sweep

Once your opponent stands in your open guard it can be very difficult to retain effective control over him. He is in an excellent passing position and can easily attempt various locks on your legs. There is, however, an extremely effective and simple means of sweeping your opponent down to the ground when he stands in your open guard that allows you to take a dominant position and continue the fight on much better terms.

1

Royler holds Renzo in his closed guard.

2

Renzo, going on the offensive, begins to stand.

3

As he comes up on both feet, Renzo breaks Royler's guard open. With his staggered (side-on) stance, Renzo is in good position to pass. Royler cannot reach Renzo's rear leg with his hand. As Renzo prepares to pass there is a danger that Royler will lose control of the situation.

4

Wasting no time, Royler places his foot on Renzo's rear hip while retaining good control of Renzo's arms by pulling at the sleeve cuffs. If Renzo were not wearing a gi, Royler would pull on the wrists.

5

Royler transfers his hand from Renzo's sleeve cuff to Renzo's forward ankle, attaining a good grip. At the same time Royler pushes his free leg under Renzo's forward leg and around toward the back of Renzo's rear leg close to the ankle.

Here is the same movement seen from the other side. Note how Royler grips Renzo's ankle without using his thumb for a more secure grip. His leg has gone under and between Renzo's legs to finish very close to the floor behind the ankle of Renzo's rear leg. Royler retains the sleeve-cuff grip with his other hand.

6

To perform the sweep, Royler pushes with his foot on Renzo's hip. At the same time he pulls with the hand on Renzo's ankle and sweeps with the leg behind Renzo's rear leg, cleanly clipping Renzo's leg out from under him. Think of your sweeping leg as a sickle that cleanly cuts out your opponent's supporting leg. Renzo has no choice but to fall backward.

7

As soon as Renzo begins to fall, Royler comes up and forward. He is sure to use his grip on Renzo's sleeve cuff to assist him up by pulling as he rises. Note how Royler retracts the sweeping leg back under his own buttocks to make the sitting action easier.

8

To ensure that Renzo does not get up Royler pulls strongly upward on the ankle, keeping Renzo flat on his back. It is thus a simple matter for Royler to push forward and finish in Renzo's half guard. This is quite a good position in itself. From here Royler can go on to pass Renzo's guard and take an even more dominant position.

The hook sweep

The problem of controlling an opponent who is standing in your open guard is a difficult one. One particularly effective means of coping with the problem is the hook sweep. It provides a simple and very effective means of sweeping your opponent down to the ground from where you can take a top position and gain control of the fight. *This sweep combines* extremely well with the sickle sweep outlined elsewhere in this book. In combination they provide a formidable means of attacking a standing opponent while you are on your back. If one of these techniques should fail on a skilled opponent a quick switch to the other will almost always bring him crashing to the floor.

1

Royler begins to stand in Renzo's closed guard.

2

As Royler comes up to both feet Renzo grips Royler's sleeve cuff to control his arms. If Royler were not wearing a gi, Renzo would grip the wrists.

3

Renzo switches to the open guard by uncrossing his feet and placing a foot on Royler's hips. Note how the foot on the hip is turned toes out.

4

The key to this move is to block both of your opponent's legs behind the ankles so that he can be tripped easily backward. This is done by grabbing his ankle with your hand on the same side that you have placed your foot on his hip. To block your opponent's other leg, simply push your other leg between your opponent's legs and drop your foot down behind his ankle. Be sure to use your foot like a hook by pulling your toes back toward yourself and pulling it against the back of his ankle.

(!) In this close-up you can see very clearly the fashion in which Renzo blocks both of Royler's legs at the ankles. Renzo's hand grips Royler's ankle on the same side that he has put his foot on Royler's hip. Note that Renzo does not use his thumb to grip the ankle. This makes for a better grip. Renzo has placed his other foot behind Royler's other ankle. You can see how Renzo has turned the foot out by opening his legs apart. *The knee of this blocking leg is outside the knee of the opponent's leg.* You will have to open your legs in order to do this move. Renzo pulls the toes back on the blocking foot so that it hooks into the back of Royler's ankle forming a very efficient blocking mechanism.

5

In one simultaneous motion, Renzo pulls with the hand on Royler's ankle and with the hooking foot he has placed behind Royler's other ankle, while at the same time pushing Royler back with the foot he has placed on Royler's hip. The effect is simple. Royler is pushed strongly backward while both of his ankles are pulled forward. The only possible result is that Royler falls backward to the floor.

6

Royler falls down to his buttocks. Often your opponent will try to immediately get back to his feet. Renzo maintains his grip on the ankle and Royler's sleeve to make this difficult.

7

Taking his foot from Royler's hip, Renzo places it on the floor outside Royler's hip and lets go of Royler's ankle. Renzo's concern now is to sit up and take top position.

8

Using the arm that had previously been used to grab Royler's ankle, Renzo reaches around the back of Royler's neck to help pull himself up.

9

To finish the move, Renzo pulls himself into a half-guard position (that is, a position where your opponent has his legs around only one of your legs instead of the normal two). This is a good position for Renzo. From here he can try to apply submission holds (for example, "kimura"), strike his opponent (head butts are particularly effective from this position), or go on to fully pass the guard and get to the across-side position or the mounted position. The process of passing the half guard is shown next.

Passing the half guard

Throughout this book there has been much discussion of the guard position. We have seen various methods of putting an opponent in your guard in order to escape from bad positions, how to finish an opponent in your guard, how to sweep an opponent who is in your guard, and how to pass around the legs of an opponent who has placed you in his guard. As you train with your partner you will find that very often you maneuver each other into a position where you are not fully locked in each other's guard. Rather, *you get into a position where you have your legs locked around only one of your opponent's legs instead of the normal two.* This position, commonly referred to as the half guard, since you are controlling only one of your opponent's legs, often occurs immediately after a takedown and also as you and your opponent attempt to pass and recover the guard position. In the course of the struggle to get around your opponent's legs it is almost inevitable that you will at some point end up in a half-guard position. *As you and your training partners get better at both passing and maintaining the guard, you will spend more and more time in this complex position.* It is no exaggeration to say that the half-guard game is so complex and involved that it is a game within a game.

When your opponent is holding you in his half guard you have three basic options. You can stay where you are and strike your opponent (head butts being one of the best means of striking from this position). This is only an option in a real fight; obviously you cannot do this in a grappling match or in training. Brazilian jiu-jitsu generally does not favor this option as you can strike your opponent much more efficiently and with much less chance of retaliation from other positions. A second option is to attempt a submission hold while still locked in the half guard. This can certainly be very effective. The "kimura" lock, the arm bar, the knee bar, strangleholds, and other submission holds can all be done successfully from the half guard. The problem is that your opponent can quite easily put you back in his full guard or even sweep you over as you attempt these moves. Moreover, he can attempt his own submission holds just as easily from his position. The third option is the safest. The idea is to pass your opponent's half guard and gain a better position from where you can strike and apply submission holds with little fear of danger from your opponent. From the half guard you can move into either the across-side position or go directly to the mounted position. Here we look at the former option.

1

Royler is trapped in Renzo's half guard. That is to say, Royler's rear leg is trapped by Renzo's legs, while his forward leg is free. The position Royler has is very similar to an across-side position, only his rear leg is trapped. This can create problems. A skilled opponent can use the trapped leg to recover the guard (usually via an elbow escape) or to sweep or even finish an opponent. If Royler could somehow extract his trapped leg he would get a truly dominant position from where he could control the fight. This is the problem that confronts Royler, *how can he extract his leg and get to the dominant across-side position?* Here we see one highly effective solution. Royler places his lead arm (the one closest to Renzo's head) over Renzo's head with the elbow on the floor next to Renzo's far ear. He uses that arm to hug Renzo tightly for control. Royler extends his free leg behind him and turns his hips to face Renzo's legs. This has the effect of lowering Royler's hips, making for a stable base. Now Royler shuffles the foot of his trapped leg as close as possible to Renzo's buttocks. This makes him more stable and greatly decreases the control that Renzo has over his trapped leg.

2

Now Royler places his hand on Renzo's far knee and pushes it away and down.

3

This makes it easy for him to bring the knee of his trapped leg up to Renzo's chest. Note that Royler has the option of transferring his lead arm to a grip *under* Renzo's head. This he has taken.

4

As soon as his foot is free, Royler throws his formerly trapped leg out behind him to an across-side position.

5

This enables Royler to transfer to a regular across-side position from where he can exert much greater control than previously. Having passed the half guard Royler is in position to either strike or submit his opponent with far greater likelihood of success than before, or to move on to yet more dominant positions such a knee-on-stomach, the mount, or rear-mounted position.

Renzo puts his opponent under severe pressure with a mounted guillotine choke during the Abu Dhabi World Submission Wrestli Championship. Note how Renzo crosses his feet while mounted make escape difficult for his opponent. By pushing his pelvis forw and arching his back, Renzo greatly adds to the pressure of the chokehold.

Black Belt

The triangle choke applied from underneath the north-south position

The north-south position is a very effective means of pinning your opponent that occurs often in the course of grappling training. To apply the pin you lie on top of your opponent (who is flat on his back) with your head near his hips, facing his legs. Your hips cover his head and your legs are apart for base. Since your two bodies face in opposite directions, this position is often referred to as the north-south position. By far the most common way in which this pin is attained is from the across-side position. By simply walking your legs around his head and stopping when your hips cover your opponent's head, you have entered into the north-south position. There are some definite advantages to switching to a north-south pin. It is very stable. If your opponent does not know how to escape, no amount of wild thrashing about will help him. There are many submission attacks you can employ from the top of the north-south position. From the bottom man's perspective the north-south position is a real threat. It requires a different escape strategy than the regular across-side position. Since your opponent's lower body and hips are over your head, far from your legs, it seems difficult to put him back in the guard position by the regular means. Here we look at an interesting strategy for the man on the bottom. The idea is to create space and attack from a defensive position with a submission hold – the triangle choke. This has a good deal of surprise value as your opponent is holding a superior position and is generally not expecting you to attack with a submission hold.

1

Renzo is holding Royler down in a tight north-south pin. Royler's first concern in this vulnerable position is to keep his arms in tight to his upper chest as there is considerable danger of arm lock and stranglehold attacks. He positions his hands near Renzo's waist/hips.

2

Pushing up on Renzo's hips, Royler creates just enough space to curl up in a tight ball and bring his knees tucked in under Renzo's arms. This is the key to escape. Royler's knees can create the space he needs to either escape or attempt a submission hold.

3

Royler seizes control of Renzo's arms by gripping the sleeve cuffs. If Renzo was not wearing a gi, he would grip the wrists. At this point the pin has been broken and Royler is beginning to go on the offense.

4

Still curled under Renzo, Royler places one foot under Renzo's armpit (if he uses the left foot it goes under Renzo's left armpit and vice versa).

5

Now Royler places his other foot under the other armpit.

Here you can see clearly the position that Royler has worked himself into. Both feet are locked under Renzo's armpits, right foot to right armpit, left foot to left armpit. Royler maintains his grip on the sleeve cuffs throughout. By placing his feet under the armpits in this fashion, Royler prevents Renzo from coming back down and re-establishing his pinning position.

6

To enter into the triangle choke, Royler *comes across with one foot to the opposite armpit*. So for example, Royler will put his left foot across into Renzo's right armpit and vice versa.

From another angle you can see how Royler has brought one foot over to the opposite armpit. It is this foot being brought over that will enable Royler to spin into the triangle choke.

Having brought the opposite foot over to the armpit, Royler can withdraw his other foot.

8

Continuing his spins until he is facing Renzo, Royler throws his free leg high over Renzo's shoulder. The other foot is still tucked under the armpit. Renzo cannot defend the entry into the triangle choke because Royler is still controlling his arms at the sleeves.

7

Pushing off the foot he has brought across under Renzo's armpit, Royler spins deftly underneath Renzo. If Royler brings the left foot across, he spins to his right and vice versa.

9

Royler begins to curl his legs around Renzo's neck in classic fashion for the triangle choke.

10

Trapping Renzo's head and arm between his legs, Royler sets the stranglehold in place. Note how Renzo's trapped arm is pulled across Royler's stomach for maximum strangling effect.

11

Royler pulls the foot of the strangling leg in toward himself, thus bringing the calf of the strangling leg across the back of Renzo's neck, making for a devastating stranglehold.

12

The stranglehold now locked fully in place, Royler squeezes his legs and uses both hands to pull down on Renzo's head. Royler has gone all the way from a vulnerable position to an escape and submission hold. While the move may appear complicated and involved, it is based upon sound mechanical principles and with a little training can be quickly brought into your arsenal of attacks.

101 Escape from the north-south position

We have seen that the north-south position, where your opponent is pinning you on your back with his hips over your head, presents unique problems for escape. Since your opponent is positioned over your head rather than out to your side (as he would be in a regular across-side pin), the means of escape are somewhat different than escaping the across-side position. The same general principle of creating space between you and your opponent so that you can initiate some form of escape still applies; however, the means by which you create that space are different. Here we study an escape that sweeps your opponent over and allows you not only to escape, but also to take a dominant position.

1

Royler is holding Renzo down in a tight north-south pin. Note how Renzo keeps his arms inside Royler's, tight to his chest to prevent Royler taking an easy arm lock or choke.

2

To escape, Renzo needs to create space between himself and Royler. The idea is initially to create space by bridging your hips off the floor and pushing into your opponent, then bringing your knees in to the space your have created and using the knees to push your opponent farther away. Note how Renzo curls his knees up to his chest, bringing them under Royler's chest to push him away.

3

Taking advantage of the space created by bringing his knees between himself and Royler, Renzo pushes a foot under Royler's armpit. The right foot goes to the right armpit and vice versa. As Renzo brings his foot into the armpit, he slides his hands down Royler's arms and grips the sleeve cuffs. If Royler were not wearing a gi, he would grip the wrists.

4

Having placed one foot under the armpit, Renzo pushes away to create space and allow easy entry for his second foot under the other armpit. Renzo straightens his legs, pushing Royler up straight. At this point Renzo has considerable control over Royler, in spite of being underneath him. Renzo has control over Royler's arms with the sleeve grip, preventing Royler from basing out with his hands. In addition he can use the strength of his legs to hoist Royler clear off the floor.

5

Using the strength of his legs, Renzo brings Royler's head over his hips and begins to catapult Royler over by pulling on his sleeves and pushing with his legs.

6

Royler flies! This is a *very* powerful sweep.

7

Maintaining his grip on the sleeves, Renzo lands Royler in front of him and throws both his legs over to one side of his opponent. This will allow Renzo to sit up into a perfect across-side position.

8

Renzo completes the move by coming up to an across-side pin, completely reversing his earlier position and putting himself in superb attacking position.

The kick-over sweep

For each sweeping technique there is a different "feel." While all good sweeps rely on efficient leverage and mechanics, some sweeps can be completed with power and exertion if the technique is not quite right. Some can be done regardless of the position and movement of your opponent. Others, however, rely on perfect timing and finesse. They require you to perform the move at just the right moment and are based upon reacting to your opponent's movement. When moves like this are done well, they are among the most beautiful and satisfying in Jiu-jitsu. There is an aura of complete effortlessness in their operation since they rely upon the opponent's movement and strength for their success. This is the nature of the kick-over sweep.

1

Royler is locked in Renzo's closed guard.

2

As Royler goes to stand up, Renzo gains control of Royler's arms by gripping both gi sleeves at the elbows. If your opponent is not wearing a gi, simply grip the elbows. As Royler puts one leg up to stand to his feet, Renzo waits for the perfect opportunity to perform the kick-over sweep.

3

As Royler makes the move to stand with the other leg, not before, not after, Renzo pulls strongly forward with both hands. *The key here is to pull your opponent's arms forward and out, thus opening his arms and destroying his forward base.* At the same time, uncross your feet and hug the sides of your opponent's stomach with your lower legs. As you pull your opponent forward with your arms, *kick your legs over your head to help bring him forward.* Timing is essential here. You want to perform the move as your opponent comes up to his second leg. At that moment he is very vulnerable to being swept forward. By combining the pull with your arms with the kicking-over motion with your legs, you completely break your opponent's balance forward.

(!) From another angle you can see very clearly the initial sweeping position. Note how Renzo pulls the arms forward and out. This opens Royler's elbows and makes it very difficult to resist the sweep. Renzo's knees come together as he uncrosses his feet and uses his legs to help Royler over.

4

The next crucial step of the move is to take advantage of the initial unbalancing movement and take your opponent completely over. To do this, push your hips and buttocks off the floor and punch them up and over your head. It is as though you were trying to roll your hips over your head from a supine position.

5

The result is a beautiful sweeping motion that takes Royler cleanly over Renzo's head. If the pull with the arms and kick-over with the legs is timed well, there is little your opponent can do.

6

Royler is carried over completely, landing flat on his back. Renzo immediately follows him and comes up in the mounted position.

7

Renzo immediately stabilizes his mount. Now he is ready to attack with strikes and submission holds.

Spider guard sweep

Grappling technique from the guard position is usually broadly divided into open and closed guard. We have seen that the closed guard involves holding an opponent between your legs while lying on your back. The guard is "closed" insofar as you cross your feet behind your opponent's back. There are some advantages to closing the guard. It is a simple to apply on an opponent and can be used to tie him up and stifle his offense, especially in a real fight. Your opponent cannot simply stand up and walk away since your crossed legs hold him in. The open guard is any situation where you have an opponent between your legs but your feet are not crossed. The guard is "open" insofar as your legs do not hold your opponent in. There are many variations of the open guard. We have seen a number in this book. You can place your feet on your opponent's hips, chest, on the ground, under your opponent's thighs, and so on. There are many more attacks from the open guard than from the closed guard.

One very interesting form of open guard is the spider guard. This involves placing one or both feet on your opponent's biceps. Usually you also grab the wrist of the same arm as well.

This gives you great control over your opponent's arms and allows you to control your opponent's movement through his arms the same way a spider controls the movements of its prey through its web. The spider guard makes offense, whether it be guard passing, striking, or leg locks, extremely difficult for your opponent. In addition it is a great offensive tool for the man on bottom. Control of your opponent's arms sets up many submission holds (especially the triangle choke demonstrated elsewhere in this book) and sweeps. Here we see one sweep that is set and completed through the use of the spider guard. Often the spider guard is thought to be a purely sportive technique, useful for tournament Jiu-jitsu where competitors wear a gi, but of little relevance elsewhere. This is not the case. The use of the foot in your opponent's bicep is extremely useful in any situation where your opponent is in your guard and trying to strike you. Simply pushing your foot into his bicep is an invaluable means of preventing him from punching you. This kind of control can be developed through the use of the spider guard in training.

1

Royler is holding Renzo in his closed guard.

2

Looking to go into a more offensive mode, Royler opens his guard by uncrossing his feet and initially placing them on the floor. Royler gains control of Renzo's arms from the beginning by gripping the cuffs of his sleeves. If Renzo were not wearing a gi, Royler would grip the wrists. A wrist grip is not nearly as strong as a grip on the gi, nonetheless, useful work can be done with the spider guard with a gi to grip.

3

Scooting his hips out to one side creates the room Royler needs to bring a knee up inside Renzo's arms.

4

Royler brings his other knee up inside Renzo's arms.

5

Now it is time to enter into the spider guard. Royler's hips are out to one side, giving him the room he needs to bring his foot on the opposite side up onto Renzo's bicep. Say that Royler's initial hip movement is out to the right, then this makes it easy for him to place his left foot on his opponent's right bicep.

6

Pushing Renzo's arm back with the foot on the bicep creates the space to bring his other leg inside Renzo's arm and place that foot on Renzo's other bicep. In using the spider guard you want to keep one leg extended out straight, the other bent. You can see Royler using the classic spider guard in exactly this fashion. Do not extend both legs at the same time, or bend both at the same time. Rather keep one leg extended, the other bent.

7

To off-balance his opponent, Royler extends one leg (the one on the same side from which he initially scooted his hips out) and pushes it up toward the ceiling. At the same time he drops his other foot off the bicep and puts that leg down on the floor outside Renzo's leg as shown. Throughout all this Royler has maintained his control over Renzo's arms by gripping the sleeve cuffs.

(!) Here is the classic position for this particular spider guard sweep. The foot in Renzo's bicep is pushing up, Royler is pulling down and across on Renzo's other arm, creating a big wheeling motion that brings Renzo off-balance. Royler's other leg has dropped to the ground just outside Renzo's leg at the knee. Note how Royler's leg on the floor is turned out, putting it in an optimal position to sweep Renzo's legs out from under him.

8

Sweeping strongly with the leg on the floor while bringing Renzo over with the foot on the bicep, Royler takes Renzo down in a very strong sweep.

9

As Renzo crashes to the floor, Royler uses the grip on Renzo's sleeves to help pull himself up to a mounted position.

10

Royler climbs on top of Renzo.

11

Still holding onto Renzo's sleeves in order to make escape very difficult for Renzo, Royler stabilizes his mounted position.

Passing the half guard into the mounted position

We noted earlier that the half-guard position, where your opponent is underneath you with his legs wrapped around one of your legs, is one of the most common in actual sparring and combat. This is because every time you go to pass his guard and get around his legs, he is trying equally hard to keep you in his guard. The result is often that you get past one of his legs and he hangs on grimly to the other, preventing you from cleanly passing and getting to an across-side position. Another common occurrence that often puts you in the half-guard position is the struggle to take your opponent down to the ground. It is relatively rare for a takedown to flawlessly place you in a perfect across-side or mounted position. In the heat and pressure of sparring and combat, your opponent usually tries desperately to place you in his guard as he feels himself going down in order to prevent you from landing in a really dominant position. Often the result is that you end up in his half guard. In addition, failed submission attempts often

result in a scramble where neither of you has any decisive positional advantage. More often than not, you end up in a half-guard position as a result.

The sheer frequency with which this position occurs makes it essential that you know what to do when your opponent has trapped one of your legs with his. While it is quite possible for you to attack with submission holds and strikes from the half guard, bear in mind that your opponent has a large number of submission holds and sweeps that he can use on *you* from this position. It is generally safer to extract your trapped leg and get to a more dominant position from where you can launch your attacks with near impunity. We saw earlier that one can pass the half guard into the across-side position. This is an excellent strategy and can be done in many ways, one of which was demonstrated. It is also possible to pass from the half guard directly into the mounted position. This is what we shall look at now.

1

Royler is held up in Renzo's half guard. In order to establish a stable base from which to pass, Royler places both his arms over Renzo's body and sits on the floor on the hip of his free leg. His forward arm is over Renzo's face, his elbow on the floor next to Renzo's ear, hugging Renzo in tight.

2

Having established his base, Royler begins to pass. He begins by shuffling the foot of his trapped leg toward Renzo's buttocks, going as far as he can. This greatly weakens the grip Renzo has upon his leg. He then places the hand of his rear arm on Renzo's far knee and pushes, further weakening Renzo's grip.

3

Sitting on his forward hip, Royler pulls his trapped leg straight forward by bringing his bent knee up to Renzo's chest.

(!) Here you can see the stable position that Royler employs as he passes. He sits on his side, resting on the hip of his free leg. The knee of his free leg is drawn up to Renzo's buttocks.

4

As his leg becomes free, *Royler switches direction and begins to drive his knee across Renzo's stomach and down to the floor.*

5

This takes Royler directly to the mounted position, bypassing the usual pattern of passing to the across-side position and then working to the mounted position.

6

Having gotten to the mounted position, Royler *immediately* posts both his hands out wide on the floor, preventing Renzo from attempting to roll him over the moment he gets mounted. Royler has gone from a good position to a truly dominant one. Now he can attack with little fear of counter.

The front shoulder choke from the guard position

The front shoulder choke is one of the very best submission holds. It works on the same principle as the triangle choke only you employ your arms rather than your legs to implement it. By placing your opponent's arm across and under his throat and then wrapping your arms around his neck in a way that shall soon be explained, you prevent blood being transported through the carotid arteries to the brain. The result is either submission or your opponent being rendered unconscious. Interestingly, it is your opponent's *own shoulder* that is used to close off one of the carotid arteries. One of the chief advantages of the front shoulder choke is that it defeats two of the most common street defenses to any strangulation at-

tacks from the front. Most people react to being strangled by someone in front of them by biting and eye gouging. In the case of a front shoulder choke, this is impossible, since your arm is pushed across in front of you. The only thing you can bite is your own shoulder. Nor can you eye gouge effectively, since your arms are trapped. This makes it one of the safest frontal attacks to employ in a street-grappling situation. The front shoulder choke can be applied when you are across your opponent's side, when you are mounted, and when he is locked in your guard. Here we see an application from the guard position.

Renzo is holding Royler in his guard. Royler leans forward and places his forearm across Renzo's throat, trying to choke Renzo. This is actually a very inefficient means of choking someone. Only an inexperienced opponent would attempt it. It is, however, very common among street brawlers and therefore worthy of study. Renzo is not all perturbed by the pressure on his throat. He places his hand on the elbow of the choking arm.

To relieve the pressure on his throat, Renzo pushes Royler away with his hips. At the same time he grips Royler's head with his other hand.

By pushing Royler back with his hips, Renzo makes it easy to push Royler's choking arm across his chest. As Royler's arm slides across, Renzo jerks Royler forward with his legs and with the hand on Royler's head.

4

The result is that Royler's arm is pushed across Renzo's chest. Renzo brings the arm that was holding Royler's head around Royler's neck. This traps Royler's arm in place. Royler could not pull it out now even if he wanted to. *A crucial detail here is that the arm that goes around Royler's neck goes under the trapped arm before encircling the neck.* The bicep of the arm encircling your opponent's neck cuts off one carotid artery. Your opponent's own shoulder, pressing into the side of his own neck, cuts off the other.

5

Renzo places the hand of the arm wrapped around Royler's neck on the bicep of his other arm.

6

To finish the choke, Renzo places his free hand on Royler's forehead. To strangle, squeeze your elbows together.

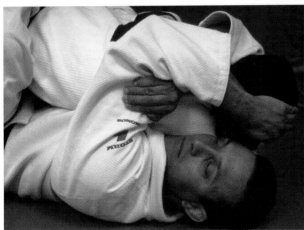

(!) Notice how the arm that goes around Royler's neck first passes *under* Royler's trapped arm, *then as far as possible around Royler's neck.* At that point the hand of the choking arm folds into the bicep of the other arm. The hand of the other arm is placed on the opponent's forehead. Royler is trapped in a very tight stranglehold. He cannot bite or eye gouge Renzo. Should the stranglehold fail for any reason, Renzo can easily slide around behind the trapped arm and get to Royler's back. This is a great move in both a street fight and in grappling tournaments. There are *many* ways to slide your opponent's arm across in front of you in order to enter into the move. You can experiment with different ways to do so.

Transition from the mounted position to the side-mounted stranglehold

One of the chief advantages of grappling as a form of self-defense is that it allows you to practice all your grappling techniques at full power on a resisting opponent on a daily basis. In the case of boxing and other striking arts, sparring cannot be done at full power at all times. The training is simply too damaging. Protective equipment must be worn and hard sparring time limited. The grappler can keep going at full power as long as he or she has sufficient strength to go on. This is a tremendous advantage. It makes you very familiar with the sensation and feel of restraining and overcoming an opponent who is doing everything he can to resist and defeat you – which of course, is exactly what you can expect in a real fight. When you are mounted on an opponent in a real fight, striking and trying to make him submit, you can expect him to be doing everything he can to get out of the mounted position.

No doubt he will be twisting, pushing, bridging, even scratching and clawing, in a frenzied attempt at escape. By training with resisting partners, each of you trying as hard as you can to overcome and defeat the other, you will become very familiar with the movements required to keep an opponent pinned under your mount no matter how desperate his attempts at escape. Since there are no potentially injurious striking and foul tactics in grappling training you can go as hard as you can every time you train with little fear of injury. As you train very often at close to full power you will become so familiar with the "feel" of overcoming a struggling opponent that real combat will not hold many surprises for you. A good example of dealing with the resistance of a live opponent and turning it into victory is offered here: a transition from the mounted position into a stranglehold.

1

Royler is mounted on Renzo. By reaching across into the collar, Royler sets up the beginnings of a stranglehold.

2

Anytime you are mounted on an opponent and you begin to attack, whether it be with punches, head butts, joint locks, or in this case, a stranglehold, *you can reasonably expect your opponent to try as hard as he can to escape.* Real opponents do not sit passively under you as you attack them. Here Renzo tries desperately to bridge and roll out from under Royler's mount. *The key point here is that Royler opens his leg out wide and gives Renzo room to roll.* This is a crucial point. Failure to do so usually results in your opponent rolling into your leg and dragging you over until he finishes in your guard. This is not totally disastrous (your opponent is still in your guard after all), but it is much better to retain the mounted position. It is important that you open your leg out to create space for your opponent to roll into.

3

Having opened his leg out, Royler allows Renzo to roll to his side. Royler is still mounted, but you can see that the nature of his mounted position has changed, Now he is out to Renzo's side. From this position Royler opens Renzo's collar, making it easy for Royler to reach in for the stranglehold with his other hand.

4

Royler's strangling hand grips thumb inside the collar, fingers outside, high up on Renzo's collar.

5

Royler's other hand goes under Renzo's armpit and around to the back of Renzo's head.

6

The hand in the collar pulls across the throat and up to the opposite ear. The hand behind Renzo's head pushes forward. This creates a very strong stranglehold. If Renzo does not submit he will pass out.

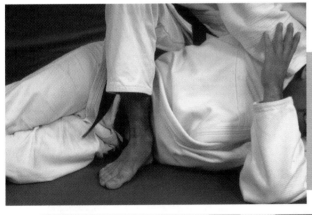

(!) A very important point is the switch in the mounted position that occurs as Royler gives Renzo room to roll. As Royler opens his leg he posts out the foot of that leg on the floor, placing it at his opponent's hip. Royler is now sitting on one knee out to Renzo's side. This is still a mounted position (he still straddles Renzo's upper body) but he is now in a side-mounted position. Note how Royler keeps his foot close to Renzo's hip to make escape difficult.

(!) From the other side you can see how Royler sits on his knee. His lower leg is drawn up alongside Renzo's back. This side-mounted position is ideal for dealing with a wild, twisting, rolling, bucking opponent and getting into an offensive position from where to attack with strangleholds and joint locks.

Defense against a one-handed choke against a wall

On several occasions we have pointed out the need to take into account your surroundings whenever you are in a potentially violent situation. Often your immediate environment plays a crucial role in determining the outcome of the situation. For example, the way you might approach a fight with a stranger would be radically altered if it were to take place on slippery ice, on a dance floor strewn with broken glass and beer, next to a busy road, or on board an airplane. Perhaps the single most common environmental factor in real fights are walls. Most fights take place in urban and indoor settings since this is where people most commonly interact with each other. Accordingly you can reasonably expect a wall to be nearby whenever you fight in such a setting. If the fight should take you up against a wall or any wall-like obstacle (such as a

parked car, fence, or tree), this may well play a crucial role in the outcome. In mixed martial arts events many otherwise experienced and skillful martial artists were unable to cope with the complications provided by the fence of the arena in which they fought. Some competitors pushed others up against the fence, using it to severely limit their opponent's mobility and to inflict heavy punishment, just as so often happens in a street fight. It is vital that you practice defending yourself in the presence of obstacles such as walls for street realism. Here is a defense to a common use of walls in real fights. Your opponent pushes you up against the wall with a one-handed chokehold. This is both uncomfortable and dangerous. Your opponent can strike you with his free hand while controlling you with the other.

1

Royler, against the wall, is approached by Renzo, who lunges forward to grab Royler by the throat.

2

Contact! Renzo grabs Royler and pushes him hard against the wall.

3

Royler does not wait. Once your opponent has made contact in this way he can easily strike you with the other hand. If he is aggressive enough to grab you, he is almost certainly aggressive enough to follow up with strikes. Royler quickly comes across with his hand and shoves Renzo's grabbing arm at the inside of the forearm. If Renzo grabs with his right hand, Royler will come across with his right hand to strike the forearm and vice versa. It takes little strength to knock the choking hand off your throat in this fashion. This is because you are fighting only against the strength of your opponent's thumb. The strength of your arm and rotating upper body can easily win this fight.

In the close-up you can see clearly that the only thing preventing Renzo's grip being broken out to the side is his thumb. This makes it easy for Royler to come across and knock the choking arm to the outside, striking at right angles to the choking arm.

4

Having come across and knocked the choking hand off his throat, Royler simply comes back with the same arm he used to dislodge Renzo's choking arm and strikes Renzo's jaw with his elbow. This is a very hard blow. Your elbow is a superb close-range weapon, and this is a great context in which to use it.

Breaking out of a headlock and going into an arm bar

We have seen several escapes from various kinds of headlock attacks both standing and on the ground. Many inexperienced opponents retain their grip on your head even after you have escaped their pin and are on top of them. If you are stronger than your opponent this is not a problem. However, if your opponent is extremely strong it can be quite difficult to break his grip around your head. He simply holds on to you, making it tough for you to go on and finish the fight. What is needed is an efficient means of breaking even the strongest headlock so that you can finish the fight. This is exactly what we are about to see.

1

Royler has used one of the various headlock counters shown in this book to get a top position on Renzo. However, Renzo has retained his headlock grip and is still squeezing hard. *Even though Royler is on top he cannot take advantage of this until he frees his head.*

2

Royler's first move is to place the foot over Renzo's hips on the floor. He is sure to keep it tight to Renzo's hips to ensure that Renzo cannot escape under it. Royler keeps his hips low to make it very difficult for Renzo to use the headlock to roll him over.

3

Should Royler feel any danger of being rolled he throws his hands out wide on the floor to widen his base.

(!) You can see here how Royler positions his foot on Renzo's hips. Note how tight it is to the hips.

(!) From the opposite angle you can see how Royler kneels on his other knee. This lowers his center of gravity and makes him hard to roll.

4

Renzo is still grimly holding on to the headlock. Royler places his forearm on the side of Renzo's neck and grabs his wrist with his other hand.

5

Initially Royler leans forward into Renzo, putting pressure on Renzo's neck and jaw.

6

To break the headlock, Royler pushes with his forearm on Renzo's neck and straightens up. This breaks Renzo's hands apart, breaking the headlock.

7

The arm that was holding Renzo's head is now straight. It is thus very vulnerable to an arm bar. Royler takes advantage of this to go straight for a submission hold. He grabs the straightened arm and places his other hand on the floor over Renzo's face. This prevents Renzo from sitting up as the arm bar is being applied.

8

Royler swings the leg upon which he was kneeling over Renzo's face, putting him in perfect position for an arm bar.

9

At this point, Royler simply falls back on his buttocks and lies down. He is sure to squeeze his knees together and uses both his hands to grip the wrist of Renzo's trapped arm. To put breaking pressure on Renzo's elbow, Royler pushes his hips up toward the ceiling.

The star sweep

The most practical and useful moves in Brazilian jiu-jitsu are not very spectacular to observe. No one would claim that an elbow escape is exciting, yet it is probably the most utilized move in Jiu-jitsu and success or failure in its application often means the difference between victory and defeat. Other moves are very spectacular but are either very difficult to carry out against a skilled, resisting opponent, or opportunities to employ them come along only rarely. In general, the more exotic-looking moves are less suited for real fighting. There are a few exceptions to this general rule, however. The star sweep is both very exciting to watch and yet quite practical and simple to perform. It can be done on any opponent standing in your guard. Thus opportunities for its use come as often as your opponents stand up in your guard. The move can be used as an independent technique in itself, or as a combination with the handstand sweep described earlier in the book.

1

Royler stands in Renzo's closed guard.

2

Renzo immediately hooks one arm inside and around one of Royler's legs at the ankle. He places the palm of his other hand on the floor close to his own ear as shown. At this point Renzo's movements are the same as for the handstand sweep (described earlier in the book).

3

Pushing his hips up into Royler, Renzo tries the handstand sweep but cannot take Royler down.

4

Rather than fight with strength, Renzo quickly opens his guard and brings his leg (the one on the same side as the hand pushing off the floor) in a wide looping motion around toward his other leg.

5

You can see how Renzo's leg whips around in a wide arc, blasting through Royler's arms. You can see also that Renzo grips Royler's ankle very tightly throughout the move.

6

Still gripping Royler's ankle, Renzo lands on his knees outside of the leg he is gripping. Now he is facing the same way as Royler.

7

Posting his free hand on the ground for leverage, Renzo begins to straighten up, still gripping Royler's ankle.

8

Renzo pulls Royler's ankle off the floor as he straightens up all the way. His upper back pushes back into Royler's thigh and hip as he does this, aiding in taking Royler down. For Royler there is no choice – he is forced down to his back. This sweep is done in one quick motion.

Here you can see Renzo's grip on the trapped leg. One arm is around the ankle, the other at the bend of the knee. The arm around the ankle does most of the work in taking Royler down. Renzo pulls Royler's ankle forward and up.

9

Still holding Royler's trapped leg up high, Renzo takes his arm from around Royler's ankle and puts it around Royler's head, enabling him to secure a tight across-side position. While the move looks spectacular, it is really quite simple and based upon sound mechanical principles. With a little practice you will be able to perform it easily.

110 The knee bar from the closed guard position

Whenever your opponent stands in your guard it becomes more difficult to attack with the standard submission holds like the arm bar, "kimura," collar chokes, the guillotine choke, and the triangle choke especially if your opponent has a good, upright posture. This is because you have to lift your hips high off the floor to catch a standing opponent with arm bars and triangles. Your opponent can make it hard for you to come up. *When your opponent is standing in your guard his legs are the closest target for submission holds. Moreover, since he is standing his legs will be relatively straight—ideal for leg lock attacks. One of the best leg locks to use on an opponent standing in your guard is the knee bar. It is simple yet very hard for your opponent to resist if well applied, moreover it does not expose you to much danger from strikes as you perform it.*

1

Renzo is standing in Royler's closed guard.

2

Upper-body submission holds will be difficult on a standing opponent. Royler switches his attention to the legs. He brings one arm inside and around Renzo's leg at the ankle as shown, pulling his upper body closer to that trapped leg while at the same time opening his guard by uncrossing his feet.

3

In one smooth motion, Royler drops his foot (the one on the same side as the arm he is using to grab his opponent's leg) to Renzo's hip, the toes pointed out. *The knee of that same leg slides to the inside of the knee of Renzo's trapped leg.* This is a crucial detail. Failure to do so will make the move far less likely to succeed. Royler uses the arm holding Renzo's trapped leg to pull himself around toward Renzo's trapped leg. Royler then swings his other leg around in an arc toward Renzo's trapped leg.

4

Royler swings his other leg all the way around Renzo's trapped leg until his foot reaches the back of Renzo's buttocks. Now Renzo's trapped leg is held between both of Royler's thighs. Note that Royler's arm never relinquishes its grip upon Renzo's leg at the ankle throughout all this movement.